D0630664

Person and Myth

PERSON AND MYTH

Maurice Leenhardt
in the Melanesian World

James Clifford

University of California Press

Berkeley • Los Angeles • London

University of California Press
Berkeley and Los Angeles, California
University of California Press, Ltd.
London, England
© 1982 by The Regents of the University of California
Printed in the United States of America

1 2 3 4 5 6 7 8 9

Chapters 5 and 8 have previously been published in slightly
different form in *The Journal of Pacific History* and *Man*.

Library of Congress Cataloging in Publication Data

Clifford, James, 1945-
  Person and myth.

  Bibliography: p.
  Includes index.
  1. Leenhardt, Maurice, 1878-1954.
  2. Ethnology—New Caledonia.
  3. Anthropologists—Melanesia—Biography.
  4. Anthropologists—France—Biography.
  5. Misssionaries—Melanesia—Biography.
  6. Missionaries—France—Biography.
  I. Title.
  GN21.L373C57 306′.092′4   81-4509
  ISBN 0-520-04247-6   AACR2

For My Father

Contents

List of Illustrations   *viii*

Acknowledgments   *ix*

Some Misleading Terms   *xi*

Introduction   *1*

PART ONE: *Do Neva*
    I.   The Education of a Missionary   *13*
   II. La Grande Terre   *30*
  III. Getting Involved   *45*
  IV. Do Neva   *59*
   V. Translations   *74*
  VI. War and Rebellion   *92*
 VII. Evangelical Horizons   *105*

PART TWO: *Do Kamo*
      Introduction to Part Two   *124*
 VIII. The Making of Ethnographic Texts   *129*
  IX. The Canaque Professor   *145*
   X. Gens de la Grande Terre: New Caledonia, 1938-1940   *158*
  XI. Structures of the Person   *172*
  XII. The Colonial World   *189*
 XIII. Participation and Myth   *200*
 XIV. Plenitude   *216*
      Afterword   *225*

Abbreviations   *229*

Notes   *231*

Bibliography of Works by and about Maurice Leenhardt   *257*

Index   *265*

Illustrations

MAP OF NEW CALEDONIA   *9*

1. Franz Leenhardt   *16*

2. Maurice Leenhardt in 1902   *25*

3. The fiancées, Maurice and Jeanne Michel in 1901   *28*

4. In the valley of the Houailou River   *37*

5. & 6. The traditional village, men's and women's houses   *39*

7. New Caledonian colonialism   *49*

8. Do Neva, first pastoral students   *64*

9. Protestant missionaries   *67*

10. The farm at Do Neva   *72*

11. Maurice and Jeanne Leenhardt in 1909   *75*

12. Do Neva, a Christian marriage   *101*

13. Grand Chef Mindia Néja in 1878, 1892, 1912   *132*

14. A page from Boesoou Erijisi's notebooks   *143*

15. Paul Rivet, Maurice Leenhardt, Lucien Lévy-Bruhl   *151*

16. Maurice Leenhardt and Eleischa Nebay, 1938   *162*

17. The ceremonies at Coulna, 1939   *167*

18. Esthetics and *mythe vécu*   *211*

19. Maurice Leenhardt in 1953   *218*

Acknowledgments

Of those who remember Maurice Leenhardt in their rather different ways, I am principally indebted to his son, Raymond Leenhardt, pastor and professor in his father's tradition. M. Leenhardt has been most generous in giving me access to his father's unpublished papers—letters, journals, and lecture notes—the large majority of which are in his hands. He and Mme. Geneviève Leenhardt have read and corrected my text in matters of fact at various stages of its development. M. Leenhardt has been admirably open in encouraging me to interpret his father's life as I have seen fit.

Mme. Roselène Dousset-Leenhardt, herself a well-known historian of New Caledonia, has made available to me some of her own holdings, principally her transcriptions of passages from her father's letters in the years 1917 and 1923-1925. In discussions, she has provided me with valuable insights into his character and work, reflecting the general viewpoint recently expressed with passion in her short autobiographical text, *La tête aux antipodes*. This *"récit autobiographique"* includes many poignant portraits of Maurice Leenhardt and the extended family during the early 1920s. It arrived during the editing of the present study, and I have thus not made specific use of it. It is not, nor does it pretend to be, a source of dispassionate fact, but is an honestly subjective cry of protest—a taking of distance from many of the constraining contexts, imperial and Protestant, that I have indicated in the pages that follow.

Anyone dealing with the history and ethnology of New Caledonia owes much to the writings of Jean Guiart, Maurice Leenhardt's most distinguished successor. From the beginning of this project, Professor Guiart has provided valuable advice and documentation; the frequent citations of his works will indicate my debt to him.

Father Patrick O'Reilly, in his incomparable documentary collections and in conversation, has deepened my understanding of colonial New Caledonia.

Mme. Hilda Danon, herself engaged in writing a philosophical study of Leenhardt, has helped me in many way. As friend and collaborator, she has shared with me her insights and problems. M. Claudio Rugafiori was most generous in providing information from the Mauss archives and hints on Leenhardt's work, of which he has a deep understanding. M. Jean Cadier, former *Doyen* of the Montpellier Theological Faculty, provided me with invaluable background information on the Leenhardt family milieu. Mlle. Léonard, librarian of D.E.F.A.P. (the former Société des Missions Evangéliques), 102 Bld. Arago, Paris, gave generous advice and archival assistance. Father Coste of the Marist Archives in Rome was kind enough to search out documents relating to Leenhardt. Pastor Jean Paul Burger provided a lucid and detailed assessment of Leenhardt's visit to the upper Zambeze.

In New Caledonia, more people than I can mention here made me feel welcome and *en famille* on the occasion of Leenhardt's centennial celebration at Houailou during August 1978. Among scholars based in Noumea who helped me with my inquiries, I would like to thank Mme. Dominique Bourret and M. Jean-Marie Kohler. M. Gorohuna Firmin Dogo of Poindah kindly explained to me a considerable amount of local history and custom relevant to Leenhardt's work; and M. Jean-Marie Tijibaou of Hienghène, both in person and in his writings, has been an incomparable guide to things Melanesian. The New Caledonian land, in its complex, vibrant beauty, has been an inspiration and ally.

My thanks also to the following individuals who have shared with me their memories of Leenhardt: Mme. Henry Corbin (née Stella Leenhardt), Mme. Jean Gastambide (née Francine Leenhardt), Mme. Eric Dardel (née Renée Leenhardt), Pastor Charles Monod, M. Michel Leiris, M. Pierre-Henri Chombart-de-Lauwe, M. Georges Condominas, Pastor Etienne Kruger, Mme. Germaine Dieterlen, the late M. Robert Delavignette, and the late M. Henry Corbin.

The following have read and criticized the text at various stages: Virginia I. Clifford, H. Stuart Hughes, Vincent Crapanzano, Jane Kramer, Gilbert Lewis, Connie Higginson, Michael Ignatieff, Gustaf Sobin, Karin Lessing Merveille, Richard Sieburth, Anna Cancogni, Frederika Randall, Geoffrey Kabat, David Koteen, Robert Schulzinger, T. N. Pandey, Joan Larcom, and my tactful editor, Dan Dixon. Donald Beggs prepared the index. I thank and absolve these, my friends, in the usual ways: a life is written, as it is lived, plurally.

Some Misleading Terms

Ethnology—I use the word loosely, as the most common French equivalent for what has been called "Social Anthropology" in Britain and "Cultural Anthropology" in America. Its use shades into "ethnography" when designating empirical research. Although it is convenient to make the distinction between "ethnology" and "ethnography," I do not wish to imply that they are sharply dissimilar intellectual undertakings.

Canaque—An indiscriminate name applied by white settlers to native New Caledonians. In its English form, kanaka, it exists widely in the Pacific, usually with a disparaging connotation. However inaccurate and offensive the term may appear, I have not eliminated it from this study (1) because Leenhardt used it, without prejudice, throughout his life, (2) because its use is common in French ethnological circles to designate specifically the Melanesians of New Caledonia, (3) because it has been adopted as a term of national pride by Melanesians. I have left *Canaque* untranslated.

Pagan, Savage—Leenhardt commonly used *paien* neutrally to denote only pre- or non-Christian. He sometimes invested the pagan "stage" of moral development with the dignity of classical antiquity or that of the early Hebrews. The French *sauvage* is more ambiguous than the English "savage," for it implies "wild," "undomesticated," or "natural" (as in *La Pensée Sauvage* or "le camping sauvage"). "Pagan" and "savage" are not necessarily pejorative.

Introduction

I first encountered Maurice Leenhardt through his intriguing, unorthodox study in religious phenomenology, *Do Kamo: Person and Myth in the Melanesian World*.[1] Then, in the course of general research on the history of French anthropology between the world wars, I became aware of an extraordinary ethnographic experience underlying *Do Kamo*'s moral speculations (its title, in a New Caledonian tongue, means "the true person"). I began to wonder about this anthropologist who as a missionary had spent more than half his adult life in the field. My interest grew as I delved into Leenhardt's unpublished letters and journals, spanning twenty-three years in Melanesia and one and a half in Africa. I found a complex, ambiguous struggle—within and against the colonial system, within and against the ideological forms of a Western, Christian world view. A better acquaintance with Leenhardt's research convinced me of its continuing value as a methodological model. The author of *Do Kamo* began to emerge as a provocative combination of ideas and practices, at once old-fashioned and prescient. I have tried to make sense—or at least a story—out of these conflicting impressions.

The shape, also the enigma, of Leenhardt's life are nicely caught in an anecdote, perhaps apocryphal, told to me by one of those who attended his lectures on New Caledonian ethnography during the 1930s. In a classroom at the Sorbonne, a skeptical student confronts the missionary-anthropologist: "But, *M. le Pasteur*, how many people did you *really* convert during all that time out there?" Leenhardt strokes his finely combed, abundant grey beard, then replies with a shrug: "Maybe one." His blue-grey eyes often contained a hint of amusement; he liked to provoke. There can be little doubt that the "one" in question was himself, for Leenhardt had been powerfully influenced by his years in the South Pacific. In his later teaching and writing, until his death in 1954, he thought and rethought a difficult and inspiring involvement with the Melanesian world.

As an evangelist Leenhardt worked on the large island of New Caledonia from 1902 until 1926. Thereafter, an academic anthropol-

1

ogist in Paris, he taught at the Ecole Pratique des Hautes Etudes, the Institut d'Ethnologie, and the Musée de l'Homme. During these years he continued his life's work of extensive field research in Southern Melanesia. The founder of modern French oceanic studies, first president of the Société des Océanistes and of the Institut Français d'Océanie, Leenhardt held Marcel Mauss's influential teaching chair at the Ecole Pratique des Hautes Etudes during the late 1930s and the 1940s before the post was passed on, in 1951, to Claude Lévi-Strauss. He advocated an important theoretical countercurrent in French anthropology and sociology between the world wars.

Leenhardt was the brilliant fieldworker one does not expect to find in the French university tradition before 1950. Anglo-Americans, at least, tend to think of twentieth-century French anthropology as essentially philosophical in orientation—a tradition whose strength lies in the production of powerful explanatory paradigms and whose weakness is a tendency to overintellectualize and explain away the incongruities of lived experience. If there is truth in the stereotype—applied primarily to Durkheim and Lévi-Strauss—it should not blind us to the fact that this "tradition" has always been contested. Leenhardt, Arnold Van Gennep, Alfred Métraux, Charles Le Coeur, Marcel Griaule and his school are important counterexamples.

Leenhardt stood for a lifelong commitment to empirical, firsthand research. He attempted, moreover, to emphasize cultural expressivity and change over structure and system, experience over formal laws. He resisted the separation of phenomenological and sociological approaches—a distinction that had tended to define social anthropology since Durkheim. Leenhardt's theoretical stance, it seems to me, has become newly significant in a post-structuralist context. Indeed, his entire life of research, in the widest sense of the term, addresses itself to the present concern with more "open" cultural theories—modes of understanding capable of accounting for innovative process and historical discontinuity, for the dynamics of the person, and for reciprocity in ethnological interpretation.

≥<

In 1978, the centennial year of Leenhardt's birth, a monument was dedicated to his memory in the Houailou Valley of New Caledonia at the site of his mission station, Do Neva. It was an event of local political importance. Leenhardt's name stands for something in the region. Once seen as a radical, he has now been reclassified as the island's greatest liberal. New Caledonia remains an Overseas Territory of France, heavily settled by Europeans and exploited for its considerable nickel deposits. For many Melanesians and liberal whites, Leenhardt's name signifies the valorization of tradition and cultural authenticity. Among a number of older colonists it evokes a dangerous, "pro-native" radicalism. (Leenhardt was, in fact, frequently embroiled with colonial authorities and with his own mission society.) And among an emerging group of nationalists, the name stands for an outmoded brand of reform. The missionary-ethnographer's long-term practice of "applied anthropology" is far from insignificant in New Caledonia today. His example stands, also, to be of wider interest as fieldworkers everywhere—both ethnographic and evangelical—reexamine the consequences of their participation in exotic communities.

Leenhardt's research experience was not, of course, a typical one. Indeed, that much of it—though not all—was accomplished in an evangelical context may render it suspect, especially to those who see the roles of missionary and ethnographer as irreconcilable. A certain friction between science and religion is frequently at issue in my account. I had come to Leenhardt with well-formed opinions about the missionary enterprise, something I had dismissed as culturally destructive, a spiritual aggression inseparable from colonial domination. Had I not first become interested in Leenhardt as an ethnologist, I would probably not have considered the experience of an evangelist worthy of extended, sympathetic attention. But to understand Leenhardt's work more than superficially, one cannot separate its scientific from its religious aspects. Although he devoted himself increasingly to university-based research, Leenhardt should not be thought of as a missionary-turned-anthropologist. Ethnography was, from the beginning, an integral part of his mission work; and his anthropology continued to be shaped by the fundamental goals of his evangelism. While his peculiar combination of careers imposed limits on Leenhardt's academic production, it also contributed to its originality in a secular university milieu. Thus, at times, I have been led to argue for the value of "religious" modes of interpretation in a comparative science of human culture.

The word "religious" needs to be kept, implicitly, in quotation marks, for Leenhardt at least did not see it as a separate, clearly definable category of experience. Rather, he assumed that "religion" referred to a basic and universal mode of knowledge, an access to transcendence permeating all realms of human experience. If he was sometimes troubled by the old Christian ambiguity of a divinity both transcendent and immanent, his deepest instincts were on the side of immanence. In this he derived constant support from Melanesian religious attitudes—pitched, literally, at ground level and inscribed in immediate socio-mythic relations. But Melanesian myth and the Christian person represented two distinct—often conflicting—ways of experiencing divinity. Leenhardt worked heroically for their mediation; through his struggles I have tried to indicate certain structures and limits of liberal Protestantism—and ultimately perhaps, of the montheistically organized self.

In August 1978, I was in New Caledonia to attend the celebration of Leenhardt's centennial. A few days after the ceremony at Do Neva, I had occasion to accompany Pastor Raymond Leenhardt, the missionary's son, to a Protestant Sunday morning worship service at Gondé, a village set in the narrowing Houailou valley near the geographical center of the large, mountainous island. (I shall return to Gondé more than once in retelling Leenhardt's life.) M. Leenhardt preached a sermon in the Houailou vernacular, a tongue he had learned as a young boy at Do Neva and which he spoke with an old-fashioned grace. He urged the people of Gondé to hold to their traditions, which he said were in profound harmony with the essential Christian message. After the service M. Leenhardt, his wife, and I were guests of the village at a sumptuous meal. We sat at a long table beneath a corrugated iron canopy placed beside the small church at the center of the village. Following custom, the chief and the men of Gondé sat with us at the table, while the women served and reclined on colored mats nearby, eating the same food, listening in, and occasionally commenting. Around the open sides of the canopy was a feathery screen of vegetation: palms, pines, mandarin orange trees. Through the foliage, stirred by the breeze, one saw the outline of the nearby mountains. We ate ceremonial *bougnas* made of yams, taro, meat, herbs, and coconut juice, all wrapped tightly in banana leaves and baked in earthen ovens on hot stones. The *bougnas* were supplemented with fish, squash leaf salad, and an array of other cooked vegetables. Conversation was relaxed, in French and Houailou, centering on the old days. Everyone seemed pleased when—the group being unable to recall a pre-Christian Houailou term for circumcision—M. Leenhardt was able to find it in his father's translation of the New Testament. Local coffee was served in English china set out especially for the guests.

A theological discussion ensued. One of the men at the table spoke to us about the food we had just eaten. He said that this food was not just food, physical nourishment, but was filled with significance. Everything we had eaten, he told us, came from specific places nearby. Its history was known. The food was local sustenance, a source of life; it had been touched by certain powerful stones to make it grow. The speaker wondered whether in our country we had anything similar to this. (Politically anticolonial, he was putting us on the spot—gently, stubbornly.) Did our Western food hold this kind of meaning?

I made the first attempt at a reply, speaking of supermarkets and of produce wrapped in plastic. Mme. Leenhardt agreed that our food had generally lost its local, sacred meaning, but she added that in certain parts of France bread retained a significance similar to that of the yam in New Caledonia. Pastor Leenhardt then suggested a religious interpretation. He said that Europeans had perhaps forgotten what was remembered here—that the Holy Spirit could be present, concretely, in everything. But our interlocutor politely refused the explanation. The other men at the table and a few of the older women reclining nearby supported him with gestures and an occasional word. He told us that for them it was wrong to speak this way of the Holy Spirit being everywhere. Our food, he said, is not "sacred." It has particular virtues based on particular circumstances. Foreigners come here, he insisted, talking about "sacred" stones and so on. It's not true. A stone is not sacred. A stone is a stone for making yams grow. Or it's a stone for human fertility. You wouldn't apply a stone for yams to anything else. Its meaning is in its application, *dans son application*, he repeated. People talk of "sacred" stones, of the "Holy Spirit" . . . . It's not true. "Ce n'est pas vrai. Ce sont des pierres *pour*." Stones *for* . . . .

Later I told another Melanesian friend of mine about this exchange among Protestants at Gondé. My friend was raised a Catholic and had attended seminary, all the while retaining a belief in his ancestors and habitat. He laughed. "Oui, le dieu chrétien c'est une fille publique!" The Christian God would do anything, anywhere, with anyone.

I was, by then, prepared for my friend's sally. I had come to a similar conclusion in working through, struggling with and against, Leenhardt's example. I admired his attempt to rediscover his God concretely in Melanesian religious experience, but I wondered whether this could represent anything other than a personal solution. I have not, at this moment, attained much certainty on the matter. Most important, I have had to question seriously what it now means to be a "Melanesian Christian." In following Leenhardt's complex experience, I have come to a more concrete understanding of the dynamics of the colonial encounter; I have had to recognize, too, that Christianity— globally articulated—is an indeterminate, open-ended process.

There seems, in fact, to be a growing general confusion over what counts as cultural "authenticity" and as significant cultural "difference." Appeals to the supposed continuity of tradition are increasingly suspect. And Jean Duvignaud argues in *Le Langage perdu* that "real difference is not merely something connected to the strangeness of ethnic or cultural traits. Rather it is something which results from the original invention of a change, from the capacity to face the new, and experientially to define unprecedented forms of relationship, organization or expression."[2] To be profoundly Melanesian, one need not, of course, wear a penis sheath or live in a round house. One can wear a "UCLA" tee shirt or a brightly colored mission dress. One can, in fact, be a Christian *and* something else.

I hope that the reader of these pages will derive from them, at least, an informed uncertainty about cultural identity and difference, avoiding especially the easy recourse to dichotomies and essences. Such an attitude has the merit of leaving the future open and of not equating cultural change too quickly with modernization or global homgeneity, with history or with entropy. In political contexts such prophecies—whether of doom or development—tend to be self-fulfilling.

>€

The present book is a sympathetic, though not uncritical, account of Maurice Leenhardt's experience and writings. It takes, inevitably, his side of things. My main sources have been Leenhardt's private papers—an extensive collection of letters, journals, memorabilia—and his many scattered publications. These I have quoted, except in a few specified instances, in my own translations. Following conventional biographical practice, I have also attempted to portray a variety of lived contexts, the most important of which—colonial New Caledonia, French Protestantism, Paris anthropology between the world wars—are unfamiliar to Anglo-American readers. I have relied here on archives and standard secondary sources, also on interviews and participant observation in these contexts as they persist.

I trust I have not, in striving for a biographical closure, smoothed over the rough edges of Leenhardt's life—the clashing milieux, the dicontinuous personae that made up an engaged, active, confused existence. Nor have I tried here to reveal an inner life or to portray a "real" or "essential" Leenhardt. In talking with those who knew him (and who do not agree), in considering the multiplicity of situations in which he acted, I have concluded that to mark off a true Leenhardt, to reconstruct the workings of an intimate self—assuming this could be done by working largely from written records—would be inappropriate to a life that I take to have been an experience of relationality and participation. In some degree, therefore, I have applied to Leenhardt his own theory of the Melanesian person, a person seen as decentered, "outside" itself, continually rising to occasions. The notion of an "inner" life is probably best understood as a fiction of fairly recent, and far from universal, application—even in the West.

Here it is worth looking ahead to Leenhardt's mature conception of myth, a "mode of knowledge," as he put it, accessible to all human experience whether archaic or modern. Myth, in this view, should be freed from the status of a story or even of a legitimating social charter. Myth is not expressive of a "past." Rather, myth is a particular kind of engagement with a world of concrete presences, intersubjective relations, and emotional participations. There is nothing mystical, vague, or fluid about this way of being; it does not impede logical, empirical, or technological activities, as Leenhardt's colleague and friend Lévy-Bruhl tended to assume. Myth is a valid mode of present knowledge fixed and articulated by a "socio-mythic landscape." Place assumes here a density inaccessible to any map, a superimposition of cultural, social, ecological, and cosmological realities. Orienting, indeed constituting the person, this complex spatial locus is not grasped in the mode of narrative closure by a centered, perceiving subject. Rather, the person "lives" a discontinuous series of socio-mythic times and spaces—less as a distinct character than as an ensemble of relationships. This *mythe vécu* calls into question a Western view of the self coterminous with a discrete body, a view that values identity at the expense of plenitude.

Ideally, perhaps, a biography seeking to evade its built-in tendency to deliver a coherent whole should not be written in a realist mode, as a *Bildungsroman*, a fable of identity, and so forth.[3] In the present instance, however, I have not felt at liberty to engage in formal experimentation and have written from within the culturally defined biographical genre—while trying, occasionally, to hint at its constraints. Charged with introducing Leenhardt to an English-speaking audience, I have thought it necessary to present his public acts and writings as a continuous historical record, in chronological sequence. What follows is therefore a European-style biography. It delivers a self, but a self ambiguously involved in a Melanesian landscape. And it tries to construct a personality open to the following:

> I leap and I stand upon the wood
> heart of the iron wood trunk from the tree *apa*
> and *apiatyau*
> I'll be the tongue of men
> fathers, sons and grandsons of Mwanapo
> the master of Gotipu and Nanyaka Rawe
> the man who will speak and reply
> the sons and grandsons of Bwae Bealo and Bolo
> and Kadyatu
> the man who disperses the country

the man residing in the home of the Bay Meedu. . . .

I, the vine, enormous phallus that stretches
out and crushes
I, the milky-sapped vine, ornament of the house
that sucks, standing on the thunder mountain
I will cry out a song
I will beat the bamboo. . . .[4]

This is the sort of speech the missionary had to learn to understand—
and to love. The voice is that of one of Leenhardt's early pastoral
students and ethnographic informants, Eleischa Nebay. As late as the
1950s, long after New Caledonia had become wholly "Christian," this
pastor and devout Protestant was still in demand to recite his orations
for festivals. Within the orator's speech is the eloquence of his clan
and his habitat; his words, gestures, and breath express the Melanesian sense of local pride, of mythic attachment.

Leenhardt came to believe that the Christian God spoke in these
accents. Not only could God speak this vernacular, but in so doing, he
revealed himself, to the European able to listen, as a source of life as
well as of power. In doing so, "He" could become more relational—
closer to land, stones, people. The Word, for Leenhardt, was flesh
again, Jesus reborn in androgynous concreteness, present in Melanesian society and mythic habitat. This—as will be shown below in
more ambiguous, lived detail—was Leenhardt's belief. The reader need
not, of course, adopt his religious conclusions to admire and gain
sustenance from the missionary-ethnographer's openness of spirit,
his scientific probity, his great loyalty to a land and its people.

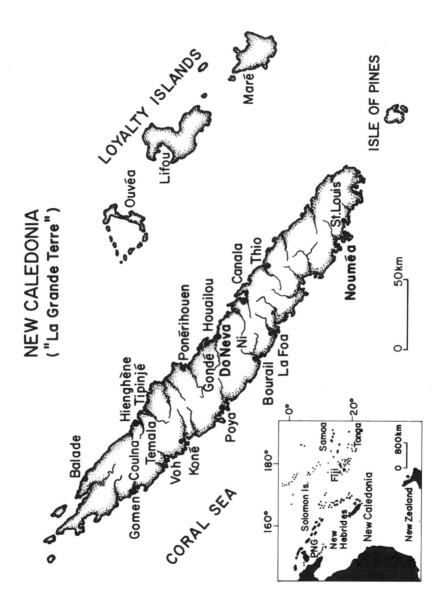

NEW CALEDONIA
("La Grande Terre")

LOYALTY ISLANDS

Ouvéa

Lifou

Maré

ISLE OF PINES

Balade

Hienghène
Tipinjé
Coulna
Gomen
Temala

Voh
Koné

Poya

Ponérihouen

Houailou
Gondé
Do Neva
Ni

Canala
Thio

Bourail
La Foa

St. Louis

Nouméa

CORAL SEA

0   50km

0°

20°

160°   180°

PNG
Solomon Is.

New
Hebrides

New Caledonia

Samoa

Fiji

Tonga

New Zealand

0   800km

PART I

Do Neva

When a European has been living for two or
three years among savages he is sure to be fully
convinced that he knows all about them; when he
has been ten years or so amongst them, if he be an
observant man, he finds that he knows very little
about them, and so begins to learn.

—L. Fison, missionary in Fiji,
    quoted by Codrington, *The Melanesians*, 1891.

We na a na Bao ro poe kamo roi merea re na ji
rai pani e ma, na wi a.

God speaks to a man's heart in the language
he has sucked from his mother.

                    —M. Leenhardt, "Lettre aux
                    Pasteurs de Nouvelle-Calédonie,
                    11 Oct. 1938"

CHAPTER I

The Education of
a Missionary

Maurice Leenhardt was familiar with proud, small cultures. His family, Scandinavian in origin, had been well established in the French *Midi* since the late eighteenth century. They intermarried with other bourgeois Protestants around Montpellier and Marseille—Westphals, Castelnauds, Monods. France's peculiar Protestantism, though it had gained legal status with the Revolution, retained the outlook of an embattled minority. Since the middle ages, Languedoc had been a home for heretics; it was a country of spiritual "springs," in André Siegfried's words, a band of rugged land where the religious life seemed traditionally "to have burst from the soil."[1] Maurice Leenhardt grew up close to this land, in a small pious world full of cousins, uncles, aunts, grandparents. Family loyalty meant a great deal to him. But he was affected also by the expansive world of the late nineteenth century, a time of opening horizons—geographical, cultural, scientific. Leenhardt knew both the support and suffocation of kinship.

His father, Franz Leenhardt, had been the first of the family to turn away from trade. Born in 1846 at Marseille, Franz spent his childhood at L'Isle sur la Sorgue in the Vaucluse, where his father, Henri Leenhardt, owned a thriving dye manufactory. After the Franco-Prussian War, the family business was ruined by the advent of chemical dyes and by the belated realization of their chief client, the French military, that bright uniforms made excellent targets. (The Leenhardts specialized in red trousers.) Beginning with Franz, the family inclined toward the liberal professions, showing, however, a marked attraction for the pastorate.

Henri Leenhardt had wanted his son to take up engineering, a career that could contribute to the family business. Franz was, in fact, gifted in science. But it was the biological and earth sciences that fascinated him most, and as a boy in the Vaucluse he was an ardent collector of plants, animals, and fossils. He followed his father's wishes until, as a young man, he became convinced that technology without

13

faith must be an empty exercise.[2] At mid-century, Wesleyan revival-ism had already swept much of the Protestant south. Franz Leen-hardt's piety was nourished by the newly fervent climate. He gave up engineering and decided on the vocation of a pastor, marrying Louise Westphal, a woman who shared his piety and aspiration to a life of service. His wife, an enthusiastic churchwoman, was a member of one of Montpellier's influential Protestant families.

At the time of their marriage, a split in the Montpellier church was becoming final. The group to which both the Westphals and Leen-hardts belonged was commonly known as "The Chapel." This impor-tant faction had abandoned the city's established congregation, "The Temple," because they did not feel that its rationalism, restraint, and general "liberalism" could accommodate the new winds of fervent "orthodoxy." With orthodoxy went philanthropy, social work, educa-tion, and foreign missions. More than a few individuals like Franz Leenhardt, whose restrained personal style and taste for science and philosophy placed him nearer to liberalism, instead allied themselves with the orthodox camp primarily because its style was engaged and activist. They felt it necessary to abandon the staid elitism into which much bourgeois Protestantism had settled since the late eighteenth century.[3] Louise Westphal Leenhardt, for her part, was a true mem-ber of The Chapel; she vibrated with ecclesiastical élan. A strong-featured woman with animated, sparkling eyes that Maurice would inherit, she was lively, enthusiastic ("Oh, comme c'est beau. . . . Comme c'est intéressant!"), and rather sectarian. Her son would later take a certain ritual pleasure in shocking her puritan sensibilities. Overall, the Leenhardt household was relentlessly high-minded and pious. This cast was set by Franz Leenhardt's somewhat distant, dominating presence.

Having pursued his theological studies in Germany, Franz was about to engage himself in local pastoral duties when he received an unex-pected call. The principal theological faculty of French Protestantism, located at Montauban, had decided that the faith needed to become closer to modern scientific methods and trends of thought. In 1875 Franz Leenhardt was asked to set up a curriculum in modern sciences for the pastors-in-training.[4] With some hesitation, for he and his wife were loath to give up the all-encompassing life of a pastorate, Leen-hardt accepted the assignment. Thus it was at Montauban, a small provincial city just north of Toulouse, that the Leenhardts made their home. There, on March 9, 1878, their fourth child, Maurice, was born. His older brother, Camille, was six years of age, and his two sisters, Aloyse and Amélie, four and three. Three years later, the

Leenhardts' last child, Paul, was born. Professors at the Theological Faculty lived apart yet in the same neighborhood. And since Montauban possessed no other institution of higher learning, the scholars were rather spoiled by the local populace, accorded a special deference. Franz Leenhardt fit the professorial image, for he possessed a natural *hauteur* and distinction. But Maurice's father, if distant, was not unapproachable. His children and students learned that, once questioned, he could be a patient teacher. If asked for advice on some controversial issue or personal problem, he would respond with a simplicity and directness that soon translated the discussion to its essential spiritual and moral plane.[5]

Franz Leenhardt was an eminent geologist. His doctoral thesis, a magisterial study of the Mont Ventoux region of the Vaucluse, received the French Geological Society's prize and brought its author the offer of a Paris University chair. Franz chose to stay at Montauban, a milieu more hospitable to his ultimate life's work, a philosophical fusion of theology with positive science. "Facts," Franz Leenhardt was in the habit of saying, "are a word of God." At Montauban his teaching was exclusively scientific. He exposed his students to a wide range of disciplines, from paleontology and physical anthropology to chemistry, physics, and geography. His chief concern was to encourage habits of observation and direct experimentation: "To teach them to see, that's why I'm here." He felt that theological students particularly needed to be brought to respect and understand objectivity. It was too easy to dismiss scientific facts, like evolutionism, as un-Christian. Leenhardt believed that theological speculation must always begin with the experimental evidence. The pastor-naturalist saw the material world, scientifically revealed, as God's expression, and he labored to communicate this attitude to the students at Montauban. His demonstrations were practical. "In any area whatever," he would write, "whether physical or moral, as long as one has not seen and touched, one's knowledge is of an inferior order, a dead letter, something learned by rote, faith in authority. . . ."[6] Leenhardt organized field trips during which he passed on the geologist's method of energetic and minute observation.

At the Faculty his teaching centered in the laboratory. The "Musée Leenhardt" was a well-lit room equipped with benches for chemistry experiments; the walls were lined with glass cases full of rocks and bones of all descriptions; a complete skeleton hung in the corner; there were tiers of specimen drawers for Leenhardt's extensive collection of fossils. After he had completed his practical demonstration, the professor would field questions from the students. Some were critical,

1. Franz Leenhardt, date uncertain.
Photo: Leenhardt

others passionate, for the relation of science to religion was becoming
an inescapable issue. Franz Leenhardt had eloquently defended Dar-
winian theory before the Montauban faculty.[7] In his laboratory, speaking with calm precision beside a row of plaster busts showing the
development of cranial capacity from ape to man, the pastor-naturalist
elaborated his views. Christian morality, he argued, is not old-
fashioned or in conflict with science. Its essential requirements may
be formulated in the language of the most modern of the sciences.
Physically, man is inferior to the animals, his body undeveloped, except for his brain, tongue, and hand. The course of evolution reveals a
tendency toward the development of "higher" capabilities, as man
learns to master his body and environment. Freedom is independence
from material, animal, dependences. The attainment of warm blood,
the progressive centralization of the nervous system—every development points towards a being who will be entirely master of himself,
will be what he wants to be. This, in short, is the moral goal set for us
by evolution; we fall short. But one man's example has opened the
way. This man, Jesus, could say "I am the father." Through every trial
and temptation, Christ remained "in full possession of himself, enjoy-
ing absolute self-mastery. [Jesus] attained the triumph of the spirit,
constantly and without compromise; he was free, truly free."[8]

    Franz Leenhardt's reputation among his colleagues was consider-
able; and his influence on his son was, from the beginning, immense.

As a model of scientific open-mindedness combined with unshakeable personal faith, he was an inspiration. Indeed, something of a paternal cult formed around Franz Leenhardt, observed, primarily, by Maurice and his younger brother, Paul. Paul, the family poet, composed effusive, religious lyrics in honor of the patriarch. And Maurice, even in his late thirties, writing from the Pacific, tended to address his father as a humble student does his teacher, dwelling on his own innate intellectual "nullity" and his inability to attain the "heights" to which his father's thought aspired.[9] True, there was a double edge in this kind of repeated profession of incapacity. Maurice Leenhardt felt a life-long ambivalence—suspicion mixed with awe—regarding eminent professors and scholars (feelings that continued even when he had become one himself). His own early academic career was a series of frustrations and failures painfully accentuated by the rigid lock-step of the secondary education system.

An anecdote, certainly apocryphal but still told in the extended family, recounts that Maurice Leenhardt, a troublesome student, once provoked this angry warning from a teacher: "You'll end up in New Caledonia!" In the late nineteenth century, the island's sole reputation was that of a penal colony. Maurice Leenhardt would, more than any other person, change that image. But to certain of his family, whatever his ultimate reputation as a missionary and university ethnologist, he would always be thought of as a failure and misfit sent off to the ends of the earth. Family reputations tend to be unfalsifiable. it did not matter that Maurice Leenhardt was, in fact, seldom rebellious or that his scholastic performance, though mediocre, did contain real successes. He was judged by a rigid set of standards and found wanting.

Leenhardt's difficulties began during his late childhood. He developed an infection that was discovered too late to prevent the permanent loss of hearing in one ear. His attention in school was impeded. At the age of thirteen he had to repeat a grade. His parents sent their adolescent son away to a Protestant boarding school in the Dordogne, and there, according to his later account, he engaged in his first serious spiritual questioning.[10] Maurice hated the various boarding schools to which he was consigned. This was his first experience of exile from the family, and during these months his missionary vocation took shape. Previously at Montauban he had listened with fascination to accounts by a visiting Moravian evangelist of work among the Eskimos of Labrador and the islanders of the Pacific. During the years that followed, the boy's "dreams wandered over white ice and blue ocean. . . ," an immaculate vision of opening horizons and freedom.[11] Prior to his boarding school experience, the idea of evangelical work was linked to adventure and escape. This was the heyday of Livingston, Stanley, Brazza, and the romance of exploration. But during this first long separation from his family, Maurice identified the mission career with a personal, religious need. It sanctified the pathos of separation and transmuted a general desire for adventure into an image of approved work in the service of Christ. It was through the idea of missions, Leenhardt said, that he came to love God. The idea provided a clear spiritual direction for his unruly, adolescent energies. While away at school he began to contribute some of his pocket money to the Paris Evangelical Mission Society.[12]

His studies improved. Back in Montauban he continued at the local lycée while pursuing a course of religious education. But school was never easy for him. The pace was too rapid; he was not rhetorically gifted and was a poor memorizer. Moreover, he was enthusiastic and enjoyed shocking and arguing with people. This bent did not help him with his teachers. By the age of eighteen he had already failed his "bachot" twice. The entire secondary education system was oriented toward this exam. In the late nineteenth century the Classical Baccalaureate was the mark of the educated bourgeois.[13] The students who could not manage to pass, or even those who took the relatively new and less "considéré" Modern Baccalaureate, were marked for life. After the second of his failures, Maurice was sent away again for individualized tutoring in a "boîte à bachot" in Toulouse. Here he crammed his head with mathematics, practiced endless Latin compositions, found his teacher uncouth and crude, and was generally miserable. His fantasies turned again to freer spaces:

> The weather here is dark and sad [the 18-year-old wrote to his parents]. It's the same climate [as yours], but to me it seems more sombre and unhappy because I'm living in a narrow street. This is the first time I've lived in a street with facing houses. It's suffocating when one wants to get some fresh air at the window. The houses become sad and dark. One is not so much melancholy as annoyed. Enervation circulates in the streets: the coming and going of carriages, busy people, school children, and beggars. And then one becomes enervated oneself, and thirsts for a whole sky, to see trees, expanses. . . .[14]

Maurice's need for nature had been acquired at the family center of Fonfroide, in the vicinity of Montpellier. The children spent their vacations there in the company of the paternal grandparents and a constant flow of cousins, uncles, aunts, and maternal kin. Fonfroide was a cavernous Neo-Gothic mansion built by Henri Leenhardt as a residence closer than L'Isle sur la Sorgue to the family center. He, and later Franz, retired there, and it soon became a family reunion site and symbol of paternal order. In an ambience of high piety, the children enjoyed considerable freedom to roam the grounds and surrounding country. Fonfroide was set on a gentle rise surrounded by rolling, open land, fertile orchards and vineyards. The ensemble of its buildings and grounds created an atmosphere of intimate space enveloped by a tall, light canopy of Alep Pines. Maurice Leenhardt's primary feeling for the proper "scale" of life—a habitat set in an open, familiar countryside—was formed at Fonfroide. "Nature" never carried the connotation of wildness, isolation, or retreat; it was an inhabited space, structured by social and religious attachments. (We may note, in anticipation, his "New Caledonian" orientation.)[15]

The anomie of Toulouse did not prove conducive to work. Maurice failed again. He was despondent; his mission career seemed blocked. His father, much worried, arranged for him to go to the pastoral Collège des Batignolls in Paris. There, while working on his Latin, he could, at least, participate informally in the activities of the Paris Mission Society under the patronage of its director, Alfred Boegner.[16] But the Leenhardts were somewhat chary of Paris. Boegner would have to watch out for their son. "Maurice," his father noted, "is very fond of art, and I would rather that he didn't, at first, have too much stimulation from that quarter." Boegner quickly inquired further concerning his prospective student's (dangerous?) esthetic proclivities, and Franz Leenhardt provided the following account of his son's character:

> You were concerned with what I said concerning Maurice's taste for art; it's not a question of the theatre, but simply of a preoccupation and exaggerated enthusiasm for works of art, painting, sculpture, and certain literature. But I don't think there's anything here to be preoccupied by, especially once put on the alert. You will surely have a great influence on him, especially if you take hold of him in the name of missions. But you have to know how to approach him, because he's quick to protest and gets his back up easily. You'll be shocked. But I don't want to give you the wrong idea of Maurice, for I'm certain you will become fond of him once you've recognized his devoted and cooperative nature. And anyway, what can you do? He's a missionary towards and in spite of everything.[17]

Maurice became a boarder at the Collège des Batignolls, a place he sincerely detested. The students' time was rigorously programmed; studies were competitive, long, and lonely. Leenhardt did not make any close friends, and—the son of an exceptionally pious family—he was repelled by the adolescent vulgarity of much around him. He yearned for a companion of solid faith and elevated sensibility.[18]

He was encouraged, however, by the contacts he made at the "Maison des Missions" in the Boulevard Arago, headquarters of the Mission Society. He was delighted to be a member of what was commonly called the "mission family." Activities at the society were eagerly attended, especially since they could justify release from Batignolls for an afternoon or evening. If the boarding school was suffocating, the Maison des Missions provided glimpses of an exciting, wider world. Looking after a table at a mission fair, Leenhardt sold and wondered about a collection of African "fetishes"; he was avid for news from the society's mission fields, LeSotho, Zambeze, Gabon, Madagascar. He was moved by the astonishing eloquence of two visiting Malagasy native pastors. He eagerly absorbed the experiences of veteran evangelists on vacation and wallowed happily in the romance of departures —young, dry-eyed missionaries on trains, the fluttering handkerchiefs of the "mission family" on the receding platform.[19] An opposition began to form in this thinking between the roles of "the pastor" and "the missionary." The former's more settled life might be appropriate for a person like his elder brother, Camille, who by this time was responsible for a parish and was at ease preaching and playing a traditional role. He, Maurice, would be the spiritual explorer who would sow his faith on virgin ground instead of pruning and coaxing tired old roots.[20]

Maurice presented a brave, sometimes combative, front in the face of his repeated "failures." But the specter of the *bachot* was to haunt him for almost two years at Batignolls, where he dutifully crammed his head with the rules of Greek and Latin grammar (confessing in a letter that he retained only the poetic "genius of the language").[21] He practiced endless compositions, managing to conjure up a real but, alas, "not very classical" enthusiasm for subjects like "Corneille's theatre is a school of the soul's greatness," a typical baccalaureate quotation from Voltaire. Finally, by July 1898, he had absorbed enough appropriate answers, rules, and flourishes to be deemed worthy of the title "Bachelier de l'Enseignement Secondaire Classique." His career was at last open before him.

꘎꘎꘎

Maurice Leenhardt's letters from Paris show him to have been a high-minded and independent, basically agreeable, and rather sentimental young man. A mixture of sublimated feeling and traditional morality characteristic of the period's brand of official romanticism turns up in his letters, especially those to his brother Paul. His parents need not have worried about the corrupting effect of Parisian art and letters. He read poetry, but it was that of Hugo, Lamartine, and Musset, writers already venerable; he did not seem to know of Baudelaire's existence; Mallarmé inhabited another universe. Maurice responded to the pathos of noble renunciations. His enthusiasm for Corneille's "school of the soul's greatness" found echoes in his own century—in books like Fromentin's *Dominique*, the beautifully written story of a romantic triangle, rich in evocative landscape and thoroughly moral. Maurice devoured this work passionately. "You'll find in it," he wrote his brother, "a natural, true love" and "will emerge edified, seeing [the illicit lovers] at the abyss, with fortitude enough to part from each other forever."[22]

Maurice, while warning his poetic brother to "beware of his facility," responded strongly to some of Paul's early verses. He praised, for example, lines on the flag. (Patriotic ballads were a popular genre after the defeat of 1871; Maurice was an ardent patriot and Dreyfusard republican.) He was moved also by a poem of fraternal communion within and with nature, responding passionately:

> Your description of the night on the plain we contemplated together recalls those gentle dreams and long ecstasies in the night, the harmonies one hears that calm the heart—Oh, you make me miss all those happy pastimes. . . .[23]

And so on. A natural, familial Paradise Lost was by now well established in Leenhardt's emotional universe. It is possible that he was never closer to anyone than he was to his brother Paul in their pre-adolescent years, before Maurice's departures, first for Paris, then for the South Pacific. Paul, of a deeper piety, perhaps, than either of his pastor brothers, was always emotional and troubled. He became a businessman in Marseille, a devoted lay activist in Christian social causes. A supporter of his beloved brother's evangelical work, he died young, in 1932, not long after Maurice had returned to Europe to stay.

Maurice, as Franz Leenhardt had warned Boegner, was "excessively" attracted to art, especially to the visual, architectural arts. His childhood difficulties with hearing probably accentuated this sensitivity to gesture and spatial form. The Louvre to him was a sacred site. The elder Leenhardts worried, perhaps, that their son might receive the wrong kind of stimulation from certain of its contents—for example, the works of Montauban's most famous son, J.A.D. Ingres (sumptuous, bejeweled nudes like *La Grande Odalisque*) or Delacroix's exotic harems. But their son was probably more attracted to the sublimated eroticism of a monument like the famous *Winged Victory of Samothrace* or to the warm, feminine tenderness in Da Vinci's *Virgin and Child with Saint Anne*. Maurice was especially moved by Leonardo, a genius of science, art, and, as the young theology student discovered on a trip to Milan in the fall of 1899, "a great Christian." Maurice stood for a passionate hour (dizzy with a toothache) before the disintegrating frescoes of the *Last Supper*. And in the nearby Brera Palace he was deeply touched by Leonardo's study for Christ's head, a photograph of which hung in his parents' dining room. "It's what the most elevated humanity is capable of dreaming as a model of gentleness, if you analyze this word not in terms of delicacy, but of firmness and goodness, energy and forgiveness. . . ."[24]

During his student years, Leenhardt thought seriously about the relation of esthetics and religion. He wondered whether "art alone might not suffice to establish the worship of God . . . for a certain elite."[25] In "pure esthetic feelings" he had experienced on earth the reality of heavenly "harmony" and "tenderness." These views, expressed in a letter home, provoked one of the rare long replies he received written entirely by his father. Franz Leenhardt cautioned his son against mystical elitism. The human world is by nature a fallen, imperfect world. Too much estheticism in religion (a reflection of late-century trends toward art for art's sake) could distance one from concrete activity in a corrupt actuality. It would also dilute and disperse the religious experience, removing one from primary communion with Christ. At this time, Maurice accepted his father's criticisms. He believed that his choice of a down-to-earth career in missions would protect him from the danger of estheticism.[26] But he continued to wonder whether the esthetic sense might not be the essence—or at least the earliest manifestation—of religious experience. As a missionary-ethnologist he showed himself willing to recognize authentic transcendence outside the person-God couple. And as an old man, in his last years of teaching at the Ecole Pratique des Hautes Etudes, he would return to his youthful preoccupation in his discussions of the phenomenology of Melanesian art.

In Paris, Alfred Boegner took Maurice in hand. A man rather like Franz Leenhardt in his high seriousness and simplicity of manner, Boegner presided over French Protestant missions during the period of their most rapid expansion.[27] The Société des Missions Evangeliques had been founded in the 1820s, a product of revivalism's growing interest in converting the heathen. The society was a nondenominational, multinational body drawing its support chiefly from France, but also from Switzerland, Holland, and northern Italy. Its governing committee, training center, and general headquarters were located at the Maison des Missions in Paris. When Maurice Leenhardt was preparing for evangelical work during the late 1890s, the society was principally engaged in two major African fields—in the South African Kingdom of LeSotho and in the upper Zambeze region. It also maintained a smaller mission in Tahiti. Around 1900 the society took on a series of important new commitments in Gabon, Cameroon, Senegal, Madagascar, and as a kind of afterthought, New Caledonia. These were years of enthusiasm for evangelism in the "Dark Continent."[28]

French and Swiss Protestants had their own Livingston in the explorer-evangelist François Coillard, founder of the Zambeze Mission. The vigor of his propaganda and personal charisma had brought him rapid success—measured in donations, stations, and staff, if not in the creation of independent African churches. He embodied an evangelical "imago" that never failed to move the faithful: the lone man in white, paddled by blacks up an infested African river, bringing the Gospel to lost souls. Coillard passed through Montauban on one of his fund-raising tours, and Leenhardt, an eighteen-year-old dreaming of missions, was much impressed.[29] But with experience he became suspicious of the Coillard style, which tended to center the mission on the heroic personality of the missionary. (Much later he would visit the Zambeze field and compose a stinging report on its failure to create solid local congregations.) The young man was more inspired by the example of LeSotho, the society's oldest field of activity.

The LeSotho mission stressed education in the Sesotho language and translation of the Bible into the vernacular. It also trained a large corps of African evangelists and teachers. Local congregations demanded and received a considerable measure of control over their own finances and the election of elders. The two lessons that Leenhardt learned from the LeSotho example—which remained, throughout his career, a model for him—were the primary role of native Christian pastors and laity, and a commitment to linguistic sophistication and translation.[30] At the Maison des Missions, Leenhardt was much influenced by Herman Kruger, a veteran familiar with Madagascar and LeSotho. Kruger liked to deflate young theology students by asking whether they knew how to pour cement or frame a window.

He advised mission trainees arriving in their field to "do nothing" for at least six months. Their first duty was to keep eyes and ears open, and above all, to become competent in a local tongue.[31] From Kruger, as well as from his father, Leenhardt derived the notion that mission work should be rooted in a "method." And as a student influenced by positivism, he believed in a possible "science of missions" with "laws."[32] He mistrusted the emotionalism that tended to obscure mission discourse, and later he would analyze the conversion process with considerable coolness and relativism.

As a theology student at Montauban during the years 1899-1901, Maurice Leenhardt edited the *Almanach des Missions*, a publication of the local "friends of missions" society. Once, with the "audacity of youth," he later put it, the student-editor dared "to challenge (though unsuccessfully) a missionary who in an article had put under the rubric 'devil' all the genies, spirits, and gods of paganism." In another article, Leenhardt mentioned in passing the kinds of questions that were beginning to interest him. "One of the most serious concerns of the missionary lies in the task of discovering what among the customs of the people he is working with can coexist with the Christian faith, and what is clearly sin." He concluded diplomatically: "Methods to this end are varied and controversial."[33] During these years Maurice cautiously managed to go his own way. There were no more scholastic crises. His relationship with Boegner and the Mission Society was properly filial. If abstract theological studies continued to bore him (his final exams at Montauban received a barely passing grade), concrete activities, editing the *Almanach*, training himself in gynecology and basic medicine, were more engrossing. He was growing steadily in maturity, confidence, and an appreciation of the realities of mission work. These qualities are evident in his extraordinary bachelor's thesis: "The Ethiopian Movement in Southern Africa from 1896 to 1899."[34]

The example of LeSotho had convinced Leenhardt of the need for liberalism in allowing the spontaneous development of African Christianity. His thesis analyzed the early struggle by the new churches to find a path of authenticity between nativisim and European domination. The core of the thesis was an attempt to pull together a preliminary narrative of the establishment and early vicissitudes of the African Methodist Episcopal (or "Ethiopian") Church, founded in 1896 by disaffected pastors of South African Wesleyan mission congregations, principally Manghena Mokone and James Dwane. Ethiopianism, preaching "Africa for the Africans," spread rapidly in the late 1890s across southern Africa and the Transvaal. The response of white missionaries and governments was denunciation and ridicule. Since they were ignorant of the movement's inner dynamics and were deceived by the apparent radicalism of its slogan, whites tended to see it in a purely political light. Leenhardt made short work of these explanations. Ethiopianism, he writes, is not a political but a social movement, and it is based on legitimate complaints against repression and discrimination. Leenhardt was the first systematic historian of Ethiopianism to attempt to understand it from within. He was dealing with a movement only just beginning to make its presence felt in newspaper accounts and the mission literature; thus internal documents were few and hard to locate. Leenhardt obtained some precious sources through the Ethiopians' black American allies. Otherwise he drew on small church newspapers and correspondence with various mission societies, German, English, and French. His conviction that European missionaries had something to be ashamed of in the matter was strengthened by the noncooperation of some of the groups to which he addressed his inquiries. The mere establishment of an adequate narrative for the years 1896 to 1899, following James Dwane's travels to America and shifting alliances in the Transvaal, was a considerable achievement. Nearly fifty years later, the classic study of

2. Maurice Leenhardt in 1902.
Photo: Leenhardt

Ethiopianism and Zionism, B.M.G. Sundkler's *Bantu Prophets in South Africa*, refers to Leenhardt's work as authoritative. The thesis, a remarkable achievement for a twenty-three-year-old, has recently been republished.[35]

While Maurice was fulfilling Montauban's required semester abroad, at Edinburgh during the fall and winter of 1901, he pondered his approaching career. Africa, of course, attracted him. But during the past year he had followed with growing interest a series of pleas from another quarter. A missionary was needed for the large island of New Caledonia in southern Melanesia. The Grande Terre (or "Mainland"), as it was called, had been a French possession for a half-century, its colonial history notoriously violent. Recently, Melanesian Protestant evangelists from the outlying Loyalty Islands had begun to proselytize successfully on the Grande Terre, an area only partially converted by white Catholic missionaries. These Melanesian evangelists were encountering considerable obstruction from white colonists, and they required the protection of a European missionary. The *Journal des Missions* carried their eloquent pleas, seconded by a French Protestant on the Loyalty Islands, Philadelphe Delord. This task, in difficult political circumstances and in competition with an established Catholic mission, seemed to require a mature evangelist of proven authority. But the months passed and no one stepped forward, for the Grande Terre had little allure, with its reputation as a land of convicts, policemen, and bloodthirsty cannibals—*Canaques*, they were called. Leenhardt began to investigate the situation more carefully. He discerned a noble work of social and spiritual regeneration. Moreover, the idea of a new field of possibilities in which he would have entire responsibility certainly attracted him. In November 1901 he wrote to Boegner, asking to be considered for the post despite his inexperience. The director's response was favorable. Leenhardt forced the pace to complete all of his requirements—semester abroad, thesis defense, final exams, ordination—in time for departure by the following fall, for he would have to arrive in New Caledonia before Delord returned on vacation.[36]

Maurice had already fulfilled one of his most important "requirements" for mission work. Before departing for Edinburgh, he had become engaged to be married. Although the mission society did send out single men and *"demoiselles,"* couples were preferred. In contrast with Catholic practice, Protestants offered the heathen concrete examples—presumably edifying—of Christian domesticity. More than a few hasty marriages were arranged on the eve of departure. But in Leenhardt's moral universe the couple was sanctified, and Maurice yearned for deep spiritual communion in marriage. He found in his helpmate a woman who shared his devotion to missions and who became the friend of elevated sensibility he had been seeking throughout his rather lonely late youth. At the end of August 1901, he announced his intentions to Boegner. (The society formally reserved the right to veto any "imprudent" marriage plans by its evangelists in training—a requirement for membership in "the mission family.")

Jeanne André-Michel was the daughter of a prominent family of Montpellier Protestants; her father, curator of the Louvre, was a famous art historian and member of the Paris intellectual elite. In his daughter, high art and piety produced a personality of firm taste and determined morality. Jeanne was orthodox but not in any simple sense a conformist. From an early age she decided on a course of her own. Her horizons had been broadened by the stories of her mother, who had for a time lived in Honolulu as daughter of the French consul. Mme. André-Michel encouraged independence in her daughters, allowing them a relative freedom that was the envy of their Paris friends. Moreover, Jeanne André-Michel was well educated for a woman of her time, being among the first of her sex to pass the ("Modern") Baccalaureate.[37]

At the age of fifteen, Jeanne was deeply transformed by her reading of Calvin. Thenceforth she would consecrate herself to a life of service, and it was not long before foreign missions captured her imagination. Her family resisted for a time this extreme adolescent predilection—which matched so well that of her husband-to-be. The solid piety of the André-Michels was tempered by urbanity and sophistication. They were members of the Montpellier "Temple." In fact, Jeanne, in her personal manner of restraint, *hauteur*, and directness, was somewhat reminiscent of Franz Leenhardt. Maurice and Jeanne adored each other. Theirs was a spiritualized passion nourished by a vaguely eroticized imperative of duty and renunciation—at once "romantic" and "classical." They loved one another with an adolescent awkwardness and a desire for a totally shared life. Their piety forbade any gross physicality. When Maurice Leenhardt later wrote of the Christian family ideal set against the "raw sexuality" of primitivism and of "that sublimation which leads to the heightened and pure love of Christian couples," he was describing his own marriage.[38]

Jeanne André-Michel could be intimidating. As a twenty-year-old woman doing charity work in a children's home, she stood out among her co-workers, keeping them at "a respectful distance," as one of them put it, and impressing all by her "moral superiority and the high seriousness she devoted to the accomplishment of her task. . . ."[39] Jeanne cherished intimacy and a certain privacy. Her sense of decorum

3. The fiancées, Maurice with   *Photo: Leenhardt*
Jeanne Michel in 1901.

was more easily violated than her husband's, and often she felt it
necessary to restrain him in his various enthusiasms. During their
fifty years of marriage, she had to appear unshockable, and she put up
with physical hardships for which her background in Paris society had
ill prepared her. Late in life she allowed herself dreams of a settled life
in a rural French pastorate. But as a young woman of twenty, determined, against the advice of all, to devote her life to God and
savages, she radiated confidence. By now her parents had given their
blessings to her vocation, though some of her family still thought it a
waste, as one put it, "to make dishtowels out of such fine lace."[40]

Maurice Leenhardt's ordination ceremony took place on the eve of
his departure in October 1902, three months after he and Jeanne were
married. The Montpellier "Chapel" was filled with more than five
hundred people.[41] Three surviving grandfathers of the missionary
couple sat next to each other. Boegner preached; Camille Leenhardt
intoned the articles of engagement; Franz and Louise Leenhardt received the congregation at Fonfroide after the service. Maurice spoke
in a confident voice:

> The Christian church seems nowhere so pure as in missions,
> where it finds itself liberated from the dogmatic political
> debris with which history has burdened it. Those who have
> just laid on me their hands will understand what I mean when
> I speak of the privilege of sowing in a virgin land rather than
> incessantly pruning sprouts from sick roots. And perhaps,

> God only knows, it is the young churches in pagan lands
> who will provide us with the fresh blood needed for the
> vitalization of our tired milieux.[42]

Four days later the young couple departed. The families bade them
farewell from the dock in Marseille—Jeanne, outwardly serene, Maurice, wiping away a tear, Paul, weeping floods.[43] The voyage to the
South Seas would last more than six weeks. In their baggage was a
case of materials for the collection of scientific specimens, prepared,
on Franz Leenhardt's orders, by the Paris Museum of Natural History.

The Leenhardts departed with hearts full of faith. Their aim was to
participate in the life of a faraway land, to consecrate themselves to
whatever might be the needs of its people. Perhaps they hoped, half
consciously, for a clean slate, the pure, open spaces Maurice Leenhardt dreamed of as a schoolboy. Many missionaries have desired
such a place, a spiritual clearing where religious life can be simple and
authentic, where the Christian evangelist can lay the foundation of a
noble edifice. Such dreams receive rough treatment on contact with a
culture possessing its own prior historical and religious traditions.
Nor do such dreams leave much space for a very clear idea of the
colonial milieu and the agonies of culture contact. The Leenhardts
were not naive, and they probably entertained fewer illusions than
most beginning missionaries. But one wonders what their feelings
were when, on their arrival in Noumea, the New Caledonia capital,
they were greeted sardonically by its mayor: "So what have you come
here for? In ten years there won't be any *Canaques* left!"

CHAPTER II

La Grande Terre

". . . A high wooded hill, burned, corroded brown by the sun. At the far end of the channel, flattened by light, the city, a cascade of zinc roofs. Here and there a coconut palm casting some shade. Flame trees show off their gleaming flowers. . . ." Thus a traveler of the late nineteenth century described the approach to Noumea. And so it would have appeared to Jeanne and Maurice Leenhardt when they arrived aboard the packetboat *Polynesia* on November 13, 1902. From some distance they could see the large military hospital, set on a rise, and the grandiose cathedral with its two towers. Across a spacious harbor, on *l'Isle Nou*, they could make out the low structures of the penitentiary.

By the turn of the century, Noumea was something more than an overgrown outpost.[1] After forty years of existence, it had become a sprawl of buildings spreading into the hills of its peninsula. The European settlement clung to an arm of land pointing seaward in the direction of Sydney, Australia, the first landfall, more than a thousand kilometers distant. As befitted a colonial capital, Noumea kept up appearances. Its dusty streets were named for Paris boulevards. Some of its public buildings had attained a certain out-of-scale grandeur. Atop the attorney general's residence, large and square, an ornate, pagoda-like belvedere perched incongruously. However, most of the area was covered with two- and one-story colonial houses, metal roofed, with shuttered verandahs. There were few trees on the streets and public squares; shade was in short supply everywhere. The various commercial depots and stores were little more than glorified sheds, and it seldom took more than a decade for Noumea's exposed wooden buildings to go seedy. With the opening of the new century, rat-catching was officially subsidized.

Apart from routine brawls and disorders in the port, excitement was rare in the small community. Daily existence was taken up with a perpetual routine of socializing, business, the circulation of political gossip. Periodic arrivals of mail boats from France were the chief events marking the passage of time. Occasionally a novelty would arrive, as on April 19, 1897, when the island's first showing of a moving picture was witnessed by the population of Noumea. The familiar personalities gathered at the town hall, a villa surrounded by coconut palms. In the bare *salle des fêtes*, where every fourteenth of July the same people gathered to drink the municipality's champagne in a swirl of gowns, uniforms, and bunting, a curious apparatus had been installed. The citizens of the capital gasped to see the flickering image of a train entering a French station. The effect on the spectators, we know from the local press, was overwhelming.

The population of Noumea was mostly European: businessmen, soldiers, functionaries, and their families. There was also the usual sprinkling of Javanese, Chinese, and Pacific Islanders. Occasional *Canaques* from the interior could be seen engaged in menial occupations. White prisoners were also very much in evidence: the island had been acquired by the French government in 1853 as a suitable dumping ground for the metropole's "dangerous classes." The streets of Noumea were dug through the hills by convict labor gangs. Its monuments, its port, were largely constructed by prisoners. In the interior of the island, parolees were encouraged to set up as small farmers.

La Grande Terre, 400 km. by 50 km., possessed good land for cattle grazing and the cultivation of coffee. By 1900 an official drive was underway to populate the territory, no longer with convicts, but with French farming families. Rich mineral deposits had been discovered, and in the capital the lure of nickel prospecting exercised many imaginations. Mining companies already disposed of considerable land and power. Inside Noumea not much was known of that unmapped, menacing area, "the interior," or *la brousse*. Denizens of the capital were more interested in the price of nickel and the perpetual political maneuverings of the Paris-appointed governor and the local *Conseil Général*. Perhaps now and then a shabby farmer, herdsman, or priest would arrive from the island's opposite coast, bearing news of a cyclone at Hienghène, Houailou, or Canala. Often there would be word of "troubles," rumors of an insurrection brewing. Then those who recalled the terrible year of 1878 would retell their gruesome tales of cannibalism and the war in which savages from the central highlands had wiped out two hundred whites. Noumea was a refuge, an ingrown European city clinging to the lower tip of the Grande Terre. At its back stood the forbidding, empty mountains of the island's southern chain. Noumea was not a gateway to New Caledonia. It looked toward the sea; one entered by boat and departed by boat. The capital could not have made a very good impression on Maurice Leenhardt. He learned to detest its hollow pretentiousness and isolation from the cultural and ecological life of the island. Imagine, having sailed for

seven weeks, only to disembark deep in the Coral Sea and find oneself
standing in a shabby Rue Solferino, Rue de Rivoli, Rue de l'Alma!

The new missionary couple was greeted by François Lengereau,
chaplain at the penitentiary and pastor of the capital's small Protestant
congregation. With him was Philadelphe Delord, a colleague stationed
on one of the small Loyalty Islands just a hundred kilometers from the
opposite coast of the Grande Terre. Here was the man whose letters
had first brought New Caledonia to Leenhardt's attention. Delord had
fresh news of the Melanesian evangelists whose work the new missionary had come to direct. These Protestants from the Loyalty Islands
were called "*natas*," meaning "messenger" in one of their vernaculars.
At Leenhardt's arrival the Grande Terre was about one-third Catholic,
the rest unconverted. Loyaltian Protestantism had led an embattled
existence there for six years and was making headway.

The Leenhardts' destination was the eastern side of the island; in a
week the coastal steamer would take them there. Houailou, midpoint
of the other coast and a Protestant foothold, would be their point of
arrival. They had many questions concerning the Houailou region.
Would it be suitable for a permanent base? Delord thought so, but
neither he nor Lengereau could be very specific. In the meantime,
during his inevitable round of courtesy calls, Leenhardt learned that
petitions were circulating among colonists in the hinterland asking
the government to expel the Protestant *natas*. These "foreigners," it
was said, were stirring up resistance to white rule and impeding the
recruitment of *Canaque* labor. The young missionary politely promised
to look into the charges. The Leenhardts were shown around the
immediate area. They did not, however, pay a visit to the nearest
center of mission activity, the large Catholic station at St. Louis just
down the coast. Relations between the two Christianities, though
officially correct, were in practice very hostile. The *natas* had too successfully challenged a half-century of Catholic monopoly. Leenhardt's
arrival as the island's first European Protestant missionary was a clear
escalation of the battle for souls. The newcomer already felt the tension. In the capital many potential friends and foes were observing his
performance. Would this young pastor play by the rules?

The Leenhardts were lodged in the presbytery. It had been decorated
in their honor by Melanesian Protestants. But it was not until their
third day in Noumea that they met these *Canaques*. A service of welcome had been arranged in the church for Sunday afternoon. After
the white congregation had departed, a crowd of Melanesians gathered, attired in their best—rumpled jackets, trousers, loose mission
dresses, and barefoot. There were short speeches, prayers, hymns.

Leenhardt's few words were translated into Houailou by a Protestant chief, Ounyna, and into Maré by Delord. The service was warm and, except for the incomprehensible languages, familiar in form. After the official gathering, ten residents of the Houailou region asked to meet separately with the new "Missi." The Leenhardts received them on the presbytery verandah and the welcome was repeated but in a rather different style. Chief Ounyna spoke on behalf of all. Then a large handkerchief was spread at the newcomer's feet, and each person approached to offer greetings, gravely placing a piece of European currency on the white square.

"There is a simplicity about these people that is wholly un-European," Jeanne Leenhardt wrote aboard the *Saint Antoine* as it rounded the desolate southern tip of the Grande Terre. Neither she nor her husband could say that the *Canaques* were a handsome race, with their thick, dark brows and muscular bodies; still, they had a grace about them that pleased her. Some of the Lifouans who made up the crew of the coastal steamer were more attractive to the European eye. These Loyalty Islanders, with their hint of Polynesian blood, sometimes possessed thin features and a pale skin. During the trip the Leenhardts were able to converse with them, young Protestants who had been educated in the schools of the Loyalty mission. They spoke a curious French sprinkled with English words.

As the *Saint Antoine* turned up the east coast, keeping a safe distance outside the ring of coral reefs, the mountains of the Humboldt Range seemed to loom closer. The Leenhardts could see why this long island was called the Grande Terre: it was an imposing mainland. Its two coastlines were quite different. Noumea's side was dry, sparsely inhabited, with mountains rising some distance back from the shore. But these eastern peaks plummeted into the sea; and further up the coast, behind a thin strip of beach and within steep valleys, the voyagers caught glimpses of luxuriant green. At Canala, two-thirds of the way to Houailou, the steamer carefully navigated a pass in the reef and entered a beautiful, fiord-like bay. As supplies were unloaded, words were exchanged in the boats—"Missi," "Houailou"—and frank, curious gazes met the two new whites.

Considerable excitement surrounded the Leenhardts' arrival. A Protestant missionary had long been promised and awaited. His presence now consecrated and reinforced the *natas'* work throughout the Grande Terre, a work that, for all its initial success, badly needed organization and protection. For many *Canaques*, the arrival of a "Missi" to establish a permanent station on the main island meant that the new "English religion" had come to stay. Its message of temperance, literacy, and social regeneration had struck a responsive chord in an increasingly colonized land.

The next morning, Sunday, the Leenhardts finally arrived at Houailou. A broad estuary and fertile valley were enclosed on either side by picturesque peaks—mountains owned, they were told, by the large mining company, "Le Nickel." A group of small craft appeared in the estuary and approached the *Saint Antoine*. In one of them, Delord recognized Mindia Néja, the most important chief of the region. Leenhardt had heard of Mindia, his personal struggle with alcoholism, then a dramatic reform during a stay with Delord on Maré. In fact, the colonial government had been threatening to divest Mindia of his chieftainship. But now, sober, influential in his kinship ties, he was supporting the work of the *natas* and combating the influence of the wine and absinthe sold by local colonists. Mindia, accompanied by Weinith, a Lifouan pastor and one of the first group of *natas* to arrive on the Grande Terre, clambered aboard the steamer. There was an awkward, emotion-filled moment. Then the chief, dressed in an improvised military outfit, greeted the missionary couple with a broad smile (Jeanne Leenhardt was struck by his "row of superb teeth") and invited them aboard his skiff. The group did not linger at Houailou, a scattering of colonists' houses, but continued directly to Mindia's village, Nindiah, not far beyond. At each turn of the pathway the crowd of people accompanying the three whites burst into song. More singing greeted them at the village. Almost at once a service of welcome was held on an open, grassy lawn near the tiny church, which could not come close to accommodating the more than three hundred who had gathered from neighboring clans. The three guests of honor occupied the only chairs. Behind them stood Mindia. Nine *natas* sat on a bench to one side. The congregation spread itself around on mats, and there was more singing (a bit too shrill for the newcomers' taste) and many speeches. Once again, the newcomers noticed in everything an oddly formal simplicity. The greetings lasted the entire morning. Again, a rectangle of cloth was placed at the Missi's feet and the speeches and handshakes were again accompanied by gifts of money. But this time there were also yams, taros, and chickens. It was a long, emotional morning, and the Leenhardts thought they sensed real joy and hope in the welcomes. Many orators spoke of a new dedication to "life" and to the "Word."

Delord concluded with a few well-chosen comments for the benefit of the five or six curious whites on hand—colonists, parolees, and the local gendarme-syndic. The new missionary's ends are spiritual not political, Delord promised. We Protestants are not interested in tribal

or governmental affairs. An atmosphere of political tension surrounded the arrival at Houailou. White hostility to the *natas* was not
disguised. Two Catholic fathers newly stationed nearby were in active
competition throughout the valley. It was already clear to the Leenhardts that the Grande Terre's colonists did not have much concern
for the well-being of mere *Canaques*. The few they had met who did
seem to care spoke of Melanesians as if they were children or toys.
Many repeated the Noumea mayor's dire prediction of racial exter-
mination.

The plight of the island's Melanesians was indeed desperate. An
ever-increasing European presence—penitentiary, mines, colonization—had shaken their culture to its roots. Leenhardt was already
familiar with the litany of disaster: military conquest, disease, alcoholism, uprooting, the relocation of reservations on inferior lands. In
two terrible decades just preceding his arrival (according to the best
modern estimates), the indigenous population had fallen by fully 33
percent. There were dangerously few children in the tribes.[2]

But Leenhardt was encouraged by the vitality of Houailou's welcome and by the hopeful attitude of the newly converted Melanesians
he had met so far. Their attitude, he sensed, was not merely the result
of the *natas'* recent work, significant as that had been. At Houailou,
and with each step deeper into the island, he sensed an essential
authenticity, a locally based, cultural resilience. Leenhardt was sensitive to landscape. His father's lessons in field observation served him
well. The rugged, mystical mountains of the Grande Terre recalled
the Cevennes of his native Languedoc, and the Houailou Valley, with
its twisting river, gently sloping hillsides, and enclosing mountains,
appealed to Leenhardt's sense of scale, to his feeling for the right
balance between cultivation and wildness. Under Mindia's leadership,
the social regeneration of the area seemed to be underway. Perhaps
Houailou could become the center from which the revitalizing work
of the Gospel might spread throughout the land. Its geographic centrality and the relative importance of its language recommended it.
After talks in the area, Leenhardt found that a farm was for sale a few
kilometers inland along the estuary. He decided to make it his base.

But there was no time now to do more than reconnoiter. A conference of all the island's *natas* was scheduled to begin in three days at
Ni, more than halfway across the mountains. The Leenhardts and
Delord, accompanied by a group of *natas*, began a leisurely climb on
horseback that followed the twists and turns of the Houailou River
upward through the narrowing valley toward Gondé. The Grande
Terre, previously only an impressive silhouette, now became an en-

veloping presence. Parts of the valley were occupied by native villages, many of them Mindia's kin. Some leaned to the Catholics; more favored Protestantism; others remained uncommitted and wary. Much of the valley had been taken over by white cattlemen's free-ranging herds. These half-wild beasts could be seen grazing on slopes still marked by their former owners' carefully terraced taro fields. Every now and then the palms and columnar pines of a village came into view. Leenhardt was learning to "read" the landscape and recognize in these distinctive clusters of trees the mark of a present or former Melanesian habitat. Certain of these villages, he found, were abandoned, their occupants forced by colonial expropriations to the higher, less fertile ground. As the group climbed upwards, the nearby mountains became ever more present.

From a distance Leenhardt could see Gondé—the village, or rather, as he soon learned to call it, the *maciri* (a Houailou word translated for him as "séjour paisible," peaceful abode). Near a bend in the river, at the foot of an impressive peak, a dense ensemble of palms and feathery columnar pines stood out against the open surroundings. At one end of the grove was a small rise upon which the clan, directed by their chief, whom the Europeans called Baptiste, was constructing a Protestant church. In his first published report, Leenhardt observed: "Baptiste is busy constructing a new church, with lovely proportions, and the enormous, unrottable pillars of the *pilou-pilou* house [the traditional men's house, or *grande case*]. It's the old story of Christian architecture borrowing pagan columns for the construction of its monuments." From this vantage point, Leenhardt could take in the area— the village spread just below, the nearby mountains, the curving valley. This site was to become one of his favorite places, where he always felt oriented, in scale. All at once the village in its surrounding valley became intimate and somehow meaningful. Later, as he developed his theory of socio-mythic landscape, he would better understand why. For the moment, receptive, he could only observe: "these people have taste."

Leenhardt was experiencing the form, if not the original content, of a traditional Caledonian habitat. The village at Gondé still possessed the expressivity of an esthetic whole. From the rise where the *grande case*, towering symbol of the clan, would once have stood, Leenhardt could see that the village was carefully arranged, its trees and huts laid out in alleyways. In the space created by rows of bending palms, he felt a gracious equilibrium. He may even have heard in the rustling foliage something of the *maciri*'s voice:

4. In the valley of the Houailou River during the 1930s, a few kilometers inland from Do Neva. the palms and araucaria pines show that this site was formerly a *maciri*, habitat, "peaceful abode." The village has been appropriated as grazing land for a colonist's cattle.

Photo: Guyon

> . . . Plant, arrange, coconut palms in two rows,
>   plant, you the younger,
> so that walking, we always see these trees,
>   as in memory . . . .
> So raising our heads and looking to their tops,
>   walking, we see the palm growing,
>   Weep,
>   Speak in its leaves,
>   It grows, it is very tall,
>   The leaves speak,
>   The palms speak,
>   Continuing the wind . . .

—a fragment from a funeral lament for a chief, and a favorite of Leenhardt's.[3] It is heard in a context of fragility, impermanence, cyclical transition between life and death. The chief's disappearance is traumatic for the clan. He is its "elder brother," who mediates with the power of the dead ancestors. A new alleyway of palms must be planted; for the coconut palm like the person is an eloquent but fragile plant, breaking in a strong wind. Though it was much later that Leenhardt transcribed and translated this song, the novice missionary may have sensed its mood beneath the trees at Gondé where he passed his first evening in the New Caledonian "*brousse.*"

Around the campfire the Leenhardts were charmed to find members of the clan singing Christian litanies combined with multiplication tables. The *natas* had brought basic Western education with their message of temperance and "life." Many set up schools and taught literacy and arithmetic. Indeed, "writing," "counting," and "praying" were commonly used as synonyms for the Reformed Faith. This sort of education was a threat to colonists who were primarily interested in an uninstructed, docile labor force. The *natas'* schools were frequently forbidden, and formal instruction was limited to Sundays—thus the campfire recitations continuing long into the night. Leenhardt in his early enthusiasm called them a form of "endless worship." Beneath the palms life seemed intimate, familial, orderly. Could these be the people of whom Delord had written, in a letter to the Paris Mission Society, that "family life" existed only "to a very inferior degree," the people whose "moral sense" he had called "degraded"?

Leenhardt, more ethnologically minded, would come to have a very different understanding of "pagan" New Caledonia. In *Gens de la Grande Terre*, he provided a systematic analysis of the precontact habitat, a densely meaningful space laid out in an expressive form that translated itself to the missionary-ethnographer in terms of an almost classical esthetic. A broad central alleyway bordered by coconut palms leads up to the *grande case*, a towering hut covered with an immense thatch roof, surmounted by sacred sculptures. Running parallel through the village is another alleyway lined with different plants. Every detail of the scene is symbolic. The main alley is masculine; the parallel one (in complementarity, not in opposition) is feminine. At one end of the ensemble, near the *grande case*, a hardy dry vine is planted, the *diro*, recalling the male essence in its continuity. At the other end grows the *doro*, a succulent. Dry is male, wet female. The couple is "inscribed on the earth." This union represents a joining of the two essential lines of cultural inheritance. This society as Leenhardt came to conceive it is not to be classified as either matriarchal or patriarchal. "Life" flows from the totem, via mother and maternal uncle, to the child. "Power" passes from the paternal ancestors or gods through the political organization of the clan to the child. Thus the coupling of male and female expressed in the village layout is not the meeting of two individuals, man and woman, but the patterned interaction of two constituent cultural complexes. Within this pattern a person is

5 and 6. The traditional village, 1899. "The round house is the house of life. Everything takes places there: sleep, rest, conversation. The grande case, so-called *pilou* hut, is a house which represents the strength of the group. It is the men's house, where they live together and receive their guests. The small houses belong to women; each has hers" (M.L., *Notes*, p. 6).

Photos: M. Devambez, Musée de l'Homme

the locus of a variety of dual relations, either with kin or mythic beings.[4]

All of this Leenhardt learned with time. His first impression of the Caledonian mode of life was essentially esthetic. He was charmed by the peaceful village alleyways:

> . . . Straight, smooth, carpeted with soft grass, bordered by bending coconut palms which are set out in regular terraces when the terrain allows, all leading to the summit of the *grande case* which dominates the whole—these alleyways appear as avenues possessing rare esthetic qualities of sobriety and design. They reveal the profound good taste and feeling for wholeness characteristic of the people of the Grande Terre. . . .[5]

Leenhardt's immediate sympathy for the New Caledonian "style" opened his eyes to the subtleties of its cultural expressions. And as the years progressed, he came to understand Melanesian life as a dynamic interweaving of nature, society, myth, and technology. The village was at the center of an ensemble, a surrounding "mythic landscape" where the notable mountains, rocks, trees and animals were familiar, endowed with totemic life or the power of an ancestor-god. Such natural bodies were not memorials or even representations, but discrete presences in which the living were implicated. The landscape was mediator between the invisible and visible worlds, an arena of "lived myth." The living could enter myth-times with—for Europeans—disconcerting frequency. The traditional Melanesian was a personage engaged in relations of participatory dualism with mythic "others."

Leenhardt came also to understand traditional Caledonia as a culture in transition. The most archaic experience, radical participation in the environment structured by totemic myth, was, he thought, giving way to a more "rational," more objective ancestor worship and an appeal to personalized "gods." The entire archipelago, even before white colonization, was a crossroad of cultural influences. The Loyalty Islands were more Polynesian in political structure and racial type than the mainland. Ouvéa had been largely settled by immigrants from the Wallis Islands. Loyaltian influence on the east coast of the Grande Terre was marked and increasing. Moreover, as Leenhardt pursued his ethnographic research, he became increasingly aware of a complex history of linguistic and cultural borrowings. The northern portion of the island showed evidence of recent influences from the direction of Indonesia, whereas the southern portion seemed more

archaic, perhaps culturally linked with Australia. Although each localized political unit occupied its own region and spoke a distinct tongue,
of which there were more than twenty on the island, there was a
continual process of borrowing and influence. Cultural patterns were
alive to change. The pace, however, was slow, rhythmic; and in the
late nineteenth century it was uncertain whether traditional adaptability would be able to accommodate the abrupt transformations
brought on by colonization.

Social life in traditional Caledonia rested on a system of matrilineal,
patrilocal clans imprecisely designated as "tribe" or "village." Within a
single linguistic area, regular patterns of exchange linked clan to clan.
The rhythm of gift and countergift included marriage (the exchange
of "life" in the person of a woman) and the circulation of goods,
services, and "money" (strings of shells serving not as value-equiv-
alents but as seals of agreements). Functioning in complementarity
with the totemic life force of the maternal lineage was the paternal
political structure. This "power" was associated primarily with the
ancestors, the *grande case*, and the chief. The chief was a nonautocratic
"older brother," who mediated between the world of the living and
the parallel world of the dead. His effective power was limited by the
council of elders, who controlled the succession (a role that the colonial
government would try to usurp), and by the clan's uterine relations.
In general, the small-scale political structure of the clan in New Caledonia was egalitarian and minimally hierarchical ("Melanesian" in
style, as opposed to the Loyalty Islands' more hierarchical, "Polynesian"
structure). Although a number of clans in a given area could be united
by a larger and looser "tribal" organization presided over by a *grand
chef*, the principal ties were still the direct ones of dialect and kinship.
These groups, varying considerably in size and coherence, lived in
semipermanent hostility, a state of "war" tempered by custom and
alliance. The colonial hegemony reduced, but did not eliminate, such
rivalries.

There existed, nonetheless, a marked homogeneity of custom
throughout the island. The life of every group was guarded by its
totems and ancestors immanent in the landscape. And everywhere,
the culminating moment of social life was the celebration of the *pilou*
ceremony. This important occasion frequently required years of preparation. Through it a clan expressed its vitality with displays of verbal
eloquence, dances, and ostentatious distribution of food and gifts. The
event varied in size from the regional *grand pilou* organized by a *grand
chef* to more intimate, familial rituals. The vitality of social life found
expression in the *pilou*, especially in its carefully ordered gift distri-
butions that consecrated alliances between clans.

Pilous and traditional marriage practices would present a thorny problem to Leenhardt and the *natas*. Could New Caledonian Protestantism preach social regeneration and at the same time oppose the most important "pagan" manifestations of social health? *Pilous*, especially their religious aspects—dances to the dead and other "savage excesses"—seemed the epitome of a tradition that could not be reconciled with Christianity. And the kinship system, though it was the principal guarantor of social order and personal morality, conflicted directly with the Protestant ideal of individual autonomy based on the vertical, person-God dyad. Before Leenhardt's arrival these obstacles had not posed a serious practical dilemma; the *natas* had tended to compromise without a great many second thoughts, grafting their new literate "word" onto existing structures, performing their prayers at *pilous*, and living as much as possible within the life of custom.

These Melanesian pastor-evangelists were the backbone of New Caledonian Protestantism. Theirs were complex, transitional mentalities; Leenhardt would often call them—inelegantly, but accurately—"pagano-protestants." In 1902 at Houailou and around the campfire at Gondé, he made contact with some of them. Before long, at the village of Ni, nestled in the highlands just across the watershed, he met them all as a group. Leenhardt's first *nata* conference lasted a week and included Delord and two dozen evangelists stationed on both coasts. Leenhardt was, in fact, somewhat intimidated by these Loyaltian Christians. As a young theological student he had read their letters asking for a missionary. He remembered lying awake at night wondering if he, an untried evangelist, might be the person God had chosen for this work. Now he wondered if he would ever acquire the authority needed to guide such men of experience, some more than twice his age. Already, near Houailou, he had stood mutely beside the deathbed of Haxen, an old Lifouan evangelist—sixteen years in New Guinea, now six in New Caledonia. During his last eight months, despite failing strength, Haxen had stayed at his post—until he could lay eyes on the new Missi.

Waina, Waibo, Mathaia, Owhan, Wakuba, Ipeze, Ninyima, Washitine, Joané: Leenhardt had trouble keeping the *natas'* names straight. Some were timid in manner, others seemed prideful and perhaps overbearing; towards him all were agreeable, too agreeable. Sometimes everything about them became suddenly impenetrable—their manner of speaking, the way they stood planted on the earth in their shapeless European clothes, the way they gestured, or remained strangely silent. But they could be reassuringly direct at times; and most seemed sincerely consecrated to the work. The *natas* were not Europeans, and the

Loyalty Islands had been Christian for only half a century. Sixty miles windward of the Grande Terre, these small islands had long been linked to the east coast of the larger body by ties of ritual exchange, marriage, and trade.[6] Lifou, Maré, and Ouvéa had been won for Protestant Christianity in the 1840s by Samoan evangelists under the auspices of the London Missionary Society. English missionaries followed to organize the young churches and begin translating the Bible into local vernaculars. English political influence soon gave way to French, but the "English religion" remained the principal faith in the Loyalty group.

By the 1890s, the Loyaltian churches were relatively mature. Perceiving the cultural chaos and demographic emergency on the Grande Terre, Loyaltian pastors (Nata in Maré means messenger) began evangelizing among the unconverted tribes of New Caledonia. Their efforts were initially successful. In the eyes of many Caledonian clans, embattled and confused, the new "Life-giving Word" seemed to hold a promise, literally, of cultural existence. It was known that the Loyalty Islands had been spared a heavy colonial presence, and alcoholism had been checked there. Protestantism took hold in New Caledonia during the years of the greatest expropriations of native lands and the highest rates of European immigration. The native evangelists were untainted by association with the immediate exploiters, and they knew how to adapt their Christian message to local conditions. The natas followed already existing paths of political and social alliance in spreading their message, and their initial appeal was in those areas where traditional society had been most damaged by recent white encroachments.[7]

Within each clan, the nata worked through accommodation with the chief, who often adopted the "English religion" for political reasons— perhaps because a traditional rival was Catholic. But since the political structure of the clan was not centralized and autocratic, the natas enlisted other figures of authority in setting up their young churches. The nata himself adopted a key political role (depending on his energy and talent), and he shared his authority with "deacons." These were not appointed by the nata or, later, by the missionary. They were elected by members of the church. More often than not, a person of established "pagan" prestige was chosen to fill this "Protestant" position—a jau (divine or healer), a kavu ("master of the land"), an elder, or the representative of an important lineage. Thus the natas coopted (or were coopted by) much of the deepest local, familial authority structure.

The early evangelists' message was simple: learn to read, learn to count, give up drinking, and attend prayer meetings. Among the sur-

rounding colonists, however, such a message was construed as an
encouragement to insurrection. Literacy, aside from initiating a profound psychological revolution, was an important immediate means
of cultural self-defense. It provided a useful method of communication between reservations (free travel was forbidden). It gave an independent access to the white world—to the religious power enclosed
within the holy scriptures, to the law, and to a wide range of the white
man's knowledge. Arithmetic was a check on commercial cheating.
And to reject alcohol was to disarm one of the chief weapons used to
keep the native population in a state of docility and confusion.

The Loyaltian *natas* were, to the *colons*, a new kind of native: independent, mobile, accustomed to operating in a milieu where whites
did not represent a crushing force. The Loyaltian pastors stepped on a
variety of toes; for if they were diplomatic in their dealings with
native political structures, they were perhaps too openly aggressive in
opposing New Caledonian Catholics and colonists. One of Leenhardt's
first acts at the *Ni* conference was to urge the *natas* to be more careful
in their dealings with Europeans. But he had no illusions that there
could be any real accommodation between basic conflicting interests:
"The *natas*," he wrote in his first report, "badly informed of the complexities of the white soul, have acted as they do in their more liber-
tarian [Loyalty] islands, occasionally missing opportunities to be com-
promising. In the long run they can't avoid this, for they will always
fall short of the only compromises which can appease a colonist—that
is, to drink with him, or to make their skins white."[8]

During his first weeks on the Grande Terre, Leenhardt saw his
feelings alternate between familiarity and abrupt disorientation. There
was an immense amount to understand all at once. On one occasion
the new missionary lifted up the end of a large gift yam to test its
weight and then let it fall log-like to the ground. A gasp of shock
pulsed through the crowd. Leenhardt had not yet learned that a yam
must be cradled like a tender infant. Confused, charmed, he would
keep his eyes and ears open. He was prepared for rigor and struggle,
but was he ready—he wondered in his first report—for the "delicacy
of evangelical work?"

CHAPTER III

Getting Involved

I believe that the Caledonian mission is one of the most discouraging there is . . . everything is nuances; the existence of the *Canaques* must be affirmed, maintaining tribes dislocated by forced labor; and one must not be afraid to find one's influence counterbalanced by terrestrial authorities for a time more powerful; one has to walk as if seeing something invisible.

Leenhardt was writing to his parents after three years in the field.[1] He had, by then, begun to accept that real Christianity could not be forced on Melanesians, but had to be allowed to take shape voluntarily in their "pagano-protestant" hearts. (In a later chapter we will follow the development of his thinking on the conversion process.) The "something invisible" upon which *Canaque* survival depended was a local socio-religious orientation capable of prospering in a colonial world, a world whose power seemed only to be increasing. People needed to find *new* ways *not* to be white.

They had much to overcome—to resist and, selectively, to assimilate. The colonial impact on the Grande Terre had been unrelenting, and for Melanesians in 1905 the immediate problem was simple physical survival. Colonization produced a state of demographic emergency. The best rough estimates of population suggest that there were about 50,000 people living in the New Caledonian archipelago around 1855. By 1900, only about 28,000 were counted. A recent authority speaks of a precipitous drop of fully 33 percent during the two decades after 1887.[2] New diseases took their toll, and alcoholism was used as a weapon by some unscrupulous whites. The disturbance of traditional agriculture aggravated problems of nutrition. Infanticide, use of abortives, and the simple decision not to bring children into a hostile world, though elements of the traditional demographic/ecological equilibrium, now took on dangerous proportions. The shock of defeat was aggravated by separation, physical and spiritual, from the moorings of mythic geography. The colonists had established a system of reserva-

45

tions in the wake of extensive land expropriations. Distinct groups were thrown together with chaotic results. Political conflict between insiders and outsiders was matched by generational friction between traditionalists and frustrated youth. The latter, if they wanted to adapt to the new conditions, found few avenues both honorable and legal. The immediate choice was between wage slavery outside the reservation and submission at home to authorities whose prestige had been undermined. As coffee growing became an option, there was potential competition within the reservations for the little appropriate land. In such conditions, political intrigue and sorcery increased.[3]

Leenhardt arrived on the island at a critical juncture. The years around 1900 were ones of accelerated colonization. The whites were at last firmly established, having defeated the bitter resistance of the preceding decades. For the Melanesian population it was a period of defeat, despair, confusion, and prideful resignation. "Just let me drink and die," the chief at Canala had told the visiting missionary.[4] Leenhardt wrote to his parents:

> We had been given the picture of a people throwing itself into the arms of a good Jesus; but I find little except the proud *Canaque* of the insurrection who, defeated, would rather not have children at all than see them exploited by the whites.[5]

The situation was serious, but it was not without hope. The crucial word in the young missionary's account was "proud." It recognized a recent *Canaque* experience of autonomy, resistance, and defeat—not of capitulation.[6]

⊃⊂

The early Catholic Marist missionaries, who arrived in 1843, were chased off the island. There ensued a period of "massacres" (Melanesian acts of violence) and "reprisals" (European acts of violence) resulting in the Marists' definitive installation, backed by the French navy. During the 1850s the missionaries warily extended their footholds on the island, faced by resistant warrior societies. With a few exceptions the early evangelists were incapable of understanding this viable culture in relativistic terms.[7] Their tactics included the usual evangelical repertoire of cajolery, eloquence, mistranslation, and death-bed conversions (the only sure way to send a Melanesian to heaven). In the early years of colonization, the Marists accumulated considerable land holdings and exercised what minimal European political power existed.

This pattern changed with the arrival of the penitentiary regime. With the penal colony came more strenuous administration in the person of Governor Charles Guillain, who held office from 1862 until 1870. This energetic naval commander set up the major structures of white government. He encouraged European immigration, and during his administration the total number of colonists increased from 400 to 1,300. Guillain also developed the capital city of Noumea, put down frequent *Canaque* uprisings, and founded a Fourierist *phalansterie*. His colonial vision is summed up in the motto he proposed for New Caledonia's coat of arms: below figures of a Melanesian and a convict— *"Civiliser, Produire, Réhabiliter."*[8]

As a result of the official policy encouraging *"colonisation pénale,"* a great many of the early settlers were convicts. Twenty thousand prisoners were sent to New Caledonia before 1895. They ranged from professional criminals to idealistic political deportees from the Paris Commune. (Among these latter was the famous *"vierge rouge,"* the anarchist Louise Michel, who during her stay became one of the first ethnographic champions of native New Caledonians.)[9] The prison regime was a mixture of brutality and leeway, providing for varying degrees of liberty for its inmates. Convict farms were established at various points on the island, and parolees had the option of setting up as farmers or herdsmen. The Catholic church arranged accelerated marriages between male and female prisoners (additional boatloads of women were freed from metropolitan prisons for this purpose), whereupon the newly regenerate couples were staked to tools and land. The latter commodity was not, of course, imported from France. Colonization on the island thus began on a shaky basis. Property whose title was uncertain was supplied to colonists whose commitment to the land was questionable and whose behavior towards its legitimate inhabitants was frequently, to put it politely, irresponsible.

The growing friction between settlers and natives was a major source of the uprising of 1878-1879. By the time peace was restored, 200 Europeans had been killed. Losses among the Melanesians are unknown but may be assumed to have been at least several times higher.[10] A variety of sources testify to the brutality of the repression, a series of campaigns in which the French made use of traditional tribal rivalries in gaining military assistance from Melanesian auxiliaries. The causes of the uprising were not in much dispute at the time. *La Nouvelle Calédonia*, the newspaper of Noumea, published the following cogent, though rather fatalistic, analysis:

The Main Causes:—
    (a) They are black. We are white. They were the first occu-
pants of the island. We arrived later.
    (b) Formerly the vast land was free. Now the stations move
closer together and the colonists increase to crowd the natives out. They revolt.[11]

The newspaper went on to list a variety of more specific causes,
including penitentiary land expropriations, forced-labor recruitment,
violation of native burial sites, provocation by colonists and gendarmes, and (an irritant throughout Leenhardt's long career in New
Caledonia) the devastation of Melanesian gardens by unfenced cattle.
La Nouvelle Calédonia's analysis of the 1878 war's causes has remained
unchallenged until recently. Modern versions tend, however, to view
the native side sympathetically, viewing rebellion as a justified response to aggression. Indeed, today as we read this list of "causes" it is
hard to see them as anything other than a justification of the rebel
side. But it is important to realize that in 1879 a dichotomized "they
are black, we are white" attitude could argue for policies of extermina-
tion against the native race. The confrontation was not, in fact, so
stark; some indigenous groups sought dignified accommodations with
the whites.[12]

    The rebellion was the Melanesians' last chance to inflict a signifi-
cant defeat on the invaders. Its defeat signalled to all the permanence
of colonization; subsequent "troubles" were small-scale and sporadic.
The uprising's long-term effects were to restrain somewhat the government and colonists in their impositions on the natives, who were
for a time regarded as "unassimilable." The administration looked to
convicts for its labor supply and then to nonwhite sources elsewhere
in the Pacific. The bloody conflict also acted to retard the immigration
of farming families from France, convincing people that the Grande
Terre was a dangerous land. Even a half-century later, memory of the
great rebellion was strong, a permanent feature of white colonial psychology. This legacy was a constant problem for Leenhardt, for any
show of collective initiative by Melanesians tended to be construed as
revolt and was punished as such. The colonists were nervous and, in
periods of tension, trigger-happy.

    By 1900, however, the steadily growing numbers and confidence of
the whites, combined with Melanesian population decline and disarray, had led to increased pressure on remaining *Canaque* lands and
more attempts to recruit cheap indigenous labor. The decade preceding Leenhardt's arrival was dominated by the governorship of Paul
Feillet, an energetic innovator, an anti-Catholic, and a man who, if he

7. New Caledonian colonialism: gendarme's station in the back country, La Foa, 1874.

Photo: Hughan

could, would have turned New Caledonia into an ideal little rural France.[13] Feillet, who held office from 1894 to 1902, was convinced that penal colonization was ruinous for the land. He managed to convince the Paris authorities to, as he put it, "turn off the tap of dirty water," that is, to end penal transportation. Then he set about "opening the spigot of clean water" with an aggressive campaign to attract stable families of French settlers. His goal was a rural democracy of small, independent landholders. His means to this end were brusque and not always democratic. Lands were required to accommodate the new families. All cultivable areas were therefore surveyed, and those particularly suited to coffee culture—the governor's favored innovation—were set aside. A new Bureau of Native Affairs began "regularizing" (and seriously reducing) the boundaries of the native reservations.

As early as 1855 the government, which claimed "sovereignty" over the entire island, recognized in principle the "ownership" by local clans of the lands they "occupied." All the words in quotation marks represented foreign legal conceptions and were highly problematic in practice. The principal effect of setting up native reservations was simple expropriation to free the so-called unoccupied land for white use. Over the next half-century, however, the reservation system, which instituted a tradition of inalienable collective ownership of land, was an important right for those natives who survived the traumatic early dislocations. The reservations were, at least, a refuge where clans could regroup. For this reason Leenhardt in 1902 supported Feillet (who was also an anticlerical and political ally), believing that *Canaque* lands had to be legally established. He subsequently opposed any further "regularizations."

The reservations tended to be relegated to the poorer areas, rocky and unfit for extensive agriculture or high in the island's remote central valleys. Villages were "fixed," and a district system was established in which local rule was to be by white gendarme-syndics and by chiefs acceptable to the government. Melanesians were legally restricted to their territories, needing the permission of the gendarme to travel. In practice this permission was accorded only when a native was to enter service with a colonist in another locale. The terms of *Canaque* employment were governed by a system of indentured service, a regime designed for immigrant labor, one that Leenhardt would later denounce as a form of "slavery."[14] Restrictions on native travel were a recurring source of friction with local authorities. The success of the Protestant mission depended on freedom for native pastors to circulate and for students to attend school at Do Neva.

The missionary found himself enmeshed in a complex field of political conflicts involving land, labor, tribal politics, Catholic competition, and native education. In October 1903 Leenhardt became involved in the grievances of certain Protestants on the island of Ouvéa. In reply to official reproaches that the affairs of the Loyalty Islands did not concern him, he rashly replied that all injustices should be his concern. In the Ouvéa case he employed a tactic he would use again, a threat to publish the facts of the matter in France. This strategy attacked the weakest point of the governor, who was normally a career bureaucrat stationed in the colony for a few years only. Such tactics could hardly have increased the young missionary's popularity in Noumea. He was aware of the probable impact of his protests, reassuring his parents who had expressed concern over his "impudent" style: "No, dear parents, I'm cultivating a style which is always judicious and firm, with all the qualities I don't possess in my ordinary letters. And I'm beginning to make a habit of it."[15] The adopted style probably did not fool many people. Leenhardt was too evidently a man who could not always be counted on to play by the rules of cooperation among whites.

⊃∈

It was not long before the young pastor developed the reputation of a "pro-native," *"indigènophile."* Such labels, which were anything but compliments, brought with them insecurity and isolation. A tone of suppressed violence runs through his letters. This tone resonates with the surrounding context of social and racial conflict—where violence was not suppressed. Forced labor and beatings were frequent. And Leenhardt had not been long on the island when one of his mission's best *natas* was assassinated. In the letters we read casual references to "the colonist who has vowed to send me to the bottom of the sea," and so on. The danger was real. In the opinion of Professor Guiart, who knows the Caledonian climate well, Leenhardt's life was at certain times seriously threatened—not by natives, but by whites.[16] Law and order was far from secure in the territory. In effect, both legal and not-so-legal land grabbing was encouraged by official policies of colonization. Rivalries could flare into violence at any moment—colonists against natives, Catholics versus Protestants, official against traditional tribal authorities. The white *colons* and paroled convicts found themselves in a state of minimal law. Leenhardt, endeavoring to act as a moral force against decadence, was alternately enraged and saddened by the erosion of personal restraint he observed in the behavior of his countrymen.

Nevertheless, New Caledonia was governed by the French legal system. And the law was not entirely imaginary, merely difficult to reach. Although the Melanesian was not formally a citizen, he did, in theory, possess definite rights. With courage, pride, and perhaps the discreet help of a sympathetic Frenchman, a native Caledonian could sometimes obtain redress of grievances. Maurice Leenhardt had no choice but to work within this frame, however uncertain he knew it to be. A patriot, he believed in the ultimate justice of French law. Extralegal tactics were not only extremely risky; they were unthinkable. The colonial regime was not, in any case, monolithic. In Noumea there existed an informal network of possible allies—liberal, republican, anticlerical. By playing one local interest against another and by using influence in France, Leenhardt might oblige the authorities to live up to their nobler pretensions. He might also succeed in protecting his vulnerable mission while its work took hold. However, the rules of the game forbade any show of radicalism or intransigence, and Leenhardt was a young man with an instinct for honest confrontation and plain speaking. He had to learn how to be patient, how to compromise and act indirectly: his fifty years of effectiveness as a political agitator in a treacherous colonial milieu were purchased with an always painful restraint.

Leenhardt was fortunate during his first years on the island to be dealing with friendly colonial governors. Feillet was, in fact, a distant relative. A climate of Third Republic anticlericalism resulted in early

government support for the *natas* in their challenge of entrenched
Catholicism. The friendly governors, Picanon and Rognon, both tried
to impress upon Leenhardt the limitations of his role in the colony.
His work was spiritual and educational, not political. Native policy,
affaires indigènes, was the business of the secular administration. Picanon and Rognon tried to domesticate the idealist; their successors
moved to open harassment and attack. From the home front, too,
there was pressure not to get involved. The received wisdom of French
Protestant mission experience held that activity in politics was playing
with fire. Their long history of isolation and persecution had developed habits of caution in the Huguenots: "The anvil outlasts the ham-
mer. Concentrate on spiritual matters." Leenhardt rejected this stand.
It violated his instinct for a religion that participated in all areas of life.
He argued repeatedly against his parents' and colleagues' caution, and
by 1905 he was quite clear on the question of getting involved in
affaires indigènes:

> While chafing at the bit and pondering my tactics towards
> the government, I assume an elevated point of view with my
> natives. I show them that elsewhere we shall make an excel-
> lent tribe, and that the essential thing is not to be so con-
> cerned with a permanent abode here below. True. But I would
> think myself profoundly egocentric if I didn't try to get jus-
> tice for these poor people. And anyway, how can I, in simple
> everyday morality, oppose the natives' stealing of coconuts if
> I accept their expulsion from the coconut groves to which
> they are attached like mistletoe to its tree.[17]

Leenhardt did get involved and he was a stubborn agitator. But he had
to learn, also, how to ask for favors rather than demand rights.

It was, of course, impossible to separate "legitimate" mission business from political organizing. For example, what was the point of
teaching arithmetic without also nurturing the confidence to use it?
One day a vacationing student returned to Do Neva sporting a black
eye: "a [white] merchant had given it to him for pointing out that
9-4=5 and not 3."[18] Would this young man speak up the next time?
Leenhardt hoped that a general movement of assertion by Melanesians
was underway. He saw himself aligned with it, as did his enemies:

> 2 natives, day before yesterday in front of the Justice of the
> Peace, declared that they would pay their small debt to an
> exploiter if he would provide them with a bill. For natives
> there are no accounts; a citation is issued and collected by
> seizure, without bills. This recent demand is something new,

a fruit of the general development of which we are accused. And the merchant, Mayor of Houailou, said to the *Canaque* who asked for his accounting: "I'm going to denounce M. L. and P. L. to the Attorney General."[19]

There is satisfaction in this accounting to his parents, but there is also frustration. Leenhardt went on to predict that his rivals would have a much better chance of being heard in Noumea than he would.

In the capital the Native Affairs Bureau tended to be interested only in the most flagrant abuses of the Melanesian population. Its chief concern was for good order and manpower. Various thinly disguised forced labor systems were in operation aimed at coercing reluctant Melanesians to bring in the coffee harvest or work on roads in the nickel mines. The head tax, levied on able-bodied males, was designed to be paid off in days of labor. The right to requisition natives for public works (a right frequently and illegally applied to private service) was lodged in the hands of the local gendarme-syndics. It became a common tool of arbitrary punishment against which the victim had no legal recourse (a *"lettre de cachet,"* in Leenhardt's words). The missionary later composed a sharp analysis of this regime and its abuses for use by a visiting colonial inspector.[20]

The early honeymoon with the administration did not last long. Leenhardt's view of his work too often put him in direct conflict with colonial interests. Though he wished to function as loyal opposition, he was regularly forced into the dangerous public role of a subversive. This was particularly true in the years after 1910, when an activist governor, Charles Brunet, encouraged police harassment of the *natas* and the Do Neva mission station. In the Noumea press, the Native Affairs administrator attacked the Protestants, "who preach open revolt and keep the *Canaques* from working."[21] During this period the administration attempted to undermine Mindia Néja's authority as chief in the Houailou Valley by dividing his district into three parts. The two new chieftainships were conferred on men less qualified by lineage and owing everything to the government. This practice had become common throughout the island, and such chief-creating policies introduced new forms of politicking and intrigue into the already disorganized clans. A chief, as the government defined him, was responsible for order, and not the least of his functions was to provide regular supplies of indentured and requisitioned labor. He received a percentage of each laborer's wage. It is not hard to imagine the potential abuses of such a system and its corrupting effect on delicately balanced traditional patterns of authority.

Leenhardt resisted as best he could all moves toward direct rule, notably in the spring of 1914, when Governor Brunet introduced a bill that would have placed all clan authorities, chief, council of elders, tribal court, under the immediate control of the local gendarme.[22] (Fortunately the plan was scuttled by the outbreak of the First World War.) Leenhardt lobbied against the proposal in Noumea and in Paris, and his letters criticized strongly the new style of "government anthropology" that was being used to justify the measure. Brunet had argued that clan politics was in such a state of chaos that *Canaque* survival depended on the authorities' setting up an efficient tribalism and bringing order into "traditional" structures. The governor's brand of official traditionalism was suspect to the missionary, who was by now thoroughly conversant with colonial realities. The new plan envisaged a further "revision" of reservation lands to bring them into line with what the governor called the "true needs" of their possessors.[23] This plan could only mean further reduction of the sanctuaries supposedly guaranteed by Feillet. Although changes in tribal life were inevitable, Leenhardt believed, they could not be legislated by people who had no understanding of native culture. Customs, he wrote in a letter, must not be "frozen."[24] The life of culture is change—at its own pace and on its own terms. The government's brand of "applied anthropology" threatened Leenhardt's own practice, which was based on a sophisticated cross-cultural hermeneutic. His letter spells this out in a striking passage:

> The greatest sacrifice required of the missionary is that of his own culture; not that he should scorn it, but rather, it has to be taken as a given, so as to acquire a new one, a native culture—they'd call it prelogical at the Sorbonne— and this is not easy. We've accomplished very little with the natives because we've hardly begun to penetrate their mentality, to recast the data of our concepts so as to obtain concepts fitted to theirs, using our own notions, but purifying these notions, retaining only what is the human inheritance, not commentary by Westerners. . . .

A government's clumsy interventions may render customs incapable of authentic evolution or may cause them to "evolve askew. . . . For there will not have been enough critical judgment to develop in native custom what is properly the patrimony of mankind, and even to introduce elements which are new, but appropriate to the native mentality."[25]

One may certainly question the evangelist's ability to identify and develop the "patrimony of mankind," and one may have doubts about

the ultimate neutrality of this kind of cross-cultural humanism when
one culture dominates another. At the same time, one must take
seriously Leenhardt's contention that customs must not be frozen,
that they have a right to evolve, appropriating new elements. Leenhardt saw that as administrators became more ethnologically aware
they would use ideas of cultural relativism to justify keeping subject
groups backward and "traditional." The more the New Caledonian
government talked ethnologically, the more Leenhardt became suspicious. For its relativism was shallow, and its real goals seemed to be
the maintenance of a well-ordered, desacralized tribal life—with a
level of education appropriate for a docile proletariat.

There was also, of course, a direct political conflict involved. As the
colonial government became more active in tribal affairs, it came into
conflict with the *natas* residing in the clans. And frequently the Protestants' Catholic competitors would take advantage of the situation
to make common cause with gendarmes and the new "government
chiefs." In the tribes, Leenhardt wrote, "it's the reign of denunciation
and exile."

> It's gone far enough for the natives to come asking my
> help. I support them with advice and direction, teaching them
> to act on their own and not to be broken by punishment. For
> two years now the *Warai* and *Ba* chiefs have been sending
> their subjects to complain at the police station where [the
> messengers] get drunk. This time they've decided to come
> themselves. It's progress I'm pleased with. Naturally our ad-
> mirable sergeant doesn't transmit their requests; and since
> their former letters to the Government were ignored on
> arrival they are writing to the Governor by way of the law-
> yer, Brunschwig, who has already done so much for us. The
> Governor will know very well that we're behind it all, but
> we're less there than he thinks. We're in it only by influence,
> which will make him even madder.
>   . . . What will come of this crisis we're going through? I
> hope, more self-consciousness for the natives.[26]

>〓<

Everything the missionary did had political repercussions. He was in
continual conflict, latent or in the open, with gendarmes and colonists
over questions of land, labor, and civil rights. He cooperated warily
with the government's occasional gestures in the direction of native
education, mistrusting the official bush schools' purely secular emphasis, which he feared would rob Melanesians of their religious souls.

And he was, of course, constantly at odds with the Marists and their allies.

Leenhardt's relations with Catholics were proper—and intensely hostile. The relativism he was cultivating with respect to "paganism" did not extent to papism, not at least at this point in his career. His embattled Huguenot mentality saw the Church of Rome, especially its authoritarian hierarchy, as a corruption of true Christianity.[27] His letters are full of denunciations of the Marist's "intrigues," sometimes conducted in alliance with the Noumea government. (His opponents' letters to their own superiors make the same complaints of the Protestants, especially during the Feillet years.)[28] It is impossible to resolve the rights and wrongs of local cases in which the two contestants accuse one another of trickery and excessive zeal. It is clear, however, that the style of the two missions was significantly different. The Marists relied heavily on European staff; forty to fifty fathers were active in the island, seconded by a number of sisters. The Protestants depended on native evangelists and teachers. By 1913 it was admitted among the Catholics that their opponent's method was the more effective. A visiting Marist inspector's report, urging the use of more native catechists, cited without contradiction Leenhardt's contention that a single European missionary seconded by *natas* could do more and better work than an army of dedicated European priests.[29] But it was not until the 1930s and '40s that the Marists began to make extensive use of indigenous "married cathechists," and the first Melanesian priest was ordained only in 1946.

The Marist fathers were, for the most part, from rural backgrounds, simple, devout, tough believers. Most did not have the intellectual training of Leenhardt. To many he was, simply, the devil. His energy and skill made him a feared figure. But more detached Catholics appreciated Leenhardt's example and were moved to emulation. He was described in one of their reports as "not very popular with the Europeans; but feared, and of a zeal worthy of a better cause. . . ."[30] Leenhardt, for his part, occasionally recognized the work of individual fathers, those who protected their flocks from forced labor and land encroachments. Later on he collaborated with the Marist mission in obtaining legislation against the sale of strong drink to Melanesians.

In his letters Leenhardt frequently complained of the isolation his role conferred upon him. On one occasion, for example, he was unable to converse with a young priest whose work he admired, because (or so he suspected) the man was under orders not to communicate with him.[31] Sometimes he playfully made the most of his evil reputation, this time aboard a coastal steamer:

> I was chatting with an old nun, who just wouldn't stop talk-
> ing. So I very politely revealed to her my title. Confusion;
> her head bows in contrition; she has seen the devil and spoken
> to him with enjoyment. As soon as she could, she left the
> bench, and I didn't see her again.

But Leenhardt's isolation was a serious matter. On another occasion,
in a letter to his wife from the bush, he blurted out the accumulated
tensions of his public role:

> It's certain that when I'm speaking about the natives I'm
> doing so as a man who loves them . . . but my hearers don't
> see in me the man, only the pastor, the strange ecclesiastic,
> with a secular air, yet serious, hard to understand, thus Cal-
> vinist, seductor, perfidious sectarian, dangerous, agent of
> the devil, suitable for the stake.[32]

In the capital, anti-Catholicism had diminished. The Marists, numerous, endowed with extensive land holdings and influence, were well
placed to exert political pressure. Protestantism was still looked upon
as a "foreign" religion (a reputation that clung to it even in France).
Leenhardt knew how easy it would be to lose effective influence,
perhaps to be expelled. His role called for delicate maneuvering.

Once, while still inexperienced, he "let himself be caught in a trap."
In anger he publicly accused a gendarme of lying and was hauled into
court for contempt. Nothing came of the charge, but Leenhardt was
hurt and confused. He vowed never to lose control of himself again.[33]
As a seasoned missionary, he took on a more "Melanesian" political
style. Having often been frustrated by the fact that *Canaques* cus-
tomarily avoided any open show of disagreement, now he himself
learned to be agreeable and act indirectly. Much later he advised a
group of young missionary students: "When you go up to a horse to
stroke his neck you've got to approach gently and flatter; it's the same
with an administrator; he can kick like a horse."[34]

Leenhardt learned not to publicly attack his political enemies. He
went to great lengths to stay on his proper terrain (the direction of his
mission's practical affairs) while continuing to act in the *affaires indigènes* that officially did not concern him. A typical example: on one
occasion Leenardt got wind of a secret, illegal plan by a colonist to
acquire land from an individual Melanesian, who was betraying his
clan in making the sale. The missionary made no direct public fuss,
knowing that in the capital such a protest, coming from him, would be
discounted. Instead, he wrote naively to the governor asking when
the group in question was to depart from its land so that he might be

able to move the Protestant church in good time. His query provoked
an inquiry by the governor, who himself "discovered" the illegality,
and the people remained.[35]

   This sort of careful, "inside" political work became something of a
second nature to Leenhardt. In his private letters, however, he vented
his frustration and pain at not being able to denounce injustice openly.
Getting involved in colonial politics had its price; correcting the system's abuses presupposed an acceptance of the system's basic rules. In
the early century, the colonial relationship enjoyed an almost "natural"
status. It would be decades before colonialism could be called, prac-
tically, into question. Leenhardt functioned as a French republican,
champion of a French invention: "the rights of man." Later we will see
the full ambiguities and strains of the missionary's involvement in the
colonial world when, during the First World War, he will act as a
pacifier of native rebellion. The ambiguities are already clear to him in
1905, when he reports on his efforts, successful in this case, to prevent spoliation of reservation lands at Temala: "Land problems are
our daily burden. And it's one of our most painful tasks to be working
to bring people to Christ without being able always to assure them
their place on earth, and," he adds unhappily, "without ever being
completely free of complicity with their enemies."[36]

CHAPTER IV

Do Neva

The core of Leenhardt's work was the maintenance of a mission station and the supervision of a network of pastors and teachers. "Do Neva," "the true country"—so christened by a local chief—soon became a center of island-wide influence. The station occupied a narrow strip of farmland along the south bank of a large estuary. The area running back from the coast into the mountains was scattered with native reservations. In this large system of valleys the important language of Ajië, commonly called Houailou, was spoken. The *grand chef* of the region, Mindia Néja, was a Protestant; Houailou had been an early focus of *nata* evangelism.

By setting up here, Leenhardt was entering the thick of the fray. The combative young evangelist established his base on the doorstep of his Catholic rivals. The early successes of the *natas* in the region had, by 1902, provoked a Marist counterattack. Two fathers had been sent to the region, and the political maneuvering was intense, sometimes ugly. Protestantism's growing local power was actively opposed both by the Marists and by the area's colonists. Some of the latter had long had their eyes on reservation lands. Moreover, the pioneer *nata* Mathaia had set up a school near Houailou where arithmetic and writing were taught. He encouraged natives bringing their copra to sell at the store to take along a student with a slate on which to reckon weights and prices. This was unheard-of insolence. The whites, Leenhardt was convinced, cheated the natives systematically. Moreover, certain local colonists made a practice of sowing tribal discord by providing free alcohol and deliberately provoking interclan jealousies. When the Leenhardts arrived they were met with threats, along with petty harassments—refusals to sell Mme. Leenhardt eggs and milk, and the like.[1]

Catholics and colonists had good reason to be worried about the work of "les teachers." During the first two decades of Leenhardt's involvement, New Caledonian Protestantism was extraordinarily successful. In 1899, Delord had listed nineteen *natas* on the island, all Loyaltians. In 1908, forty-one pastors participated in the conference of Koné, six of whom now came from the Grande Terre. By the time of Leenhardt's departure in 1926, the number of active pastors had risen to forty-nine, of which fifteen were Caledonians.[2] By the late 1920s the island's native population had been largely divided between the two Christianities in a proportion of about two Catholics to one Protestant, a distribution that holds true today.[3] Much of the early adherence to both camps was partial or merely formal, but the achievement for the reformed faith was nonetheless considerable. A score or two of Melanesian pastors backed by a single missionary couple (who had only occasional European assistance) had counterbalanced a half-century of Marist effort.

The reasons for the Protestant success are complex, and a full explanation would have to take into account a variety of local contingencies. Overall, however, the timing of the *natas'* arrival was certainly critical. In the first half-century of European presence, native response had evolved from active rebellion to passive resistance, and finally, by the late 1890s, to a recognition of defeat that triggered a state of cultural disarray. Catholicism was usually too much associated with the conquest to win over native Caledonians searching for a specifically Melanesian way to participate in the new world dictated by the whites. The *natas*, Melanesians teaching a literate "Life-giving Word" based on a powerful new source of knowledge, brought to the Grande Terre a system of beliefs originating with the whites but not primarily identified with the French. Local attachments were not immediately threatened.[4] Here Protestant practice contrasted with that of the Marists, who encouraged converts to move their villages to the vicinity of mission stations manned by white priests. The *natas* brought their religion directly into the villages; they took up residence there with their wives and children, assuming a role in the total social life.

Leenhardt's understanding of the *natas* and of New Caledonia's specific form of Christianity went through various stages. At first he rather uncritically admired the pioneer evangelists. But as he began to know their individual shortcomings and to measure the extent of their compromises with "paganism," he entered a period of disillusionment and pessimism. His first detailed local reports published in the *Journal des Missions* were not particularly edificatory. They do not tell of dramatic religious transformations or depict the work of God advancing confidently. Rather, they recount a series of halting experiments, slow changes, backsliding, and many defeats. They speak of the need for ecclesiastical discipline. Leenhardt concludes that the mission in the Grande Terre has not resulted in conversions. The *natas'* work has been superficial. They have confused the pagan and Christian gods, have devoted themselves too exclusively to the social rehabilitation of the tribes without attempting to change customs fundamentally. To the extent that the *natas* have tried to make changes, they have limited themselves to preaching an exclusively negative code. "Thou shalt not drink, thou shalt not have more than one wife, thou shalt not make sacrifices to the totem. . . ." In sum, the *natas* have brought nothing positive spiritually; the *Canaque* does not "know Christ."[5]

Leenhardt was speaking with a certain bitterness. He had just terminated a pastoral conference in which his exhortations had met with passive resistance and incomprehension. This conference, held at Do Neva in early 1904, marked the end of the young Missi's early period of restraint. In the field now for fourteen months, he came down hard on the *natas*. Some of them had recently declined to support his attempts to intervene in traditional marriage practices. In his notebooks on the 1904 conference, Leenhardt records a number of instances when he is obliged to impose rules of conduct by authority rather than by consensus. His pastors are called to account for failing to keep Christian marriages independent of traditional rituals and kinship rules. Leenhardt outlaws what he terms the "purchasing" of brides (he has not yet understood Melanesian social structure with its reciprocal exchanges), and he requires all Protestants to break off any matrimonial arrangements made for them as children. Marriage in the new church, he insists, is "religious" and not "political"; it is none of the chief's business. As for *pilous*, church members and deacons must not participate in any way or they will be considered to have "fallen" just as if they had begun to drink. In the event of "*chutes*," offenders who repent are to be barred from communion for a year and a half. There is also to be a trial period of one full year between first baptism and communion (final church membership). These policies—Leenhardt lists them as "decrees"—were meant to counteract the lack of rigor that the young evangelist detected in Loyaltian Christianity.[6]

Leenhardt's mood of toughness was probably as necessary for self-clarification as it was for the discipline of his *natas*. The sharpness of the new "decrees" reflected an initial need to define the limits of Christian adapatability for himself as well as for his flock. In daily practice, these limits were continually being thrown into question. Leenhardt in 1904 could see that Christianization would be a very long process. The *natas* did not take well to his strictures, and the missionary wrote of "a work infinitely beyond our strength . . . not a work of conservation but of conquest."[7] Leenhardt was passing through a period of reaction familiar to most evangelists. After a first burst of activity and a hard acquisition of knowledge, the true immensity of the task imposes itself. It is also a point common in anthropological fieldwork. As Rodney Needham describes it, the ethnographer's crisis is "that sudden and dismal conviction of ignorance and incapacity by which he is afflicted when he has learned enough to see the complexities of his task but has not yet acquired the felicitous insight which will rescue him from his dejection and revive his resolution."[8] At this critical juncture the most dangerous reaction by missionary or ethnographer is a retreat into formalism, a forcing of experience into preconceived forms. The evangelist too often responds to discouragement by embracing authority and preaching the Law rather than the Word. The result, figured in the stereotypical image of the narrow-minded, moralizing missionary, is a destructive state of bitterness leading to denunciations of "these people," their "savagery," references to "heathens," and "the devil." Leenhardt was in a bitter mood early in 1904, and some of his complaints about obstruction by his *natas* seemed to be lapsing into noncomprehension. Happily, his basic nature was otherwise. He was steadily acquiring that felicitous ethnographer's insight, which he later characterized as "simplicity of observation and a certain lightness of touch."[9]

As a veteran, Leenhardt would pose a rule of conduct for novice evangelists: they should never forbid any native custom that they had not first thoroughly understood.[10] By these standards, he was premature in his early policies, for after fourteen months on the Grande Terre he had not yet acquired a sophisticated comprehension of traditional socio-religious structures. If Christian and "pagan" essences had to be clearly identified and separated so that any compromises would be based on policy, not *ad hoc* arrangement, these discriminations could not be permitted to take the form of a merely negative code. It would be disastrous, for example, to forbid Protestant participation in *pilous* without encouraging some other ritual manifestation of social cohesion. Leenhardt made this important discovery fairly early, and as time went on, he downplayed his resistance to the *pilou*, which as a large-scale political event was, in any case, disappearing under the colonial regime. He encouraged various smaller, "family" festivals while attempting to graft Christian contents onto them— "*pilous de tempérance*," for example.[11] By the next *nata* conference, held at Temala in late 1904, his mood was less legalistic than it had been at Do Neva. The young evangelist had established his authority and had legislated clear limits to Christianity's accommodation with tradition. He was now free to play with those limits.

>€

His Melanesian pastoral corps—however "pagano-protestant"—
never ceased to occupy the central role in Leenhardt's theory of evangelism. His own function as a missionary was to protect, encourage,
and, where necessary, correct autonomous Melanesian churches. It
was the community work of the *natas* that made the difference for
New Caledonian Protestantism, especially once the school at Do Neva
had begun to train locally born pastors. Around 1900, Loyaltian pastors enjoyed the advantage of being uncontaminated bearers of a new
promise of "life" and of being relatively knowledgeable in local custom.
This combination was well suited for evangelism. But looking at the
long-term development of specifically Caledonian churches, Leenhardt
saw that the Loyaltians' adaptability to their new places of residence
was limited. They were sometimes too aristocratic in their attitudes
(formal hierarchies being more firmly established in the Loyalties
than on the more "Melanesian" Grande Terre), and they did not always
master the local tongue. Leenhardt made it his first priority to educate
New Caledonian *natas*. By 1908, six qualified pastors were ready to
take up full-time duties. Some, like Boesoou Erijisi, Leenhardt's Houailou teacher and principal ethnographic informant, were members of
influential lineages.[12] Thus the new faith began to be articulated in
contexts of familiarity. Christianity, as Leenhardt conceived it, did not
require uprooting; it could speak the vernacular.

Boesoou Erijisi was the first *nata* ordained at Do Neva. He was already forty years old, a man of knowledge and experience, qualified
sculptor of masks, member of a lineage of chiefs, and organizer of the
last *grand pilou* in the area. The first impression he made on Jeanne
Leenhardt: ". . . nothing aristocratic about him with his scruffy beard
and heavy blackness, he always seems to be dirty." And she concluded,
"his pages of writing make quite a poem, but we sense that they're
done so conscientiously that there's room for hope."[13] At the start,
Mme. Leenhardt little realized how much her ethnographer husband
would later treasure the "poem" of Boesoou's awkward writing. Boesoou was not Leenhardt's only access to the vernacular at Do Neva.
The New Testament gospel of Matthew had already been translated
into Houailou by the *nata* Joané Nigoth, from Ouvéa, Leenhardt's
right-hand man for nearly twenty years.[14]

The missionary taught Christian doctrine and the Bible, using
French with a growing admixture of Houailou. Many of his initial
student-*natas* were as ignorant of Houailou as he was. Thus the early
teaching at Do Neva was less a series of lectures than a class in mutual
instruction; the approach was language learning and translation, the
content, the Bible. Even after he became fluent in Houailou, Leen-

8. Do Neva, first pastoral students, wives and children, 1907. Boesoou
Erijisi is standing at the far left.

Photo: Leenhardt

hardt retained this form of teaching—essentially a series of practical
exercises in the comparative analysis of religious language. At Do
Neva there was none of the kind of education that has, since 1950,
been ridiculed in the all-too-real example of textbooks instructing
African tribesmen on the story of "our ancestors the Gauls." There was
no exclusive emphasis on learning the language of the *métropole*. Students were taught to read and write in Melanesian languages as well
as in French. The goal of education at Do Neva was to train literate
Protestants who would live on the land and not scramble for lower
posts in the capital. Leenhardt was suspicious of centralized, secular,
national school systems. If education was essential for successful
adaptation to the new conditions of life, it should nevertheless avoid
being an entirely foreign intrusion. It should not create citizens who
could only exist as uprooted, nonreligious *évolués*.

    As government schools began to be set up in the French colonies,
the teaching of "savage" tongues came increasingly under attack until
in the 1930s all use of native languages in officially recognized schools
was forbidden. Throughout his life Leenhardt resisted this trend.[15] As

he understood it, one of Protestantism's greatest tasks was to preserve at least a few of the island's major languages in written form. He believed that authentic cultural life was tied as much to the life of language as it was to the life of the land. Dialect and geography were interconnected expressive systems.[16] If the important transactions of existence were expressed in a shallow *petit nègre* French, the effect would be that of a cultural, spiritual expropriation. The imposition of a European language would block the free invention of vernacular forms, a creative process that soon preoccupied the missionary.

In the classroom the task was to bring Melanesians to new ways of thinking that did not partake of the worst positivist tendencies of European thought. Foreign abstractions could only impede the processes of mutual understanding. The proper kind of teaching had to be almost impossibly subtle, intuitive, and precise:

> First, you've got to know excessively well what you're talking about, and it's as in art where you're simple only when you know your material inside out. Then you have to be sure not to lead them astray by talking of sentiments which don't correspond to their own. And that requires a psychology of which I'm scarcely capable. And many other things are required which I don't know very well yet, and which I'm discovering every day, for the field is immense, and our brains, moulded in abstraction, often don't understand any of this.[17]

This kind of teaching was an intellectual challenge and a method of research. In the "mistakes" of his pupils the missionary discovered openings that led to many of his most fruitful ethnological insights.

Sometimes the students' "misunderstandings" could cut very deep.

> . . . service on the folly of the cross and the wisdom of the world. But then, they objected, where does the wisdom of the whites come from?
>
> —from observation, free of superstition.
>
> —OK, but the original idea of identifying a thing [l'idée première de trouver une chose], where does that come from?
>
> —You probably think it's revealed in a dream the way an ancestor reveals to your father in a dream the location of a stone with special powers.
>
> —Yes.
>
> The other day Jesus was a stone, today science is revelation. . . .

Leenhardt is evasive, for the Melanesians have asked him a profound question. If truth is supposedly based on sense observation, how do you know *what* to observe; and if one is to be scientifically "objective," what is to be considered an object? These New Caledonian students—who suspect that their missionary's observed world must be whispered to him by some ancestor—are in general agreement with Alfred North Whitehead, who writing a few years earlier concludes that "The physical world is, in some general sense of the term, a deduced concept."[18] Both are critics of a simplistic empiricism. At Do Neva, a less-than-convinced advocate of "objectivity" is being gently led to accept the experiential reality of "mythic landscapes" and stones that contain "life."

At Do Neva the first school room was opened—Leenhardt stressed the symbolism—in a shed that had previously been used for dispensing liquor. Aside from small pastoral classes for *natas*, the Leenhardts taught the ABCs and arithmetic to small children. Class size varied in the first years from twenty to forty, not counting the bush schools taught by *natas*. Jeanne Leenhardt instructed a group of women in basic literacy and domestic skills—sewing, hygiene, and such. The Leenhardts' vision of a Christian "person" was based on the couple. They were concerned, for example, that future *natas'* wives be ready to assume leadership roles. Sometimes these marriages went against the grain of traditional kinship, and occasionally the missionaries championed the rights of individual women to choose their husbands. Generally, however, they tried not to get involved in local marriage questions. Only in *nata* marriages did they intervene, and not always with success.

Leenhardt jots down the following exchange:

"You loved Elia?" [a *nata*]—"Yes"—"why have you dropped him?"—"I gave him up because at home they won't have him."—"Were you thinking of Michel?"—"No"—"Why do you want him [now]?"—"Because my mother wants him."—"And you can't leave him?"—"No."—"On your own, what do you think?"—"Un"—which is to say a vague, "I don't know anything about it and don't want to know."

This is the pagan woman. Nevertheless, the Christian in her was very upset, unhappy with herself, wanting to cry.

Leenhardt attempts not to judge harshly the bride's relapse. He exhorts himself towards a sympathetic understanding of his students' transitional condition.

The great difficulty of the missionary is to avoid imposing his Western judgments, and to come to understand these nonexistent personalities, potential, and becoming. On one side, the pagan, social being, social consciousness, social will; on the other, the nascent Christian, the ego discovering itself, not daring to be free, falling back frightened under the protection of the social self, swelling with pride and relapsing, or else affirming itself, leaning on God's aid and triumphing. . . .[19]

9. Protestant missionaries of the New Caledonian Archipelago, 1908: M. and Mme. Étienne Bergeret (l.), Mr. and Mrs. James Hadtfield of Lifou (c.), the Leenhardts with Raymond and Renée (r.).

Photo: Leenhardt

The problematic relationship here between the social person and the individual person would preoccupy Leenhardt throughout his career. Much of his later ethnological theorizing was a reflection on and justification of his missionary priorities. However, he would come to understand what is presented here (an opposition between social paganism and the Christian "ego") less as a sequence of evolutionary stages and more as a problem of mediation in any life of personal authenticity. This is to anticipate. As an evangelist he was preoccupied with encouraging the emergence of—as he later put it—the "person" from the "personage."

>€

Do Neva, for much of the year, was a village filled with students and their dependents from various parts of the island. The station stretched for a few kilometers in a narrow band between the estuary shore and the mountains. It was divided into two parts, with the school, church, and missionary residences separated from the student village by a large field used for gatherings and sporting events. The Melanesian section was called Guilgal, from the Old Testament Book of Joshua, referring to the sacred camp made of twelve stones pitched in a circle after the crossing of the Red Sea. Do Neva's student village was, in fact, set in an amphitheatre of rocky mountains. (In New Caledonia, as in the Old Testament, stones embody mythic meanings.) The busy mission station had to produce its own food on land that was barely adequate and subject to occasional flooding. All were required to pitch in and work. Day students from the area had to provide their own food. Leenhardt rejected any enticement of people to the station by using handouts of food or trade goods. The mission had little extra for the purchase of equipment or supplies. Nearly everything was built or repaired on the spot. The missionary found that he had to be competent in a score of trades: carpentry, agronomy, masonry, midwifery, medicine, animal husbandry.

The Leenhardts did not encourage permanent settlement at the station, and there was a great deal of coming and going. Do Neva was designed to be a center from which influence would radiate and a refuge where Protestants could come for aid. The concept of a single mission station was important to Leenhardt. Later he protested vehemently when a European colleague sought to establish a separate station.[20] As a matter of evangelical method, Leenhardt avoided the multiplication of white bases, for he thought that they tended to inhibit the development of autonomous, self-reliant Melanesian churches.

The missionary himself traveled into the remote mountain valleys to visit the *natas* in their villages. When duties at Do Neva kept him at home, he corresponded with them by letter. He used the Houailou language whenever possible, for mail was not safe from white curiosity. The trips *en brousse* were arduous but enjoyable. Leenhardt traveled on horseback, borrowing mounts along the way, fording flooded rivers during the rainy season, threading his way along precipitous trails into the high country. (Later on, he acquired a five-meter motor launch for coastal trips.) Sometimes he would receive a complaint from a *nata* about harassment by colonists or problems of interclan politics, and he would have to hurry to the scene to verify the facts before taking action—a letter to the administration in Noumea perhaps, a protest at the local *gendarmerie*, a talk with a chief. In his routine evangelical practice, Leenhardt did not attempt to "conquer" unconverted clans. Rather, he sought primarily to protect and encourage existing churches, relying on the force of example to bring others into the fold. With some frequency during these years, local chiefs would ask for a *nata* to come live with them. Backed up now by an energetic Missi, a *nata* could be an important political auxiliary.

On his *tournées*, Leenhardt took with him maps of the areas he was going to pass through, not to find his way around but to show the people he visited the legal limits of their territories. There was much confusion on this score, following the series of drastic revisions by the Feillet government. Many clans did not know where their lands officially ended and thus were prey to the encroachments of neighboring colonists, particularly cattlemen. The defense of even the reduced native holdings required constant, informed vigilance. On tour Leenhardt also dispensed advice on prophylactic medicine, hygiene, and the proper use of clothing. And in this he was not always a "modernist"; he thought, for example, that the old round dwellings were superior in cold weather to the square houses coming into use, new structures that the administration would later urge upon the natives. Everywhere he preached temperance, not only with respect to alcohol but also in the use of coffee and, of course, abortives. A principal text in all his exhortations was "be fruitful and multiply."

These *tournées* in the bush were exhausting; they lasted from a few days to a week or more. They included all the inevitable frustrations of missed rendezvous, flooded roads, long days and sometimes nights in the saddle. Leenhardt usually slept in the native village (occasionally there was a choice between this and the bed of a hospitable colonist). He camped in odd places and ate whatever food was on hand. There were limits to his adaptability. Modest, he later had privies built in frequently visited locations. (And he found them always spotless, for no one seemed to appreciate these outposts of progress except the missionary on tour!) The reward from all the travel was a growing knowledge of the island's ethnic and political history. And Leenhardt's affection for the land deepened. He appreciated its vistas and intimate rhythms. The missionary knew also how to savor village life: "I great-

ly enjoyed myself chatting all evening around the fire, in the midst of
tall sugarcanes. Shame on those who call *Canaque* life dumb, and have
never partaken."[21]

But it was always with joy that the traveler returned to his mission
station. "Home" is a possible translation for "Do Neva"—the place to
which one feels most authentically attached. The Leenhardts set about
to create such a place, beginning with the farmhouse they had acquired
with their land. It was to be filled with beautiful things.[22] The aesthet-
ics of the station were never secondary. New buildings had to be well
proportioned and constructed using the best techniques and materials
possible, for the station was to be a display of quality and peace in the
midst of the surrounding colonial ugliness.

Here the Leenhardts began their family. In 1903 Raymond was
born; three sisters followed, Renée, Stella, Francine, and a fourth,
Roselène, in 1919. Raising the children along with looking after the
extended family of students and visitors was a demanding task for
Jeanne Leenhardt, requiring all her considerable dedication and talent
for organization. Life was full and often chaotic. The only moments
available for letter writing or for any serious consecutive thought
were early in the morning or late at night. The rest of the day was
occupied by a full routine, punctuated by the usual distractions and
emergencies. Maurice was an early riser. He cherished the hour before
6 A.M., when the station was silent, when he could reflect calmly and
strive to rise above the struggle. Once the morning bell had sounded
there would be no stopping. The educational program, when in ses-
sion, included an elementary class, taught with the help of a Melanesian monitor, theological discussions with the pastoral students,
and a girls' elementary class. The afternoon was devoted to various
work projects around the station, pastoral consultations, perhaps a
trip into Houailou to pick up supplies or a telegram, or to remonstrate
with the gendarme about some dispute in the valley. Frequently the
day was taken up by visits to nearby tribes or a longer ride into the
mountains. At dinner time the family discussed the day's events. There
would also be conversation, for the children's benefit, on subjects
lacking in the *culture générale*: classical authors, art, literature. The
Leenhardts were terribly worried that the children's education would
fall behind that of their cousins on the other side of the world. And
feeling themselves surrounded by colonial shabbiness and degeneracy,
they sought renewed contact with the nobler, purer expressions of
Western culture.

With sunset there might be a moment of repose, an opportunity for
games or a walk down to the estuary. But evenings were also occupied

with mission business: reading, writing, corresponding with *natas* in the field. This was the time that students or members of the surrounding clans felt free to tap on Missi's window and consult with him in his office on tribal problems, personal complaints, and dilemmas. Since most travel beyond the reservations was legally forbidden, it was sometimes only under cover of darkness that such interviews could take place. Through the closed door of Leenhardt's study, the family in the parlor, or in bed, would catch snatches of French and Houailou.

When the daily routine went smoothly, which it occasionally did, the mood was of fullness and calm. But there were frequent periods of tension, times of open war with the local gendarme, or moments when the threat of rebellion hung in the air, as in 1917-1918. There were also devastating cyclones, difficult births at Guilgal, and illnesses. As a little girl, Stella Leenhardt nearly died of fever. No doctor was available, and for days her parents, self-trained in medicine, remained in an agony of suspense—horribly unsure of their remedy.

The children's only playmates were Melanesian: students and the children of pastoral candidates. Raymond was physically weak as a child; but to his father's delight he acquired a number of frontier skills—horsemanship, fishing with a bow, slaughtering a pig, speaking Houailou. His early ambition, Maurice reported to the grandparents, was to become a herdsman or boat captain. His sister Renée recalls, with a certain nostalgia, a vast station full of friends with whom she climbed about on the mountainside, fished in the river, rode horseback, worked in the kitchen garden, practiced dressmaking—a life rich in human contacts and experience. Once she roasted and ate a spider captured on the mountain. What could be more natural? Her father was disgusted. The Leenhardts worried about the effects of too much local influence; the children studied a correspondence course under the watchful eye of their mother. Their day was disciplined. But there were frequent exciting interruptions. Once during a tropical storm as the children sat studying on the enclosed verandah, they watched a glowing ball of lightning slide down the side of the house. And there was the ever-thrilling moment of Papa's return from a tour in the back country. The scholars might look up from their books to see him spur his horse into a gallop up the avenue of trees leading towards the house. (He was exuberant and a good horseman.) There were also "mail events," when correspondence from Europe arrived and everything stopped for the eager reading of letters or the opening of a package. Once a rather large parcel was found to contain a plaster replica of the *Winged Victory of Samothrace*, sent out by Grandfather

10. The farm at Do Neva. Milking the cow is Tnein, chief of Coulna;
Raymond Leenhardt stands beside him; Francine Leenhardt is held by
Laura, future wife of the chief of Poyes, Kowy Bouillant.

Photo: Leenhardt

André-Michel. Henceforth this symbol of the Louvre and classical
culture presided over the dining room discussions.

"I'll never have the silhouette of a saint," Leenhardt wrote to his
parents in 1914, thinking perhaps of his father's ethereal presence.[23]
Maurice was a heavy man of medium height whose body was influenced by changes of climate. In two months of heat and humidity, he
reported, his weight rose from 107 to 112 kilos. He carried himself
well, however, and possessed an iron constitution rarely immobilized
by sickness. He wore out white colleagues when he took them with
him on horseback and walking tours. His essence was movement,
activity. His letters show this. They are written in bits and pieces, in
the pre-dawn hours, on a boat's moving deck, beside a campfire. They
are constantly interrupted; occasionally Jeanne will finish a sentence
her husband has begun. The letters hurry with their author from
carpentry to theology, from family counseling to the preparation of
legal documents and Houailou translations. The present account, arranged thematically, smoothes over this confusing cascade of
existence.

Against some of his colleagues, Leenhardt defended the ideal of a "total" missionary practice. For example, when one of his temporary helpers at Do Neva complained of having to waste an advanced theological training in the teaching of the ABCs, he responded:

> When I make writing models for the children I suffer from how terrible they are, since I'm no good at printing; but I don't feel any less a missionary than when I'm explaining the mystery of the cross . . . or directing the *natas*, or building a house, or writing to the governor. . . .[24]

There is an extraordinary overall serenity in Leenhardt's accounts of his hectic comings and goings, a sense that every small task is somehow part of "the work." His use of the term suggests that he feels himself part of a larger process transcending any personal setbacks and victories. There are, of course, periods of anger and frustration. One of Leenhardt's hardest tasks is learning simply to hold his temper. He sometimes describes himself as a soldier fighting "with calm in his face, but his heart deep in anguish, pressed close to his God." We have seen the self-control required by his political role in the colony. "There are moments," he would recall later, "in one's struggles with the administration when the bad faith is so great that you have only one recourse left: you withdraw for a moment, close your door, and fall on your knees until calm returns, and through God's strength you feel yourself once more in command of the situation."[25] The letters home undoubtedly helped as outlets. And Leenhardt's anger and crises of morale seem not to last very long; the fundamental, innate optimism always returns. One's general impression is of a mature man who has found an encompassing activity and landscape, a *"do neva."* He moves in its field of involvements, social, religious, familial, ecological. He is needed.

It is difficult to form a clear image. Many who knew Leenhardt recall his booming laugh and lively eyes. But the surviving snapshots from Do Neva are posed and faded. We see the first class of *natas*, sitting stiffly in a row, buttoned up to the neck, barefoot. Boesoou's face is expressionless. Jeanne is thin in her plain dress and high boots, her head inclined wistfully to one side. Maurice, amply bearded, wears a rumpled white suit and sometimes a gigantic pith helmet (later, a broad, black hat). We see an intense bear-like individual leaning slightly forward, as if listening hard.

CHAPTER V

Translations

By 1908, the end of his first sojourn in New Caledonia, Leenhardt was in command of the situation and of himself. The struggling schoolboy was now a confident, open-minded man of thirty. He had exercised authority and had learned to be patient. Most important, he had avoided that defensive narrowness that haunts mission work. The long training process over, he was ready to learn what evangelism at its most authentic had to teach. His continuing education took the form of a long series of conversations with the people of the Grande Terre. Later Leenhardt would call the experience—when speaking of his qualifications as professor of ethnology—his "*Canaque* humanities."

The missionary's first vacation in Europe was important for his intellectual development. It gave him the freedom to reflect on the long-term work in New Caledonia from outside the fray. He composed an 80-page illustrated booklet designed to acquaint the faithful at home with the specifics of his mission.[1] It was badly needed, for the Paris Mission Society tended to ignore the Grande Terre. Throughout his mission tenure, Leenhardt would complain of the directorate's neglect, bias towards its African fields, and tendency to lump the work of the Grande Terre with that of the Loyalty Islands. (The two churches had been built on dissimilar cultural traditions and were elaborated in different historical circumstances.) The seeds of later conflict with the mission committee were already sown. Leenhardt had spent more money than was authorized. His family made up the difference, Franz and Louise Leenhardt having founded an independent support group. But their efforts were not actively supported by the society, and the support group was seldom mentioned in its journal. In 1907 an exasperated Franz Leenhardt wrote protesting the "sort of suspicion" he felt emanating from the committee. (Some apparently had accused Leenhardt of undertaking a purely personal mission.)[2] This accusation would dog the New Caledonian work. The Do Neva mission could sometimes claim to be financially independent of Paris; and in practice, Leenhardt's tendency was to act first and ask permission afterwards. (The many months required for official deci-

11. Maurice and Jeanne
Leenhardt in 1909.

Photo: Leenhardt

sions often made doing so unavoidable.) Through the 1920s, Do Neva
retained the reputation of an individual undertaking, independent and
unorthodox.

In 1908 none could deny Leenhardt's initial success. Protestantism
had made important gains among the Grande Terre's unconverted
clans. The work of the *natas* was secure; statistics of church membership and school attendance were growing. But Leenhardt, as we have
seen, harbored doubts about the thoroughness of the conversion behind the figures. To grasp the experiential processes involved, he
would have to understand traditional society and religion much more
fully. During 1909 he was exposed to the latest currents of ethnological theory—the work of Durkheim's *Année Sociologique* group and Lévy-
Bruhl's developing conception of a "prelogical" primitive mentality.[3]
Although the fieldworker was critical of both approaches, they
strongly influenced the ways he defined his field of inquiry. His father,
as usual, urged him toward more precise observation and stressed the
importance of collecting genealogies. During his next stay in New
Caledonia, Leenhardt began his scientific ethnography in earnest.
He had already written to his father that his work required him to
study the "complete psychology" of his Melanesian Christians. "I'm

astounded at all the pathways different from ours that I've discovered in their hearts. But it's not enough to discover a country, you've got to know how to map it." Melanesian resistances had to be grasped sympathetically and with considerable relativism: "We don't know how to judge others without comparing them to ourselves; and surely divine wisdom consists in weighing each according to its own measure."[4]

Leenhardt's growing relativism caused him to question seriously the notion of religious "conversion." He criticized (privately) the naiveté of colleagues like Delord. Philadelphe Delord, a veteran evangelist and innovator in the treatment of leprosy, was one of those missionaries who knew how to sway an audience with tales of dramatic transformations.[5] He believed in the existence of simple peoples desirous of the faith. Their "paganism" was for him merely a sort of natural state, not a living culture rooted in a complex reality. Leenhardt was increasingly critical of this approach. Rather than imagining a people yearning for the Gospels, it is better, he said, simply to see "various tribes, looking for a support."[6] As time went on, he became even more of a realist. In the natives' adherence to a religion, he wrote to his wife, prestige often plays a key role: they become Protestant in English colonies and Catholic in French. "Conversion" is for them a means of becoming actively involved in the white world. Adoption of a new religion can be a method of "observation" of the white. And finally, it can spring from a "need to react against the deadly breath of civilization." Religious adherence in this case involves a "judgment" of one culture by another. Moreover, the *natas*' message had been essentially "this-worldly," a promise of better explanation, prediction, and control of a changing environment. Christianity's "other-worldly" significance, concentrated in personal communion with a transcendent God, was not so easily accepted.[7] Adherence to the practical religion of the *natas* did not necessarily entail even an elementary acquaintance with Christ.

As a consequence of such views, Leenhardt had difficulty adopting the modes of discourse proper to his profession. His mother prodded him repeatedly to include more "touching stories" and "edifying conversations" in his reports. Anyone who has leafed through mission journals will know the sort of thing she wanted. But Leenhardt could not bring himself to adopt a language he felt to be fundamentally meaningless. Only with difficulty could he write using "the little touch which creates sympathy."[8] In early 1905, he expressed the radical opinion that, since his arrival, he'd seen no real conversions at all, only mass and individual "adherences."[9] He could be mordant in his deflation of colleagues:

. . . how dangerous it is to always portray the march of the
Kingdom of God as if it advanced overstriding all contingencies. It makes me think of Delord moving an audience with a
Caledonian woman's story about how prayer of a *nata* had
swayed a pagan chief. But at the same time, the *nata* had sent
2 [other] chiefs as delegates with 25F of persuasion. The
prayer stands, but so does the contingency—and the chief is
still pagan.[10]

Leenhardt's mother, in pressing him to recount stories like Delord's,
wrote not simply as an orthodox believer but also as a fund-raiser.
Sentimental stories brought in donations; her son's infrequent, long,
and rather dryly descriptive reports did not. At one point Leenhardt
promised his parents he'd write more "sentimentalism." But he added
in exasperation: "I gave myself dispassionately to this work. Why can't
Christians learn to give—dispassionately?"[11] Boegner, too, chided
Leenhardt for not writing the right kind of reports for the Mission
Journal, not including enough of his personal experience. The missionary replied: "It must therefore be the case that to interest people
in a mission you've got to be able to interest them in yourself. But I
feel myself incapable of doing for us what Delord does so well." And
he added, once more, his plea for dispassion.[12]

Important issues of evangelical method were at stake. The Delord,
Coillard style of mission, centering on the romantic figure of the
evangelist, seemed dangerous to Leenhardt. It diverted attention from
the real work, which was the encouragement of indigenous churches.[13]
His own reports tended to leave himself out of the picture and describe
political and cultural circumstances in the Grande Terre, including
frequent portraits of individual Melanesian Christians. Leenhardt,
like many a missionary, was torn between the real needs of his work
and the demands of his publicity. He had somehow to avoid sacrificing
the former to the latter. And this choice involved struggle, for missionary practice was deeply enmeshed in the fantasy systems of European religious sentimentality. Many evangelists never really chose
between their audience in the metropole and their audience in the
bush.

Conversion, for Leenhardt, was never a matter of "conquest," as it
was often portrayed in evangelical rhetoric. He felt, in fact, an attraction for "pure" primitivism. Small-scale, nonhierarchical Christianity
had always been his ideal, and in the back hills he rediscovered "the
true *Canaque* of before, . . . who has not rubbed against the White. He
is more savage, a hundred times better, and in him one sees the lost
soul to be brought home so much more clearly than among the poor

natives who have been made corrupt and cynical [*désabusés*]."[14] But
Leenhardt had to resist this taste for the primitive. He did not question the need for education and change, and traditional socio-religious
structures were, he thought, collapsing. Thus his greatest energies
were devoted to students and *natas*. These, he thought, were minds in
transition, searching for a new conception of themselves that could be
guaranteed only through a personal relationship with divinity. The
conversion process, as Leenhardt analyzed it in a number of subsequent works,[15] consists of an interrelated series of movements: from
concrete toward abstract modes of thought and expression, from a
diffuse, participatory consciousness toward self-consciousness, from
the affective domain of myth toward detached observation and analysis. The process must not, however, be accomplished in simple imitation of whites, but rather as an independent invention. It must develop as "some kind of appropriate civilization, affirming itself gradually."[16]

In experiential terms conversion was the emergence of an inter-
nalized moral conscience based on an intimate communion with Christ.
True conversion was never collective. To encourage the necessary
personal changes, Leenhardt urged his students to write down as best
they could their life stories—to testify to themselves. The missionary
and ethnologist learned a great deal from these documents. For example, in a notebook written by Eleisha Nebay at Guilgal in November 1911, we learn that the Christian God appeared to a young
convert as a new father *and* mother. Eleisha testifies also to a new feeling, something he had not experienced before becoming a *nata*-in-
training. Previously, "there seemed to be only one man in my
heart . . . ," and

> At that time my eyes saw well what they saw and my heart
> was direct [*droit*]. After a few years in God's work, I've found
> there to be two men within me, disputing in eloquence every
> day 'til the present. I used to wonder whether the first state
> was God's will. I prayed to him ceaselessly to take the other
> away. I'm opening myself, telling you what isn't clear to me;
> but that's how it seemed in my heart.[17]

The conception of conversion as struggle within a divided heart is,
of course, well known in the literature of the early Church. To Leenhardt in colonial Melanesia it was a hopeful sign indicating that his
students were growing in self-consciousness. People like Eleisha, he
thought, would henceforth be able to separate themselves from the
flux of events and make clear choices. This would make resistance to

colonial temptations possible, an active selection of alternative moral values within the new, ambiguous context. Other readers of Eleisha Nebay's notebook may be less content with the assumption that such a selection can only be made on *personal* grounds, or with what appears in the journal as the birth of modern self-alienation. And indeed, Leenhardt was aware of the danger that the newly individualized Christian might be founded on a personal experience of separations without healing communions. The person, he believed, must not abandon myth for rationality, becoming severed from passionate involvements with land and kin. If conversion involved a process of separation and self-discrimination, it had also to be based on translation, a knowing search for equivalents and mediations uniting the old and new, pagan and Christian, mythic and rational.

⋺⋲

Leenhardt believed at first that the Melanesian experience of divinity could be brought directly over into Christianity. In 1905 he began experimenting with using the *bao* (a spirit, ancestor, or corpse) to clarify in the native language the "visions" spoken of in the Gospels. The development of his translation researches will be treated more fully below. It is worth noting here that for Leenhardt this kind of activity represented a form of questioning that sometimes verged on rebellion. For example, after describing in a letter his use of the *bao* in teaching, he added: "Mama shouldn't think I'm playing the rebel. The thing is too serious here, and why rebel when there's no one to scandalize?"[18] But of course there was someone to scandalize, for at the antipodes Leenhardt remained a member of the French Protestant extended family. His father had advised him to devise a "simplistic theology" for his students.[19] Leenhardt's problem was to do more—to purify as well as to simplify the Christianity he was teaching. His faith had to be conceived as concretely as possible. This was a prerequisite of communication, with an immediate aim of subtle and effective evangelization. But more than just that was at stake. The idea of a cross-culturally translatable Christianity coincided with the sort of lived religion and morality that the young missionary was seeking for himself. From the start he was worried about the need for absolute sincerity in his classes. He was free to follow his feelings, but at the same time he felt uneasy about the great leeway he enjoyed and the resultant dangers of teaching a heterodoxy. "My entire difficulty," he wrote, "is to teach them nothing that I don't believe myself."[20]

In 1913 he sent a report to the Paris Mission Society for publication in its journal.[21] In it he hinted at the supple method of evangelization he

had for some time been practicing. The article was composed in Leenhardt's best "missionary style"; "From Shadows into the Light" was its
title. It described halting and apparently rather quaint attempts by
natas and Do Neva students to grasp the true message of Christ.
Various strange native prayers and mistaken concepts are portrayed
and explained. Then the concept of "God" is discussed. God had to
have a vernacular name, Leenhardt argued, or rather He had to coopt
the generic term for the traditional gods and spirits. Otherwise, designated by a strange, foreign word, the Christian God might be simply
added to the roster of deities as *primus inter pares*. Other missionaries,
for example, Patteson, Codrington, and the English Melanesian Mission, had opted for the European term "God." They feared the inevitable misunderstandings involved in the adaptation of a pagan
name. But Leenhardt believed that a certain confusion was part of any
process of change and education; and unless native terms could be
brought to new significances there would be no real conversion.

Thus the Christian God had to appropriate the essence of Melanesian spirits by taking possession of their generic name, *Bao*. In the
process of cooptation, Leenhardt suggested, Christianity was in fact
recovering a religious reality that preexisted the magical gods and
spirits, an affective, communal essence that he later identified with
totemism and worship of the landscape.[22] This approach to conversion,
amounting in some ways to a reversion, was dangerously close to
heterodoxy. Where did the Christian missionary draw the line in making use of archaic concepts and terms?

It is interesting to see from the private letters that Leenhardt had
already censored his own article. Writing to his father, he revealed
that he had begun with an account that would have been much more
specific and controversial than the one he finally sent. In the original
version he had discussed openly

> the heart of the question . . . which is to determine: is God
> the revelation man has of Spirit with which we are in rela-
> tion, and which man then personifies according to his men-
> tality in various spirits etc. . . , until he even succeeds in sys-
> tematizing and hierarchizing these spirits; or is God much
> more transcendent, not discoverable by man?

God is either "immanent or transcendent"; and if he is the former,

> If Jehovah is really that which is visible since the creation . . .
> then the pagans must have an obscure revelation of God at
> the heart of their beliefs. This is a minimum of experiences
> upon which the preaching of the Gospel can be based. And

thus we shouldn't reject the entire jumble of their gods in order to give them a new god with a foreign name; rather we should search for the word in their language, even the strangest word, into which can be translated the visible experience of God.[23]

The *natas*, he adds, had already been doing so, "openly adopting the pagan name." Leenhardt sympathized, but he felt himself to be walking a fine line.

We cannot know exactly what Leenhardt felt he should exclude from his original article or just how he recast its style. But we can compare a published passage with a later, different analysis of the same event. He quotes a prayer overheard on the lips of a Melanesian Protestant: "Oh God who is wholly long, you came to our Néporo and Asana families; then you stretched yourself out again and arrived in Monéo, and again stretching yourself you came to Paci." In the article printed in the *Journal des Missions*, Leenhardt cited this curious prayer merely as a poetic image for the Gospel's progress throughout the land. But the "long god" meant something much more profound to a Melanesian. It evoked the elemental flux, or life force, emanating from the totem and passing into the present generations through the blood of the maternal lineage. If the Christian God was called "wholly long," that meant it had appropriated this potent myth. In a lecture given much later at the Paris *Ecole des Missions*, Leenhardt described the relation of the "long god" to the totemic flow of "life" and added that "this god who stretches out may make us smile when we don't understand paganism. But when we are familiar with the "long god," the image is a moving one, touching the Missionary's heart."[24] This was the sort of comment Leenhardt could not permit himself in his original article, where the *"dieu long"* remained a picturesque image.

In 1913, Leenhardt was still unsure of his missionary ethnology. He asked his father whether it was permissible to affix pagan names and properties to the Christian God. And the question posed once more the basic theological problem for Leenhardt: that of mediating an apparent choice between immanence and transcendence:

> . . . so that according to whether God is transcendent or immanent (I mean glimpsed as such, for I think he is both) we translate using the foreign name or the pagan name; and who knows whether we're being orthodox or heterodox?

Was God in effect already present in Melanesian language and experience? Or did He have to be imported? Leenhardt's instincts were all on the side of immanence, but he needed encouragement:

> I wish Father would tell me what he thinks of all this; because I wrote that article as a search, and seeing that I was heading straight for heterodoxy, I began again and turned it into edification. But if Father tells me I'm on the right track, I'll feel a lot more courage in searching for God among the pagans.[25]

In the ambiguous freedom of his mission work, Leenhardt had to develop enough self-confidence to see God for himself in strange contexts. This was a problem of personal identity, or "sincerity," in the language of Leenhardt, which was that of Rousseau. However, the romantic route of introspection and confession made no claim on the activist. He looked for his "God among the pagans," among the others—and in this he opened himself personally to the conversion process.

Later, in an ethnological context, "inverse acculturation" was Leenhardt's way of describing a desirable colonial reciprocity in which the European would learn from the Melanesian.[26] Before an audience of young evangelists he put it rather differently. The missionary, he insists, keeps his mind open—but not to be influenced by primitivism so much as to be, simply, a purer Christian and man:

> The missionary is called to bring the Gospel of Jesus Christ and not the Gospel of whites. His purpose is not the founding of a white church. In remaining perfectly loyal to the mandate given him by God, not men, he must become a man, and not the representative of a civilization. Otherwise . . . his message will not be that of pure Gospel; it will contain a mixture of voices. . . .[27]

The purity required of the missionary was not a form of dogma or divine inspiration. It was an attitude of openness—a poet's negative capability. "The Gospel of Jesus," the veteran said in his lecture, "adapts itself to all peoples." As an evangelist, Leenhardt had to learn to recognize true translation when it was already at work in an unfamiliar idiom.

The *nata* Joané Nigoth had already produced a Houailou version of the Gospel of Matthew. The translation of the remaining New Testament was a collective enterprise spanning more than fifteen years that became, for Leenhardt, an intense focus for ethnolinguistic research. A letter sets out his procedure:

. . . Just a word while waiting for Boesoou, my old teacher
with whom I can't manage to find a few quiet hours to work
on translations. By now he's used to the work and gives the
correct word fairly quickly. For two hours a week I read
completed chapters to the students, and it's very interesting
to see them satisfied by a good word which makes clear in
their minds something they hadn't understood; or protesting sometimes against a word which doesn't satisfy them.
After their verdict I give the rough draft to Apou to copy....[28]

It was often almost impossible to find meaningful equivalents for
Christian religious concepts, and Leenhardt went to great lengths to
avoid imposing a foreign expression. It was important not to be in a
hurry. He would try to hold an open mind and keep discussing a
troublesome idea whenever he could, in classes and sermons, until
some Houailou speaker arrived spontaneously at a meaningful
rendition.

An example of how the process sometimes worked is given in Leenhardt's article of 1922 on translating the New Testament. He was
having difficulty rendering a key concept in the Epistle to the Romans.

While I was seeking for the meaning of the term "propitiatory," I heard a native Christian explain the text of Romans
3:25 with these words, which I translate literally, "God has
made Jesus an object *of sacrifice, and the healing and propitiatory leaf
is his blood for those who have faith.*" This confusing and
awkward expression is translated in Caledonian by a very
short word, "Demo." Its original significance is "leaf cicatri-
zation, or living leaf," the ideas of healing and of life being
connected. But this should not lead us to think that it is the
leaf which cicatrizes; in that case the phrase would be "cica-
trizing leaf," "*De Pemo.*" The leaf is only the vehicle for a
virtue transmitted through the benevolence of a divinity in
the course of a sacrifice. Without this sacrifice or an offering, the leaf does not act. This virtue, originally given to a
leaf, must have been extended later to other objects, for the
word designating it has a generic sense and is applied to all
objects provoking or soliciting divine influence. In this very
primitive idea, the medicinal value of the leaf has not been
grasped; the leaf is effective only by virtue of its propitiatory
value. When *Canaques* applied this word to Jesus Christ, they
perceived that the death of Christ modified the relations
between man and God, and took away their sin, as these

leaves in sacrifices formerly altered their condition and took away their sufferings. This is perceived from a wholly simple and concrete standpoint.[29]

Leenhardt goes on to suggest that the Melanesian—who propitiates a god or totem using the *demo* leaf as part of his everyday activities of fishing or gardening—probably grasps the expiatory role of Christ in a manner that is more alive than that of many Christians tied to a "juridical" mode of comprehension.

In the same context, Leenhardt tells how he finally arrived at a term that would express "redemption." Previous missionaries had interpreted it as an exchange—an exchange of life, that of Jesus for ours. But in Melanesian thinking more strict equivalents were demanded in the exchanges structuring social life. It remained unclear to them how Jesus' sacrifice could possibly redeem mankind. So unclear was it that even the *natas* gave up trying to explain a concept they did not understand very well themselves and simply employed the term "release." So the matter stood, with the missionary driven to the use of cumbersome circumlocutions, until one day during a conversation on I Corinthians 1:30 Boesoou Erijisi used a surprising expression: *nawi*. The term referred to the custom of planting a small tree on land cursed either by the blood of battle or some calamity. "Jesus was thus the one who has accomplished the sacrifice and has planted himself like a tree, as though to absorb all the misfortunes of men and to free the world from its taboos." Here at last was a concept tht seemed to render the principle of "redemption" and could reach deeply enough into living modes of thought. "The idea was a rich one, but how could I be sure I understood it right?" The key test was in the reaction of students and *natas* to his provisional version. They were, he reports, overjoyed with the "deep" translation.[30]

Often enough, Melanesian terms seemed to express the elemental meaning of the Bible more truly than the French or the Greek, both of which were less concrete tongues than the original language of the Gospels. Thus Leenhardt's intercultural translation was more than a simple scriptural exegesis. His "primitivizing" of the Gospel restored to it a rich, immediate context and concrete significance. An example of the kinship between the biblical idiom and the Melanesian, which Leenhardt would elaborate again and again throughout his ethnological career, was the term for "word" or "speech" (French, *parole*; Houailou, *nō*). "In the beginning was the Word . . ." was first translated by the Loyalty missionaries using the Greek and pronouncing it in native fashion. "In the beginning the logos."

Canaques are intelligent people: I've never heard them using words which have no meaning. But when a *Canaque* speaks French, he translates his thoughts as best he can. He has no trouble at all expressing himself concerning the man who has conceived good things, has said them, done them, or even accomplished the three acts at once: "The word [*parole*] of this man is good." Thought, speech, and action are all included in the Caledonian term *Nö*. Thus in speaking of an adulterous man, one may say: "He has done an evil word." One may speak of a chief whose character is uncertain, who does not think, organize, or act correctly, as—"His word is not good." The expression "the Word of God," which we limit to divine discourse or literature, here includes the thoughts and acts of God. "God spoke and it was done." We need search no farther; we translate using *Nö* this term of such richness—the *Logos* of the first verses of John that the native attempts to transpose into French using *"parole."* The term for Word takes on a broad, living meaning, worthy of the God whose creative will it must make intelligible. Things become clearer. The native has no trouble seeing the word becoming action, the word made flesh, the word as phenomenon.[31]

The opening of the Book of John was particularly effective in Melanesian vernacular. Another "improved" passage was Matthew 19:6 (New English Bible) where man and wife are said to be "one flesh . . . no longer two individuals." This section became "more expressive in Houailou," a language rich in concrete terms for relationships.[32] Leenhardt was discovering that the vernacular abounded in locutions of duality and plurality. These were substantives, and they did not imply the additive combination of separate parts. Rather, they were "one flesh," as with husband and wife. The same was true for other couplings: grandfather and grandson, nephew and maternal uncle, the relation of homonyms. What in Western languages would be seen as composites would in Houailou be expressed as ensembles, substantial entities, or "images."[33]

For Leenhardt, translation was part of the inventive interpenetration of two cultures. In the process it was essential not simply to find accurate versions, but to locate and use *meaningful* expressions. In this concern he anticipated modern, ethnolinguistic approaches to Bible translation, the search for "dynamic equivalences."[34] Imposed terminology had no place in real translation. Spontaneously borrowed and adapted foreign words were accepted, after scrutiny. Terms that once had sense but had been abandoned were left to their fate. At the same time, "those expressions which spring from the native mind in an attempt to formulate new concepts revealed by the knowledge of the Gospel or by contact with [Western] civilization, exhibit a great variety. And their value is far greater; for these are not artificial words, but truly living words."[35]

Leenhardt is attempting to grasp a moving language. He values those usages that, although they might appear "corrupt" when judged against an imagined, static, primitive standard, are the most "alive" elements of a parlance. He works within a dynamic conception of culture. Rather than a simple transferring of meanings from one cultural code to another, a dialog is created in which the language of all parties is enriched. Unlike the ethnographer, who typically concentrates on making an alien expressive system understandable, Leenhardt works at making himself and his beliefs understood—to others and, in the process, to himself. A context of exchange is initiated. By contrast, scientific ethnology runs the risk of overemphasizing the univocal translation of exotic cultures and languages as if they were complete systems (*langues*) rather than evolving expressivities (*paroles*). Perhaps to translate "them" into "us," one must be prepared to translate "us" into "them." The missionary's summary of the translator's role is relevant—in some degree—to all ethnographic encounters:

> The work of the translator is not to interrogate his native helpers, as if compiling human dictionaries, but rather he must solicit their interest, awaken their thinking. . . . He does not create a language; this is composed by the native himself; it is the product and translation of his thoughts. And the translator, he who has initiated this thinking, merely transcribes the words he has aroused, overheard, seized upon —fixing them in writing.[36]

The translator inscribes a moment of intercultural "thinking" within a language's perpetual process of rebirth in the encounter with other languages.

The importance of this process for Leenhardt was two-fold. First, in cooperation with Melanesians, he hoped to preserve an endangered expressivity, not as a static ethnological document, but in words that would be "acts of life inspired by experience." Living Caledonian culture required living languages. Second, for himself and his own culture, Leenhardt uncovered in the translation process a Christianity made newly pure and concrete:

The missionary has once more experienced the power of the Gospel, and now the natives have helped him in better understanding this power. He perceives that if psychological and theological terms are abstract and indefinite, words as they spring from the experience of the believer are concrete and precise. He realizes that the religious fact expressed in abstract terms is without active value and constitutes merely a dead formula whose spirit has departed. . . . Christianity will appear to [the missionary] stripped of the various historical garments which conceal it from the eyes of so many in Europe. And [he] will glimpse the entire beauty of the Gospel, light and life-force for those who seek it with simplicity.[37]

>⋹<

Thus the translator's credo. As Leenhardt conceived the *process* involved, there could be no simple importation of a Western divinity into a Melanesian religious landscape. For the European, "God" would take on unexpected forms. He watched and listened: "*Para bao we kei pai ae para rhe we ke mi roi powè.*" (Tous les dieux à cause des hommes, d'autre part tous les totems à cause venir selon femmes.) A phrase "overheard in the mouth of a *Canaque*" provided Leenhardt with a key to the complex structure of Caledonian religion.[38] "Gods come from men, totems proceed from women."

The *natas*, as we have seen, had translated the Christian "God" as "*Bao*." Perhaps it was disconcerting for their young missionary when he discovered that *bao* could also be a term for cadaver. (He was probably not as confused, however, as his missionary predecessors on Lifou, who for a time had translated "Bible" as "container of the Word" until they discovered that the islanders also called their penis sheath "container of the word"![39] Leenhardt considered all translations provisional; he let *Bao* stand and began looking into the term's wide variety of connotations. *Bao*, he found, could be a magical spirit of recent origin used in magic and sorcery, like the "red god," *doki*.[40] *Bao* could be a human corpse or even a very old living person; it could also be an ancestor deceased in recent memory; it could be a more distant ancestor, founder of an island or region; it could be an almost forgotten deity remembered by a single exaggerated trait or identified with an element of nature or geography. Finally, *bao* could refer to a totem that had become confused with an ancestor and was thus also a "god." *Bao*, Leenhardt discovered, was generally identified with the male ancestral lineage, heritage of the clan and the chief. Its properties were masculine, its virtue was "power." Leenhardt observed that the *bao* most actively worshipped were magical manifestations—spirits of fairly recent origin linked to present occasions. As he understood better the common usages of *bao*, he worried that the Christian deity's status might be that of one more magical "god." It might—like the *doki*, recently imported from Lifou—fail to express really ancient mythic attachments. How could the missionary-translator be sure that *Bao*, the Christian god, would penetrate to the deepest strata of Melanesian feeling and belief?

Leenhardt was at first much impressed with the power in Caledonian life of the *bao* ancestor-gods. This power was most manifest in the authority of chiefs, representatives of the masculine clan lineage, and mediators with the *bao*. But as he became more sensitive to local custom, he discovered that in practice the chiefs often deferred to maternal uncles, members of clans from which the paternal clan received its wives. The maternal uncle, or *kanya*, had to be given gifts at births, deaths, *pilous*, marriages, to ensure the countergift of female life.[41] But the *kanya* did not hold power in himself any more than the chief did. The latter was spokesman, *parole*, of the clan ancestors; the former was associated with the maternal line. The *chef* represented the heritage of masculine "power," the *kanya* of feminine "life." An elemental living force flowed as blood from mother to child; its original source was the totem, or *rhë*. The totem was an animal, plant, or mineral peculiar to a clan and recognized by a system of ritual gestures and sacrifices.[42] Prior to Leenhardt's identification of *rhë* as "totem," Caledonian culture had been classified as nontotemic. The missionary now had to explain the coexistence of two parallel sources of authority, *bao*-chief and totem-*kanya*. At first he hypothesized a society in transition from "matriarchy" to "patriarchy." But after further research he dropped these terms and with them abandoned a theoretical stance tending to explain incongruous elements in a culture as survivals, or evidence of past historical stages. Nineteenth-century evolutionism frequently posited that culture in its early periods had passed from matriarchy to patriarchy. However, Leenhardt rejected the notion of opposed, successive states. He found that in New Caledonia duality was structural, with oppositon best understood as complementarity. He came to see the lineages of "power" and "life," male and female, in reciprocal union. The missionary, in looking hard at Melanesian religion, had done more than derive a simple equivalent for "God." He had identified a coherent socio-religious system.[43]

Although Leenhardt admired the aesthetic balance of the Melanesian socio-mythic order, he nonetheless judged it to be no longer viable. New modes of thought were required to deal with new conditions. The mythic landscape in which the deeper forms of ancestor worship and totemic identification had found expression was shattered. A new person, one less externalized, more centered in an individually defined ego, would have to develop. (This Western person, Lévi-Strauss has remarked, seems to have his own personality as "totem".)[44] Leenhardt's concern was with the spiritual health of this new individual, the quality of "life" available to it. He did not wish to encourage the development of a system of beliefs reduced to merely technical, magical, or rational manipulation of an objective environment. Deeper attachments were needed. Leenhardt identified these affective attitudes primarily with totemic myth as well as with older forms of ancestor-nature worship. It seemed to Leenhardt that acculturation was likely to result in a shift away from myth in the direction of magic, the latter involving a more instrumental attitude toward the world. But he did not wish the Christian *Bao* to be simply a powerful new tool for the understanding and control of immediate events. Such a development could only encourage shallowness of belief and promote the growth of sorcery and messianism, unstable means of socioreligious problem solving.

Beneath the changing repertoire of *bao*-gods lay the more authentic attachments of myth, geographic and totemic. Something of these forces would need to be coopted into the new, personal "God" if modes of mythic participation were to coexist with, not simply be replaced by, techniques of rational manipulation. Thus, as we shall see, the missionary could be delighted, even moved, to hear an old man participating in a Christian festival address a temperance commitment to "his mountains."[45] Much of this religious essence might be excluded in naming "God" *Bao*. The Supreme Being might be thought of as just another lesser god, magical, "this-worldly," and merely useful for dealing with the white world. There was a risk, in sum, of excluding the entire female-totemic "side" of the traditional socio-religious structure.

The first Loyaltian *natas* had tried to use the name "Jehovah," but their Caledonian converts preferred "*Bao*," and Leenhardt respected their instinct, though he knew the translation was imperfect.[46] The *bao* concept would have to be reunderstood, not as a generic term but capitalized, as a personal name. And mythic depth might be added through the annexation of as much totemic language as possible. Leenhardt was encouraged by his discovery that *bao* had always been a highly adaptable concept. It could apply not merely to a corpse, recent ancestor, or magical divinity, but its masculine "power" could sometimes fuse spontaneously with the feminine-totemic principle of "life." It sometimes happened that a mythic founding father might in collective memory become identified with a totem. Leenhardt had also discovered an encouraging composite usage of *bao*, the "long god" that we have already mentioned. Here was a masculine "god" being associated with the curving flow of the female lineage.[47] If such "totem-god" associations could naturally occur, there was hope for a similar mediation in the person of the Christian *Bao*. "God" could be a "long god," a source of both "power" and "life."

The religious language of Leenhardt's Houailou New Testament (*Peci Arii*) is drawn from a broad range of sources. Totemic expressions abound. The new *Bao* is characterized in language drawn from the expressive structures of myth, of social morality, of magic.[48] The Christian God had to embrace the totality of Melanesian life. It had to coopt the all-encompassing "peaceful abode" (*"séjour paisible"* or *maciri*) so effectively incarnated in the traditional village, with its symbolic male and female alleyways inserted in a mythic landscape. Leenhardt wrote to his father that he was teaching the Melanesians that "the god to whom they give boiled yams and from whom they ask an abundant harvest (*maciri*, the kingdom, same word as kingdom of heaven, *maciri*, *re nêko*) is the same whose hand they now ask for, to help them walk in righteousness."[49] But to appeal to the traditional "peaceful abode" was to invoke immanent mythic attachments, relationships not habitually thought of as a single "god." This quotation is taken from an early letter; Leenhardt would become more sophisticated in his translations. But the general aim revealed to his father remained: somehow a localized, immediate mythic experience had to be encompassed by the "person" of a transcendent deity.

In adopting the language of totemic myth to evoke the Christian *Bao* and in identifying Him with *maciri*, the "peaceful abode" and traditional village, Leenhardt in effect broadened the God of European orthodoxy in two crucial ways. In translating his deity, the missionary made "Him" more androgynous, a totem-*bao* of feminine "life" as well as of masculine "power." He also rendered God less transcendent, expressed through myths of immediate social and religious experience —"this-worldly" and participative.[50]

The Houailou translation of the New Testament fairly successfully incarnates Leenhardt's religious ideal. But it was quite another matter to achieve as precise and nuanced a "translation" in the actual beliefs of Melanesian Protestants. When Leenhardt and his wife returned to New Caledonia in 1938, they found evidence that many *natas* were preaching the Christian *Bao* as if it were "added" onto traditional religion. The missionary's successors had de-emphasized the use of Houailou in religious instruction and ritual and were not as sophisticated as he had been in detecting when Christianity was in danger of slipping either into a syncretist or merely magical-instrumental status. It is difficult today to know precisely how much of the spiritual depth Leenhardt strove to preserve in the language of New Caledonian Christianity in fact survives. French is the island's *lingua franca*, and the young have largely forgotten the old religious words.

On the other hand, there are solid indications that an immanent attachment, at once social, mythic, and ecological, to land and habitat has in fact survived to a significant degree in Christian New Caledonia. And a passing firsthand acquaintance with Protestantism on the Grande Terre has persuaded me (in the absence of any detailed study) that there is more to "modernization" there than meets the eye. One still encounters, for example, Protestants who, during their regional church festivals, "pass along the young girl," in the form of a symbolic gift, back and forth between clans united by ancient exchanges of uterine blood (life). Moreover, the desire for a return of expropriated ancestral habitats is the most constant and profound current of political agitation among the island's Melanesians. If Leenhardt's specific Houailou translations have been superseded by events beyond his control, there has been no rejection of the spirit in which they were collectively made. For the missionary, in any event, there were no final versions. Authenticity was a process—the translation of cultures, creative and humanly indeterminate.

CHAPTER VI

War and Rebellion

In 1914, for his thirty-sixth birthday, Maurice Leenhardt received four presents from his family. By his place in the dining room at Do Neva he found Durkheim's *Formes élémentaires de la vie religieuse*, James Leuba's *La psychologie religieuse* (a critique of Durkheim), a new medical *Formulary*, and from the children, *Traité des maladies de l'enfance*.[1] The pharmaceutical/philosophical mix was typical of life in the field. And as the first titles indicate, during the years after 1910 Leenhardt was thinking in more explicitly theoretical terms. His letters contain frequent, though cursory, criticisms of Durkheim and Lévy-Bruhl. He had begun to collect genealogies in the Houailou valley and was encouraging his "pagano-protestants" to write down folklore and to describe traditional rituals. He kept a field journal filled with linguistic notations and unresolved questions about custom. But at this stage in his career he did not often have the time needed for sustained inquiry beyond his immediate evangelical concerns. And after August 1914, even his Bible translating had to be sacrificed to a growing burden of work. One after another, his younger Loyalty Island colleagues were conscripted for the war in Europe. From 1915 until 1920, Leenhardt was the sole European Protestant missionary in the archipelago.

Leenhardt was severely tested during the World War. The distant conflict had a sharp impact on the life of New Caledonia, producing in the whites a patriotic wartime mentality that did not contribute to finesse in native affairs. The island's Melanesians underwent the pressures of military recruitment and service in the French Pacific Brigades. Over a thousand saw action on the Western front in Europe. The conditions of their enlistment were seldom wholly voluntary. As the Great War dragged on, disillusionment increased among all races on the Grande Terre. Signs of unrest began to appear in the northern highlands, leading to outbreaks of fighting in 1917 and 1918. Leenhardt's role during the recruitment campaigns and sporadic revolts was a difficult and ambiguous one. Strains were placed on his stance of independent opposition within the colonial regime. A passage from the missionary's journal epitomizes his situation:

I said to them: You're angry with me because I'm always transmitting the Government's orders; but they don't come from me, they are not my words.
—a man replied: Whatever you'll say doesn't much matter. Now we'll do what we want: make war.[2]

Leenhardt was intensely patriotic. He had an ideal vision of France as a great nation extending a great civilization to her colonies, as well as bringing them the life-giving Word of God. "Liberté, Egalité, Fraternité: résumé de l'évangile. . . ."; his letter continues:

We missionaries are of course ambassadors of Christ, but our mentality, our spirit of free criticism and discipline come from France, and we are ambassadors of French culture at its most elevated. We suffer enormously in our colonies from the shameful things we see, but I never feel more French than when I'm bringing back into line a governor led astray on native matters. If this were not France, one probably wouldn't be able to talk with him.[3]

During the first year of fighting, Leenhardt was occupied with explaining the European conflict to his people. His students did not understand "how Christian nations could fight such terrible wars." The Melanesians (for whom warfare was ritually circumscribed and practiced on a small scale) were astonished at the way in which the higher civilizations could behave. For them war was related to anger; its duration was short. The whites had an extraordinary and shocking ability to engage in prolonged and destructive conflict, all with cold calculation, "and perhaps they are right in having no idea of these hatreds," their missionary concluded.[4]

When the call went out for native volunteers, Leenhardt encouraged his people to enlist. He did so, however, with some misgivings. The recruiting practices of certain administrators included false promises and crude coercion. And as one of the few whites in the colony whose word meant something among Melanesians, Leenhardt knew that his encouragement and that of chiefs under his influence could be decisive.[5] His worry was that he could never be sure of the exact conditions governing the service he was advocating. Leenhardt was not consulted by Noumea but was expected to help. Promises had been made to the recruits: they were to be given land and tools after the war. Suspicious natives asked the missionary for precise information, and he had none to give. "All this is troubling, for I don't know anything about what's going on in Noumea. They've said to the *Canaques*: you'll be like the

whites. I preach: 'you will participate in the victory and because of that
you will have a new dignity which will bring you credit in the eyes of
France.'" With some pride, Leenhardt noted that the first brigade
included 450 Protestants out of 650.[6]

The missionary breathed a sigh of relief when, in early 1916, the
order arrived to stop the recruiting. He had wanted a truly voluntary
affair, reflecting freely responsible choices by prospective citizens of a
wider France. As the recruiting continued, fewer and fewer of the
enlistments were for reasons he considered justifiable. Leenhardt's
hopes for the long-range educational effects of military service were
perhaps not entirely utopian. Although, as he feared, the lands promised to the returning riflemen were not forthcoming, and although
their wartime services for "la patrie" did not lead rapidly to full citizenship, nevertheless the veterans of 1914-1918 did acquire an important
pride and a more realistic view of the white man's civilization. In the
years before the next European conflagration, these *anciens combattants*
formed a vanguard of native regroupment and nascent political activism in the colony.[7] Furthermore, the war raised important questions
about "nationality" in people's minds. Leenhardt's ideal—a fully democratic, biracial New Caledonia—demanded the formation of a *Canaque* sense of national identity, something going far beyond the clan,
the valley, and the language group. In a wartime sermon: "I had made
as my first point this morning the vision of his suffering country,
Caledonia to be loved. But this abstraction which is Caledonia doesn't
mean much to them. They've got to be led to the notion of the unity
of their people, and to an interest in the whole of the island. I'm not
saying I succeeded. . . ."[8]

Leenhardt supported the first campaign of native recruitment,
which was in some respects "voluntary." But the second drive of early
1917 was a disaster. Leenhardt held that those clans who had given to
the first contingent of riflemen should be spared further pressure. For
them the absence of their young men constituted a serious disloca-
tion. The recruiters, thinking first of filling their quotas, returned to
these tribes, and their techniques of persuasion were questionable:
". . . and then it hurts, for this is no longer an appeal on behalf of the
nation, but an assertion of ego in the style of the pre-war gendarme."[9]
Leenhardt was also unhappy about the recruitment of "pagans." These
tribes, which had not taken steps toward conscious acculturation, could
never, he thought, enlist freely and with any understanding of the
meaning of military service. People who had not already in some way
chosen the civilization of the whites could be enlisted only by the use of
deception or coercion. Leenhardt traced the violence of the summer of
1917 directly to the insensitivities of the recruiters:

What made my blood boil in March was to see them looking for more soldiers, insisting on going to the pagans, without wanting to understand that their gods are hostile to the unhappy Christianity which the whites represent—And now the blood is flowing, and it's sad, infinitely sad to be forced into repression when a bit of wisdom would have avoided the whole thing.[10]

>€

Heavy-handed recruitment was, of course, not the only cause of the 1917 troubles. It aggravated a situation already long in existence. Some sort of rebellion had, it seems, been planned as early as 1913. The inhabitants of the central highlands between Hienghène and Koné had been expelled from their lands, their villages burned to make room for the cattle of a white settler. Although this had taken place in 1903, in 1913 resentment still smouldered. To date, the most painstaking inquiry into the "events" is that of Professor Guiart.[11] Was there a "rebellion?" Guiart concludes yes and no. There was something, on that everyone agrees. At most, eleven whites died in the entire affair,[12] and it is difficult to know just how many "rebels" perished; the repression sputtered on for at least a year. Compared with the reaction to the events of 1878, the white response was fairly restrained. This was due partly to the protection accorded to their respective flocks by the Protestant and Catholic missions. It reflected also the increased numbers and military security of the colonists. A general sense of confusion about what had actually happened and who was really "guilty" may have been a contributing factor as well. In the long and complicated legal trials, only a few real culprits were identified; and, indeed, the events of 1917 are still incompletely understood. It is possible, however, to follow Leenhardt's activities with some precision.

From the beginning, the missionary conducted his own investigation of the unrest in the central highlands. He visited key areas and received regular reports from his *natas*. He sent delegates into the rebel zones, students from Do Neva, some the sons of influential chiefs, to urge calm and to find out what was happening. The missionary guarded his independence, a position not always easy to maintain. As the "troubles" continued, he began to receive telegrams from the governor, asking him for information or empowering him to act semi-officially. Leenhardt was wary of this kind of involvement. He had always in the past made a point of keeping his distance from the government. Leenhardt sympathized with the grievances behind the unrest. But he vigorously opposed resorting to violence. He thought

—probably correctly—that it could only provoke repression and further confiscation of lands. The more rapidly the nascent rebellion was brought to an end, the less chance there would be of clumsy military campaigns with indiscriminate killing and reprisals.

The "rebellion" was certainly doomed from the start, for it was a series of small-scale attacks, not united in any overall strategy. In spring 1917, a tribal conflict exacerbated by recruitment took on anti-white overtones. A tense moment at the Koné police station when the area's recruits were departing led to gestures of defiance. An influential sorcerer began preaching war on the Europeans. A shooting incident by trigger-happy whites and a retaliatory attack on a nickel mine left four dead. Such were the initial ingredients of the affair.

Leenhardt journeyed to Koné in a climate of insurrection and conspiracy to rebel. He immediately called together his *natas*: "and it didn't take long to know all . . . I've got the names of the offenders, the grand sorcerer, etc. . . ."[13] Leenhardt, sure of his information, would have arrested the conspirators without delay. But the administration's representative in the area, Segond, who headed a force of Tahitians, was less sure of his information and proceeded more slowly. Leenhardt, it appears, gave highly selected information to the forces of repression, hints that could lead them to the few real leaders. He protected a host of lesser "guilty" intermediaries and followers. When Segond asked him, on one occasion, to report on an area he was about to visit, Leenhardt found his position very awkward. "I have been able to know things precisely because of the confidence among the natives that I don't betray them."[14] His attitude toward the government was one of loyal circumspection: if they asked, he answered—but selectively and without volunteering extra facts. Later on, as matters became worse and innocent people were arrested, he wished he had been more outspoken at the start.

In mid-June Leenhardt was again in "rebel territory," this time on a trip up the east coast of the island. His voyage, using the mission's small motor launch, lasted two weeks, the most traumatic period of the entire rebellion. On the east coast, near the Laborderie station at the mouth of the Tipije River, three Europeans were massacred a few days after Leenhardt set out. In an atmosphere of terrific tension and real danger, Leenhardt circulated among the villages between Ponerihouen and Hienghène encouraging his *natas*, urging all the clans to remain loyal, or at least neutral. He also had to calm the overexcited whites of the area while trying to find out the extent of actual insurrection. Leenhardt was increasingly convinced that rebel activity on the east coast originated in the west and specifically around the long-troubled regions of Koné and Pamale. The Grande Terre's many valleys run in east-west directions, thus facilitating a great deal of cross-island communication. The whites, sticking to their coastal roads and steamers, knew nothing of this interior traffic. Thus, if colonists were massacred on the east coast, it was assumed that the local tribes must be guilty. To follow the twisting trail of alliance and influence back and forth across the island required an intimate knowledge of geography, ethnography, and local political history.

Of course the freely circulating, "pro-native" pastor was himself an object of suspicion. His wife wrote concerning various rumors and denunciations against him that were being heard in the capital. Later, at the trial, he would be openly accused by a Catholic priest of fomenting insurrection.

As he continued up the coast toward the scene of the recent murders, the tension increased. On an offshore island a score of whites had taken refuge. Leenhardt stopped to inform them of the overall situation, since no decisive relief action from the administration had as yet been forthcoming. "In the end you've got to feel sorry for the colonists, left completely to themselves and not knowing the facts of the rebellion; this makes them see it everywhere. One must be indignant and pitying, and carry with one the sympathy and faith which can calm people down."[15]

Although Leenhardt may have presented an outward image of calm, his letters became increasingly tense. He was suspected by both natives and whites. There was danger in the air. In a letter he instructed his wife what to tell the children in the event of his death. The next few days were spent in the Tipije Valley, where the three Europeans had just been killed. The area's whites were gathered at the Laborderie station, protected by a force of Tahitian soldiers. Panic reigned. In the village of the loyal Wanas clan, Leenhardt anxiously awaited the return of Apou Hmae and Eleisha Nebay, emissaries to a nearby clan, the Weava, who had taken to the mountains. When the *natas* failed to return, Leenhardt could not sleep for fear they had been killed. Leenhardt understood that the Weava and other clans in the area were caught between the rebel band and the soldiers. There existed a variety of shifting allegiances, shades of loyalty, neutrality, and insurrection. When Eleisha and Apou finally returned after spending the night with the Weava in the mountains, they told of indecision, confused preparations for war. "As for my credit," Leenhardt noted, "it's limited: 'Missi, c'est la verité, mais la verité, un peu'."[16]

After a visit to Hienghène and once back at Do Neva, Leenhardt wrote to his parents describing the deteriorating situation: "The

causes?—Total ignorance by the administration of the physical and
ethnographic geography of the island. There are no others; and true
ignorance, strong and sure of itself."[17] Leenhardt thought that he
knew a great deal more than the government, but he was himself
unsure on key points. Another trip to the troubled north would be
necessary. But for the moment he relied on the reports coming in
from his *natas* and on the emissaries radiating out from Do Neva. The
unrest continued, but after July its form was essentially secondary—
caused, that is, by the tactics of repression.

The administration, not really knowing who the rebels were or how
to find them in the bush, was forced to rely on the mobilization of
loyal tribes. Many of these came from Leenhardt's home territory.
The troops, armed with slings and spears, fought in traditional fashion.
Leenhardt feared "a regression." The government could not, in fact,
have done more to encourage savagery. It paid its troops in captured
booty and established bounties for "rebels," dead or alive. The memory
in everyone's mind was, of course, the brutal repression of 1878,
when severed heads were paid for in hard cash. Leenhardt watched in
horror and disgust the returning volunteers, laden with booty and
retailing stories of butchery—useless decapitations and the like. Certainly the greatest number of casualties in the entire rebellion were
caused during this uncontrolled period of what often amounted to
legalized tribal war.[18]

At Do Neva, Leenhardt tried to remain in touch with the worsening
conditions. The widespread instability posed a serious threat to the
success of his work on the island. If the spiral of rebellion, repression,
denunciation, and intimidation went too far, who could tell what kinds
of barbarism might surface among blacks and whites? The liberal,
evolutionary program of New Caledonia Protestantism would suffer
a fatal setback. Leenhardt felt the need to act, but he was stymied.
The political constraints of his wartime role made it impossible to be
openly critical of the government's tactics. During the next year and a
half, troops continued to search sporadically for real or imagined rebels
in the bush. Suspects were arrested; others were assassinated for
bounty; much confusion was created; little by little, calm returned.
Leenhardt was angered by the repression. And his indignation was
increased by the fact that, the "rebellion" over, the cover-up was beginning. Denunciations became more and more a cause of worry. Who
would take the blame?

The trial of the rebels would not begin for over a year. It was still
uncertain who would be charged. At Do Neva the missionary could

only guess at the machinations underway and fulminate against delays. (Innocent Melanesians were expiring in captivity.) With the help
of his *natas*, he continued his own investigation into the course of
events underlying the outbreaks. He went so far as to induce the
"soul" of the troubles, an old sorcerer, Maurice Paetou, to give himself up for delivery to the governor.[19] Meanwhile, opinion in the
island was more than usually taken up with suspicions and rumors.
For example, the newspaper *Océanie Française* convinced itself that a
Russian agent had been stirring up trouble in the north.[20]

In Leenhardt's eyes much depended on the trial and its verdicts.
Protestantism especially was in question. For if the innocent were not
acquitted and the guilty not unmasked, then the Protestants would
have been shown incapable of protecting their people from false accusation. And—thinking in terms of his postwar utopia of biracial democracy—French justice would have been undermined and with it all
of Leenhardt's preaching of loyalism and citizenship. During 1918 and
early 1919, the process of *instruction*, the investigatory portion of the
trial, dragged on. And in the end everything went wrong. Charges
were dismissed against a great many of those whom Leenhardt knew
to have been active in the rebellion. And to the consternation of the
Protestants, Chief Néa of the Wanas was arrested and charged as
principal conspirator. Néa had already been accused at an earlier
time—accused and vindicated. The administration, in fact, had con-
templated decorating him for his services. Néa had been helpful to
Leenhardt and the authorities in pacifying the Weava in June 1917.
However, in the nearly two years between the murders and the final
trial, Néa became the victim of a complex intrigue. As the only chief in
his region to have requested a *nata*, he was an object of suspicion for
the local gendarme and priest, who became his principal accusers at
the trial.

When it became clear at the end of the *instruction* that Néa would be
indicted as principal plotter, Leenhardt redoubled his efforts to penetrate the actual conspiracy. With the help of Apou Hmae and Eleisha
Nebay, the missionary finally managed to obtain a portion of the
"black money" originally received by Kefeat, the chief who led the
Tipinje killings. "Black money," a string of shell beads, was his encouragement to undertake vengeance against a white merchant. To
send this token was to offer an alliance of war. To accept the money
and pass it on was to enter into the alliance and extend it. Various
strings of black money had circulated throughout the highlands and
on both coasts of the island prior to the outbreaks of violence in

1917.[21] The presence of this secret conspiracy, with its promises of mutual aid, had encouraged various rebels to risk violent solutions to local grievances. But who was ultimately responsible?

⇒⊂

Leenhardt's researches—and those of his *natas*—into the origin of the black money would continue until the trial. Meanwhile, the ordinary work of the mission continued. And although the general situation looked grim, there were hopeful moments. In July 1918, for example, Leenhardt wrote to his wife, in Noumea, a letter full of admiration for the way a clan had organized a *"mai"* festival. (This ceremony was—and remains today—a yearly gathering at which one village entertains the others from its area with gift-giving, worship, oratory, feasting, and song: a kind of Protestant "small *pilou*.") "The natives themselves are behind the work; they organize their celebrations, supply the orators, set up the programs. It's all done in the family and is profoundly native. Our presence is a form of witness, not of direction."[22] And a month later the missionary was again a spectator, this time at a large Temperance Festival (*"pilou de temperance"*) at Gondé. Here in the mountain village whose surroundings had first charmed him in 1902, Leenhardt was again moved by the land and its people:

> Everyone was there, *natas* from Houailou, Ni, Poya, and those from down the mountain with their families. . . . Gondé, Koné, are old Caledonia. This character reappears in the temperance festival where the local eloquence unfolds with all the volubility required in *Canaque* merrymaking. . . . In the afternoon the ceremony of pledging took place. Each tribe banded together, singing to warm up the atmosphere. Planted in the middle of the half-circle formed by the groups were the three tall poles which are pulled out of the ground by those wishing to pledge themselves. You know the ceremony. But this time individual engagements were less numerous. They signed *en masse*; after a long pause a whole tribe would come forward to pull up the poles. If these were not our people, this might be a sign of less individuality, a regression. But it's a gesture of tribal opinion; and now they'll all abstain as in previous times all drank. The individualists were, on the other hand, not lacking, and their speeches were plentiful.[23]

We see again Leenhardt's concern for the "person." Protestant Melanesians are understood to be retaining their socio-mythic attachments

and at the same time acquiring the responsibility of separate individuals. This mediation would be much analyzed in the missionary-
ethnologist's later theoretical writings, particularly in *Do Kamo*. His
account continued:

> One of the poles was made of *bancoul*. [The participants]
> evoked all the images which *bancoul* suggested to them; you
> were a wood for war with your fruit which nourished us;
> now again you are a sign of war, but it's for victory over evil,
> etc. . . . Old Poindo spoke of his ancestors, then pulled up all
> three poles and hoisted them on his shoulder: "I pull them up
> and carry them to Boexawe"—the mountain of his ancestry,
> the sacred site where his gods live. Paganism, some will say,
> but proof, proof above all that his resolution is solid and
> founded on everything most deeply rooted in him.

In later reference to this scene Leenhardt recalls that as he watched
the old man carrying his three poles in evocation of the mountain, "I
seemed to hear, like a distant resonance from the ancient psalms: 'God,
my rock'. . . ."[24]

12. Do Neva, a Christian marriage, with ritual offerings of food; the bride
and groom are seated on the mat.

Photo: Leenhardt

Looking back over the day's events, Leenhardt sees in them a lesson for colonialists:

> . . . I wish one of those who govern the *Canaques* had been present—seated near these flags, close to this well-dressed crowd, near these *bancoul* poles being uprooted as a symbol and an oath, seeing all the movements of these orators challenging to combat with sling and spear; I wish he could hear the meaning of all the responses, the elaborate evocations of the ancestors, the sermons, the adjurations, the exhortations. I'm sure he'd have left the scene less preoccupied with fiscality and repression—and not whispering to himself, "We'll bring these people better laws." But none of these gentlemen were present, and none of them will ever observe this people organizing their celebrations, encouraging one another to live . . . savages constructing for themselves a civilization adequate to their mentality and born of ours. [Administrators] see in these men only material, and if the material resists, they use it to fill their prisons—muttering to themselves, "We'll never really understand these *Canaques*."

⋻⋲

In August 1918, recalcitrant Melanesian "material" was rotting in jail, awaiting the opening of the trial of the 1917 "rebels." But when Leenhardt and Apou Hmae came into possession of the black money, they held a crucial key to the affair, for this was the sort of "testimony" that carried real weight. Another important source of evidence was the government's own dossier, which it had kept throughout the uprising. At the trial the defense had to go on strike to force its introduction into evidence. When the government yielded, its earlier vindication of Chief Néa came to light, as well as a good deal of other information tending to acquit those accused. The prosecution's case was beginning to crumble when Néa's lawyer dramatically produced in open court the powerful black money. Many witnesses were incapable of lying in its presence. Testimonies changed. A number of conspirators and intermediaries now reversed their stories, including twelve of those already cleared during the *instruction*.

The real origin of the black money, it now appeared, was Bwaxat, *grand chef* of Hienghène. His nineteenth-century ancestors had been among the most redoubtable adversaries of the whites and had, one after the other, been deported to Tahiti. Now officially a Catholic, he had apparently continued in their ways, but with more discretion. Bwaxat had been able, using traditional diplomacy, to provoke outbreaks of rebellion on the opposite side of the island and in another valley without himself appearing involved. Leenhardt was summoned to testify at the very end of the trial. Bwaxat had not been openly accused, but eyes were turning in his direction. Leenhardt himself had already been denounced at the trial by the Catholic priest of Néa's region. His Protestant testimony was thus even more than usually suspect. Nevertheless, he felt that "the issue had ripened enough for one to be able to indicate the truth without seeming blinded by *parti pris*. I write *indicate*, the word is too strong, one felt so strongly that to jar predisposed minds would be to set them against the truth."[25] Leenhardt was able, he felt, "imperceptibly to direct attention toward the place of origin of the rebellion." And the supporting testimony of the black money followed. "And now," he wrote in September, "final revelations have arrived to confirm what I indicated without being able to denounce. And so it goes; [but] will they have the courage to continue to the end?" Then, as evidence mounted, Bwaxat and an important accomplice "confessed"—by committing suicide.[26]

Even in the face of all the new evidence, Leenhardt knew that justice—especially colonial justice—might well go astray. His letters of early September reveal an agony of suspense. All of his work and reputation for the last eighteen years seemed to hang in the balance. Finally, on September 19, the long trial came to a close. Néa and a number of others were acquitted. The penalties on the guilty were relatively light. Leenhardt was exuberant, relieved. The future of a vindicated mission looked bright. At Do Neva, the new school's walls of reinforced concrete were up, constructed by Melanesians. And although the mood of despair and uncertainty during the trial had been darkened by the sudden death of Joané—Leenhardt's main assistant and hope for independent native direction of the mission station— nevertheless the Pacific Brigade was returning. The soldiers' arrival wiped away the principal bitterness left over from the war (for they had not been brought home promptly). Their return provided the mission with a body of stalwarts, strong in their experience of having fought side by side with whites.

Along with the dispatch announcing the arrival of the riflemen, an exhausted missionary also received news that a fresh couple was on its way to relieve him and his wife. The vacation was long overdue and eagerly awaited. Leenhardt had become increasingly concerned about the education of his children. He was discouraged by the isolation of his wartime role and by the fear that he might not return in time to see his ailing father.[27] Now there was hardly time for a rapid tour around the Grande Terre and Loyalty Islands, a *nata* conference, tears and exhortations, regrets for ethnography and translation un-accomplished. And then suddenly the Leenhardts were off, in early 1920, for Sydney, Liverpool, France.

The "heroic period" of the New Caledonian Protestant Mission was over. The missionary's next tour of duty—without his family this time—would be fairly short. The Leenhardts had succeeded in estab-lishing a secure and growing place for the Reformed Faith in the colony. In "native affairs" the Protestants with their educated Mela-nesian elite were a force to be reckoned with. From Paris came new white missionaries, a nurse, and a school teacher. Never again would the Caledonian mission be so understaffed. And never again would Leenhardt have such complete authority over the general direction of the work. The problems facing the mission in the 1920s were no longer those of survival. They were the more subtle problems of success.

CHAPTER VII

Evangelical Horizons

The homecoming, after more than a decade of separation, was an emotional one for the Leenhardts and Michels. There was much—everything—to catch up on: marriages, births, children grown beyond recognition, and so forth. Maurice spent a great deal of time at Fonfroide to be near his father, who was dying. It was a good death. Franz Leenhardt held on until—at the end of his son's long vacation—the entire family gathered to celebrate the grandparents' golden wedding anniversary. Franz died nine days later, having completed his testament, a short work of theology entitled *L'Activité créatrice*.[1]

During his almost two years in France, Maurice was able to finish a number of long-deferred projects. His energies revived, he plunged into work. He completed the Houailou New Testament, revised and expanded *La Grande Terre*, and composed a number of reflections on socio-religious conversion: "Le catéchumène canaque," "Experiences sociales en terre canaque," "De la mort à la vie, l'évangile en Nouvelle-Calédonie," and his article on Bible translation. Of course, the veteran evangelist gave public lectures and consulted with the Mission Society in Paris.

It was soon after his arrival that he began a serious involvement with university ethnology. In September 1920, at his father-in-law André-Michel's vacation house on the English Channel, Leenhardt made the acquaintance of Lucien Lévy-Bruhl. It was the initiation of a long friendship and marked the beginning of a new career. The missionary had earlier expressed misgivings about the Sorbonne professor's theories: *Canaques* could not be characterized as "prelogical." Their thinking was not fluid; it conformed to quite a coherent "logic," but one dealing with dreams and mythic presences rather than with objective phenomena.[2] The meeting of the two men dispelled the fieldworker's reservations. Lévy-Bruhl was eager to find out Leenhardt's views on the Melanesian mind. He invited him for a walk in the nearby fields. The missionary spoke with restraint and an undeniable authority, while the professor was surprisingly ready to question his own theories. In 1922 Leenhardt still viewed the Paris University as a bastion of Godless positivism; but there was something in the bearing of Lévy-Bruhl that opened the world of secular science to the younger man.

Leenhardt frequently paid tribute to the important encouragement he received at this time. His portrayal of the philosopher is always the same: a tall silhouette, pointed grey beard, an expression of perpetual calm, two small eyes full of understanding and humanity. "You found comfort in his smile of agreement; you felt so much strength and serenity emanating from him."[3] In 1922 Leenhardt lost his father and principal guide in science; he seems to have found a partial replacement in Lévy-Bruhl. The philosopher shared many of Franz Leenhardt's qualities: intellectual probity, spiritual elevation, and an engaging—though always rather formal—simplicity of manner. The older man served as an influential patron and loyal friend during the missionary's late entrance into the Paris University. During the long walk with Lévy-Bruhl, the talk was scientific. Lévy-Bruhl expressed keen interest in the documentation Leenhardt had begun to amass and invited him to participate in scholarly meetings. The missionary felt himself confronted by an important challenge:

> . . . As we separated I strongly felt the posing of a great problem. I had replied appropriately to his questions and, yet, I was a Christian. Christian practice had not directed my thinking into paths opposed to reason. But he never asked any questions on this point; he observed. And I too, from my contact with him, learned to strip away the shell around what I could know of primitivism.[4]

Leenhardt liked to recount that, later, when he told Lévy-Bruhl his father's *mot*, "Facts are a Word of God," the philosopher's only reply was deeply, gravely, and ambiguously to bow.[5]

During this period, Leenhardt began to establish his reputation as a fieldworker. At meetings of the Paris Anthropological Society, he spoke with the authority of firsthand experience. In 1921 participant-observation fieldwork was becoming the recognized trademark of social anthropology. In the same year that Malinowski published *Argonauts of the Western Pacific*, Leenhardt met and impressed Marcel Mauss and Paul Rivet, the organizers of French ethnography. In 1922, at their request, Leenhardt prepared a long article on the *pilou* festival for *L'Anthropologie*.[6] His treatment was free of evangelical jargon and was functionalist in general approach, showing how the *pilou* bound together traditional Caledonian society. From the article no one would have guessed that the author had worked to suppress, or at least to transform, the very festival he described with such sympathy. There was no inevitable conflict in Leenhardt's mind between relativist ethnology and missiology. Ethnology was for him the crucial missing element in evangelical practice, the "method" needed to revitalize its ethnocentric sentimentalism. It also provided him with a theoretical bridge that could draw together disparate mission experiences—the African and Oceanian fields of the Paris Mission Society. Ethnology was essential in the comprehension of cultural-spiritual change and could make Christianization less authoritarian, more a part of the reciprocal interaction of cultures.

With his interests expanding rapidly, Leenhardt was uncertain about the future. He and Jeanne had decided that it would be best for the children to remain in France now that most of them were of secondary school age. Moreover, Jeanne was less eager than her husband to return to the Grande Terre. The rigors of mission work had taken their toll on her health. She was convinced, too, that her husband had an important role to play in the direction of the Paris Mission Society, perhaps as organizer of its training programs. Leenhardt would, in fact, have liked to fill the position of his former teacher Hermann Kruger as teacher of "mission science," to which he would now add ethnology. But the immediate continuity of the work on the Grande Terre required his presence. He would return alone to Do Neva for as long as he was needed to place the mission in the hands of a trustworthy successor, or until he was joined again by his wife.

>€

Leenhardt's growing interest in comparative mission strategies led him on a roundabout route back to his post. With financial support from his brother Paul, he visited all the French Protestant mission fields in sub-Saharan Africa. The trip, which lasted a full seventeen months, was a crucial experience for the 45-year-old missionary-ethnologist. He was able to test and confirm principles he had developed in his Oceanian work. Long letters to his wife provide us with a detailed record of his impressions.

In the equatorial forests of Gabon, he experienced intense moments of participation in the ebb and flow of nature, feelings similar to those that brought Albert Schweitzer—among the same forests and lakes—to his ecological philosophy of life. Such participatory feelings were not typical of white tourists in the "Dark Continent." Similar forests in Ubangui, a few years later, would impress another traveler, André Gide, as unbearably uniform and lifeless. Likewise, Joseph Conrad, who had navigated the Congo a few decades previously, experienced

difficulty detecting a humanity behind the menacing curtains of foliage
so unforgettably portrayed in *Heart of Darkness*. Leenhardt's eye, trained
in ethnography, saw otherwise:

> . . . After lunch we departed by canoe and made a stop in a
> Bakele village. One of the charms of Africa is the multitude
> of tribes juxtaposed in the forest and different from one
> another in language, customs, and certainly in origins. . . .
> The Bakele are not pahouins, their drum is not the long
> bantu tam tam, but it has a slender point; the village is not
> formed in an alley, but in separate huts. . . . Farther along are
> the Galoas, civilized, but organized matriarchally, beside
> them the wild Eshira, etc. Here are all the varieties we have
> in Oceania, but with no ocean separating them. For the prac-
> ticed eye there is great interest in distinguishing these dif-
> ferences, and I wish the missionaries of each ethnographic
> area would put together an initial monograph. But the pro-
> fane eye can see only blacks beneath big trees, some civilized,
> others not; and Africa appears monotonous rather than
> all aquiver with particles of humanity which are dying or
> rising. . . .[7]

Lacking the time or linguistic competence to do more than note the
varieties he found, Leenhardt concentrated on identifying parallels
and contrasts with his experience in Oceania.

The coincidence of colonialism and cultural disintegration was all
too obvious:

> . . . at Akomba. The village is sparsely populated, one former
> student of the mission, married, father of 2 children, talked a
> long time; everybody complains, the administration forces
> them to produce for market every week, life is expensive,
> the whites—"You don't realize how the whites treat us. . . ,"
> few children, the old crafts, forge, art objects, are dead—
> discouragement reigns. This is the way it is practically
> everywhere . . . .[8]

In a published account of his trip, Leenhardt stressed that the most
difficult obstacle to successful mission work was not "local paganism
. . . but the activity of colonization, the drought wind blowing from
Europe."[9] The traveling evangelist sketched an ascerbic portrait of the
typical administrator in the colonial capital: "He's got his vast silver
stripes, which the civilians enlarge as the soldiers reduce theirs; his
expression is heavy, his face cynical. 'These people don't react, not

interesting, soon I'll have my retirement, should have made a career in France. One can't do anything with these people. . . .'"10

In Gabon, Leenhardt became involved in disputes with the administration over accrediting mission schools. And he was of considerable help to his colleague at Lambaréné, Charles Hermann, who was setting up a pastoral training center. The visitor's searching comparative questions provoked a series of hard evaluations of the mission's accomplishments. Leenhardt drew up an informal list of issues and queries for the Gabon missionaries. He questioned the dispersion of their effort (too many stations, each the personal domain of an evangelist) and criticized the lack of independent African assistants and pastors.11 Reactions to his critique were mixed. All seem to have agreed that a strategic assessment was long overdue, but some thought their visitor too hasty, mistaken in details, and not sufficiently aware of local obstacles such as the poverty of the land and the lethal climate. Leenhardt was aware of these factors, but he believed his role as an outsider was to provide a long-range overview.

Hermann, at least, thought that the visitor had been successful, able to fit in "as a member of the family" while functioning as "an experienced, acute observer" who could somehow always manage to see through to the truth. "He has helped us," Hermann wrote the Paris committee, "to see more clearly among our methods the positive and negative results of our work. The great goodness of his heart protects him from making any malicious or wounding criticisms and allows him to encourage any effort that has a healthy logical foundation."12 But among some missionaries, who could be thin skinned, exhausted by the heat and by personal conflicts, Leenhardt's clarity of observation was distressing. One of his colleagues at Libreville complained that the visitor had hurt and discouraged two already confused young assistants by coolly enumerating the compromises and failures of their work.13 The colleague went on to say that he had himself learned a great deal from Leenhardt.

The directorate in Paris had never been enthusiastic about Leenhardt's tour, which had been seen as personal tourism and a luxury. Informal pressure was exerted on him to proceed immediately to the field, where he was needed, and to leave overview to the committee. But Leenhardt was acutely aware of his own and his colleagues' isolation and of the need to articulate guiding principles. He thought that the Paris committee, preoccupied with immediate problems of finance and staff, had not been supplying the required theoretical overview.14 He was training himself to provide this by visiting the major Protestant mission fields in Cameroon, Gabon, Angola, LeSotho, Madagascar, and Zambeze. This last mission was in a state of internal crisis and uncertainty, and the Paris committee at first forbade Leenhardt entry. Then, reversing itself, it charged him with an official mission of inquest. The immediate issue was whether the mission in Barotseland (then Northern Rhodesia) should be ceded to an English society. In France there was a growing movement to limit the Paris Mission Society's work to "colonial missions," those in French possessions. Leenhardt was to determine whether cession were possible and desirable in the Zambeze case. But Leenhardt chose to concern himself with considerably more than this immediate mandate. In the course of his nearly three months in the area, the visitor became deeply involved with the mission's complex problems.

Briefly stated, Leenhardt's diagnosis of the situation ran as follows. Since its dramatic founding by Coillard and after thirty-eight years of existence, the mission could count only 181 Christians in six separate centers. No independent pastoral corps or local church councils had formed; white missionaries controlled everything from their personal stations. Suspicion of the Africans had hardened into authoritarianism, and the enforcement of unbending, narrow requirements for church membership. The mission's one success had been a teacher-training program; but this emphasis had sacrificed moral and religious education to the mere passing of scholastic exams. These, Leenhardt's principal judgments of the mission's failure to create viable African congregations, were, in the opinion of an informed judge, "irrefutable and finely observed."[15]

Leenhardt played an active and delicate part in the affairs of the Zambeze mission. He acted as a catalyst for reform at its annual conference, in August 1923, where internal conflict, suspicion, and bitterness reigned. The visitor's official role as reporter on the stymied mission's future did not make his task any easier. But in the end even those he criticized most severely recognized the value and honesty of his judgments.[16] As always, Leenhardt urged more confidence in Africans. He was pained by the mission's handful of black pastoral assistants. "They are pitiful to see, with their childish manners, deferring to the missionary, whereas one guesses they have their own native life on the side, and must be harsh and bitter in their moments of depression and revolt."[17] He urged the Zambeze missionaries to reduce the number of white stations to three and develop more fully a recent experiment in station "annexes," with an aim to creating a system of independent local churches.

On the question of ceding the mission, Leenhardt vacillated. He was opposed, a priori, to the idea of "national missions." He believed that Gospel and empire should never be confused. If the Zambeze field were yielded to the English, he feared that LeSotho would be next; and this mission had always served as his model.[18] On the other hand, Leenhardt had serious doubts that the present personnel in Barotse-land, in their depression and disunity, could effectively implement the reforms he had urged. Without changes, the field was a liability. Leenhardt could not give Paris a clear answer. The directors were naturally frustrated by their emissary's reports, which told everything about the Zambeze field—its history, evangelical errors, how to save it—except whether it should be ceded at the present time. In effect, Leenhardt had become so involved in trying to make the Zambeze mission work that he was unable to stand back far enough to judge it in terms of the limited questions of his mandate. This instinct for participation was, of course, characteristic. But here it got Leenhardt into trouble. Although his report on the state of the field was an acute and constructive criticism that would be confirmed by later experience,[19] in Paris the episode served only to increase Leenhardt's reputation as someone who had a tendency to get out of hand. Pained and angry letters were exchanged.[20] Leenhardt's inappropriate report was shelved.

Elsewhere on his journeys, wherever the traveler found an informed or interested colleague, he pursued his interest in ethnology and translation theory. In Henry Rusillon's biblical school in Tananarive, we find him poring over student exercise books and speculating on their marginal drawings. The doodles suggest to him that shapes from the vegetable world provide bases for thought about abstract moral issues. He is critical of his colleague's clumsiness in translation, urging him to extract the meaning of terms from their usage and not to employ the words "soul, spirit, etc. . . . these impoverished words which ruin all primary research."[21] Leenhardt's encouragement and criticism helped his colleague a good deal, as Rusillon put it in a letter to Couve:

> I saw a good deal of M.L. up there. He has helped. He sees things a bit broadly, from above, seeking method. He wants an activity based on principles. He knows how to talk to blacks, is a man who knows how to work and who believes in seeing without blinders. It worries me to think that he may give up being a missionary in a few years. Well, God bless him; he's done us all a lot of good. He brought a bit of calm into situations where hastiness might have been ruinous, and I hope that some of the ideas he expressed will not fall on deaf ears, i.e., the need not to get lost in details and to make use of the native by giving him more independence.[22]

⋙⋘

Leenhardt's year and a half in Africa was a time of personal expansion and decision. The return to Do Neva lay just over the horizon and with it the prospect of renewed immersion in the problems of a single field. Leenhardt was torn between the desire for a wider forum for his ideas and the continuing need for involvement in the life of the Grande Terre. Would abandoning the Caledonian work be a bad example, he wondered? Would long-term separation harm the children? Would he and Jeanne be able best to encourage young missionaries by returning to Do Neva? Isn't it too easy to remain in a familiar place, an evasion of the greater challenge of struggling with the general problems of the missionary movement? These are the kinds of questions that recur in his letters as Leenhardt approaches Melanesia.

"Caledonia has regressed during these three years; the Native Affairs Office has turned into a labor recruitment, the women are flocking to Noumea . . . ." It seemed to the returning missionary that he was starting from zero, but this time without the resources needed to prevail. "I'll have time enough to be newly cursed without the time to become respected and understood." The "homecoming" at Do Neva was tense. It was not easy for Leenhardt to hide his disapproval of the work of his replacement, Paul Pasteur. Overall, Leenhardt thought, Pasteur had made two fundamental errors: first, lacking faith in the native and thinking like a white, "he lived in arrangement with the Administration . . . and was dominated; second, he lacked missionary patience, which, in order to form the native church, poses its existence in principle and pushes it to act for itself, without acting in its place." Pasteur's system at Do Neva had been designed for "well-behaved children, with elimination of the *têtes fortes* (strong-minded ones) . . . ."[24] A year before, he had lost control of the Do Neva school. Two teachers walked out in a dispute, and students showed their support in obstructionism and petty thievery. Pasteur's response was bitterness, talk of a purge, increased legalism. Eventually, twenty-five students were expelled, the most independent and therefore (in Leenhardt's eyes) the most promising. On his return, the veteran found "much depression among the present students—it's an interesting example of the genesis of harmful disciplines."[25]

Everything seemed in such disarray; and Leenhardt's own long-term commitment to Do Neva was so problematic that he found himself grappling with bouts of depression. To his wife he could express his feelings of despair. In a letter he does so with a *bwiri* sentence— that is, in Melanesian parlance, an expression blurted out without coherent thought, the free expression of an overflowing sentiment.

The Houailou words break abruptly into Leenhardt's description to his wife of the Do Neva situation. Literally translated: "I stay here, I know nothing, I am without will, inert, I want to weep, I love you, the day passes, tired always, it is over, the long thought of her here it is a heaviness. . . ."[26] Feelings of isolation recur throughout these letters of early 1924. Leenhardt is cut off from his family; communication with his colleagues is frustrating; white colonial society, as usual, distrusts him. He can see that in his absence the mission will be likely to degenerate into authoritarianism and complacency. But there are strong reasons why he should leave. For one thing, he feels too heavily loaded with the past and should cede to a younger person. Furthermore, he senses that his influence in the island is too great; some of the Melanesians he encounters have come to associate him with God. In their eyes a messianic aura surrounds their "Missi," an aura that only increases during his absences and is a source of frustration to his replacements.[27]

During this period of isolation, Leenhardt seems to have been confronting a constraining historical and ideological reality that can loosely be termed "the colonial situation." His ideas were ahead of their time. The missionary movement, far from being, as he had hoped, a reforming force, was at present an integral part of the colonial problem. He could not continue the work without colleagues. Yet how could he reasonably expect to find co-workers who shared his advanced attitudes? Even if he could find them and if the Grande Terre evolved as he hoped it would, how would this have any effect on other missionary fields, all of which now claimed his interest? Leenhardt could never have broken with the evangelical movement as a whole. But he was coming to realize that it needed sweeping reform and that until the calling could be made to attract people of real intellectual, as well as spiritual, seriousness, his life's effort in a single mission would be wasted.

Leenhardt found a certain consolation in ethnography, and during the twenty-three months on the Grande Terre he pursued his inquiries with a new vigor. He continued his genealogical surveys in the Houailou region and deepened his research into traditional religion. He encouraged newly literate informants to write down in the vernacular what they knew of custom. (I will discuss these methods in Chapter 8.) Lévy-Bruhl had obtained a government subsidy for Leenhardt's research. And in July 1925 Jeanne forwarded a letter from Paul Rivet asking her husband to prepare a volume for the scholarly publication series of the newly founded Paris Institute of Ethnology. The missionary-ethnographer was not tied to Do Neva; he circulated widely in the island and, as before, had highest praise for those clans who seemed to be modernizing without rejecting too much of their past. He was stunned anew by the land itself:

> I haven't spoken to you yet about the glory of the flaming coral trees (*flamboyants*) that glisten, scattered in the Caledonian bush. If Fra Angelico had known them he'd have put them in his visions of paradise. Red would be sanctified instead of being only the color of blood and damnation, and we'd see it enlivening the blue folds of the celestial countryside.[28]

As a traveler in Africa, Leenhardt had been preoccupied with what might be called the esthetics of place. As a conscious awareness, his sensitivity to scale and spatial form would manifest itself as a sudden recognition of beauty—or its lack—often understood, like the *flamboyants*, mythically. The initial mode of apprehension is participative and corporeal. For example, one evening in Gabon, somewhere on the great complex of waterways formed by the Ogoowé River and its system of lakes, the traveler is being paddled in a dugout canoe after an all-day trek through the forest:

> . . . The body of the rough dugout slipping along the African lake, rhythm of the paddles, reflection of the firmament in the ripples, clearness of the water bordered by the dark line of the forest. I dangle my feet outside the skiff; behind me, Hermann's gentle voice wanting to find out about everything and to care for me as a friend. . . .[29]

(It is interesting that Jeanne, who transcribed these letters for distribution among relatives, thought it necessary to replace her husband's dangling feet within the canoe!) In his later writings, Leenhardt would develop a conception of "esthetic" phenomenology, by which he meant the experience of affective forms and rhythms. As he saw it, esthetic knowledge was elemental to both "primitive" and "civilized" mentalities; esthetic phenomena were proximate "events," perceived in "two dimensions," that is, with minimal distance separating subject from object.[30]

Leenhardt himself experienced the absence of this distance most fully in New Caledonia, where "one delights entirely in nature; one blends oneself into her soft forms, living in the same rhythm as she . . . ," experiencing "the well-being of a bath at [illegible] the temperature of a man and the water enveloping him."[31] There is no need to stress the feminine, maternal imagery of this myth of "life." An atten-

tiveness to the rhythms of nature was, Leenhardt thought, characteristic of native Melanesians. With a good deal of sympathy—tinged by
nostalgia—he observed the intensity of their intimacy:

> A dense rain was falling along the horizon in the direction I
> had to ride, and Kabar cups his ear: "It's coming down hard, I
> hear it." But I could not make out any sound produced by
> rain falling 4 km off. These people are more within nature
> than we, they live their intimacy with her, they amuse them-
> selves in her thousand daily variations, whereas we only
> admire her in her infinite beauties, small or large—transi-
> tory hints of a finality whose secret is with God, and of
> which we are only one modest element . . . .[32]

⋗⋐

Leenhardt's memories of Do Neva were not destined to be memories of final success. Although Protestantism was securely established
on the Grande Terre, his own dream of reciprocal religious translation was fragile and not easily communicated. In the 1920s, with the
influx of new staff, latent contradictions between New Caledonia and
the Loyalty Islands, between Leenhardt's practice and that of his colleagues, rose to the surface. In thinking about what sort of person
should take over at Do Neva, Leenhardt urged that an "intellectual"
be found for the job, "and by intellectual I don't mean [simply] an
intelligent man—I mean [someone] who sees relations between things,
who doesn't dream of a little coterie, nor of a little bishopric in Noumea, but of the race to be saved by the Gospel."[33] Looking around at
the staff currently stationed in the archipelago, Leenhardt found no
one who seemed up to the task. A new missionary was needed. But
Paris was not able to provide a replacement quickly, and this made life
difficult at Do Neva. Leenhardt knew he would need time to train his
successor.

In the meantime the veteran did his best to guide the course of
events tactfully. He failed. The weight of his authority was too great.
Paul Pasteur, along with a new schoolteacher and a nurse, formed a
pressure group against him. There was an ugly fight at the inter-island
missionary conference of 1924. Leenhardt was overridden by majority
vote: Pasteur escaped the Grande Terre for Maré, and Philippe Rey-
Lescure, a missionary-in-training, was transferred to Do Neva. Rey-
Lescure happened to be Leenhardt's nephew. His uncle strongly resisted the transfer, for it seemed dangerous to set up a "family station," especially one whose practice would have to remain different
from the others. He wondered whether the young man—who was of

an independent, but stubborn, nature sometimes given to moodiness —would take well to being second in command, first to Leenhardt and then to his successor.

M. and Mme. Emile Vincent did not arrive until November 1925, and Leenhardt was scheduled to depart at the start of 1926. The veteran took his replacement around the island and did his best to initiate him into the complexities (and intellectual fascination) of the island-wide work being pursued by the *natas*. In parting, however, he warned Vincent not to give in to the "temptation" of the Loyalty Islands. There, Leenhardt was convinced, Protestantism had gone soft, lacking the constant challenge of struggle with pagans and colonial whites. Loyaltian Protestantism was not actively experiencing the spiritual revivification of continual translation. The islands tended to attract the "pastoral" rather than the "missionary" type of evangelist, and the same type was characteristic of the *natas* currently trained there.

These two familiar figures, "the pastor" and "the missionary," recur in Leenhardt's letters during this final year at Do Neva. He complains of his own ineptitude for pastoral duties—the everyday running of a church, preaching to whites, edification, and so on. The missionary's role is more active, involving outreach, education, the clash and interpretation of religions and cultures. The missionary, for Leenhardt, establishes churches, encourages and corrects them until they are capable of self-direction; then he moves on. Thus local churches, once firmly in place, must be in the hands of Melanesian pastors. The missionary must trust the new church, not become too involved in its details, and must maintain an overview. Many of Leenhardt's colleagues, especially on the Loyalty Islands, where Protestantism had been established for half a century, were sliding into pastoral roles, usurping the proper functions of native pastors and thus reducing them to the status of mere assistants and school teachers.[34] Throughout his years in New Caledonia, Leenhardt had fought to protect Protestantism on the Grande Terre from too much Loyaltian influence. Since the first *natas* were all from the islands and since Maré and Lifou were strongholds of the reformed faith, he had to struggle considerably to develop an independent New Caledonian church. In 1910 he had resisted attempts by his colleagues and the Paris committee to unify, prematurely, the overall work in the archipelago. And he had opposed a colleague, Etienne Bergeret, in his plan to found a second station on the main island.[35]

In 1925, before departing from the Grande Terre, Leenhardt did everything in his power to clarify the ongoing organizational relationships within the field. At his last Missionary Conference, he succeeded in having a constitution of his design ratified for the New Caledonian churches. The veteran was in a strong position. A series of scandals involving illicit amorous liaisons had resulted in the recall of those who had recently led the opinion against him.[36] Rey-Lescure was beginning to understand and support his general policy, and Leenhardt was temporarily on good terms with an isolated Étienne Bergeret. The constitution of 1925 formally recognized the differences between the Loyalty Islands and the Grande Terre, differences of geography, ethnography, colonial history, and a quarter-century of evangelical practice. In the 1925 document, the separate practices were allowed to coexist, with the stated hope that, over time, with communication and exchange, the differences would disappear. It recognized Leenhardt's plan for two missionaries at Do Neva—one in charge of schools, the other of tribal churches—and it established Houailou as the language of local religious instruction.[37] Leenhardt was pleased with the result, for it seemed to guarantee continuity in the work. Although Vincent arrived at the last minute, Leenhardt had enjoyed, with Rey-Lescure, something like the fifteen months he believed necessary to train a successor. His nephew had proven himself an energetic worker and could be counted on to speak strongly for New Caledonian tradition.

Back in Paris, Leenhardt faced an uncertain future. He did not feel that he was giving up his mission vocation, and he certainly did not think he was cutting himself off from the Grande Terre. He expected to be active at the Maison des Missions, perhaps serving on its Oceanian Commission while teaching missiology and ethnology. The reception he received was disconcerting. He prepared a report on his overall work, but it met with indifference from the Mission Committee. No need for advice, he was told; one of the society's directors, Elie Allegret, is leaving for Oceania and will report on the situation. Leenhardt knew that Allegret, an African veteran, had never shown much comprehension of the Pacific. He wrote to the departing director, urging him to avoid judging the Grande Terre in Loyaltian terms. He received no reply.[38] In Paris, the New Caledonian veteran was being held at arm's length. The directors mistrusted his strong opinions and tendency to become involved in general mission business. He was suspected, in some quarters, of ambitiousness. In fact, Leenhardt was not interested in administration; bureaucratic management and fundraising were not his strong points. But he did very much want to revitalize the recruitment and training program for young evangelists. His aspirations were given only lukewarm encouragement. The so-

ciety was cutting back on its mission school during these years, dis-
persing its students to other Paris faculties. An attempt was made to
reassign Leenhardt as missionary in West Africa. When the veteran
refused, his reputation for insubordination was confirmed.[39]

Within the extended family of French Protestantism, personal rivalries and character conflicts played their part. The mission directors
knew Leenhardt well. If he were allowed to become an animating
force at the Mission Center, his energy, charm, and wide experience
would soon make him, de facto, a co-director of the society. The committee—Daniel Couve in particular (Leenhardt's cousin, to whom he
often wrote in frank, intimate terms)—was becoming tired of the
constant criticisms: The society is indifferent to New Caledonia; it
lacks a guiding method, and so on. Did Leenhardt appreciate the complex job of directing an operation with many fields and shrinking
resources? His "meddling" was received with increased stiffness, and
by the early 1930s the rupture with the more conservative Couve had
become irreparable. Leenhardt was, of course, intensely interested in
the fate of his mission. He stayed in touch with Rey-Lescure and the
other members of the field. But his interventions had to be painfully
discreet, for the Grande Terre was officially no longer his business.
The veteran watched helplessly as the mission was led in directions he
could not approve, dissolving, finally, into a chaos of internal strife.

As Leenhardt had feared, Allegret's visit to the New Caledonian
archipelago served to encourage Loyaltian tendencies. The Missionary Conference of 1927, presided over by the director, significantly
altered Leenhardt's 1925 constitution, now calling for an immediate
unification of methods in the entire field. The way was open for a
majority that favored Loyaltian methods to impose them on a Caledonian minority composed of Rey-Lescure and the absent but influential Leenhardt. Bergeret, back at Lifou since 1922, had yielded to
the veteran in 1925. Now encouraged by Allegret, an old friend, he
urged acceptance of his own plan. It included the founding of a synod
uniting the archipelago and the redefinition of natas as "pastor-teachers."[40] The new Melanesian Synod was to be presided over by white
evangelists. It would consider issues of general policy raised by local
churches and by the missionary conference. Since the majority of
pastors on the Grande Terre were still of Loyaltian origin and since
Europeans were to play a central role, the new institution seemed
destined to reflect the paternalistic style of religion in the islands.

The 1927 Conference's other change of policy, the "pastor-teacher"
issue, would be hotly debated. Bergeret and Allegret sought to generalize the Loyalty conception of Melanesian pastors. In the islands the

church was long established and hierarchical in structure, with the missionary playing a central role. The Melanesian pastor functioned as an assistant and teacher; general church administration, evangelism, and political matters tended to be left to European staff. On the Grande Terre, however, Leenhardt had always insisted that native pastors maintain a wide-ranging role. The early *natas* had been missionaries, pastors, teachers, and socio-political organizers. On the islands, where distances were short and travel easier, pastors could more safely be immobilized as heads of schools. On the Grande Terre pastoral and pedagogical duties were often incompatible. The *nata*'s varied activities required mobility and independent initiative.[41]

After 1920 the archipelago's pastoral school was located on Lifou, its normal school at Do Neva. Little by little, a schism developed between the two programs, with each one tending to encroach on the other's work. As Rey-Lescure came to dominate the New Caledonian effort, he expanded the network of "bush schools," manning them with teachers from Do Neva. Meanwhile, the pastoral school, under Bergeret, trained pastors who were Lifouans or Loyalty-influenced. As time went on, each missionary came to trust only his own students. The Grande Terre could only lose from the official division of labor. Its own pastoral candidates were trained in the language and practices of Lifou, and few Loyalty students were sent to the Do Neva normal school, because Bergeret thought that the roles of teacher and pastor should be united and because "the spirit of Do Neva" was suspect among the Loyalty missionaries.[42]

The schism widened inexorably. In 1928 and 1929 Rey-Lescure was on vacation in France, where, with Leenhardt's support, he argued against the pastor-teacher idea. He won his point—the policy's impracticality in New Caledonian conditions—but only for a time and at the cost of angry protests from his colleagues in the field, who accused him of acting behind their backs. In 1930, with Rey-Lescure back at Do Neva and Bergeret now urging his own viewpoint in France, an already tense situation exploded into open strife.[43]

There is no point in rehearsing in detail the ensuing sequence of attacks and counterattacks, recriminations, and misunderstandings. Rey-Lescure was soon isolated from the rest of his colleagues. And the young man's "ungovernable" personality became the central issue. It is depressing to read the swollen mission archives from this period; in all the letters and reports, almost nothing is said concerning the aspirations and responses of the Grande Terre's Melanesians. "*L'Affaire Rey-Lescure*" had degenerated into a confrontation of missionary egos, revealing once again the fatal tendency of evangelism to become centered on the problems of evangelists rather than on the needs of indigenous churches. The conflict deteriorated to a point where two colleagues at Do Neva, living within fifty yards of one another, communicated by letter.

Rey-Lescure had absorbed many of Leenhardt's ideas concerning cultural authenticity. His bush schools were adapted to local needs, stressing vernacular instruction. He advocated, for example, a program of reconstructing the pagan *grande case* as a symbol of regional pride. This sort of idea met with disbelief and noncomprehension from his colleagues. Rey-Lescure, in effect, took over the reputation of his predecessor as the organizer of an unorthodox church. Like Leenhardt, he was an active evangelist and political partisan. (The government in Noumea complained about his subversive activities.) But his uncle had been personally outgoing, willing to explain and to compromise, whereas Rey-Lescure, less sure of himself perhaps, was taciturn and defensive. In late 1932 the Paris Mission Committee yielded to the simplest expedient; they purged the missionary who had stood against his colleagues. Rey-Lescure and his wife were transferred to Tahiti. As a consequence, New Caledonian churches were left without an energetic defender of their specific tradition. The recent years of changing policies and ugly internal strife had been disillusioning to Melanesian Protestants. Do Neva rapidly declined as an animating center; the mission's important functions were henceforth located in the Loyalty Islands. The role of Rey-Lescure's normal school diminished; his artisanal training program was closed down. The education of pastor-teachers took place on Lifou. And significantly, the Houailou language was downgraded in a move to establish Lifou as the common vernacular of mission education and publicity.[44]

In Paris, seeing the drift of events, Leenhardt finally abandoned his attempts at informal influence and composed an open condemnation of the situation. In December 1932, he sent a fifty-page memorandum to the president of the Paris Mission Society—his version of recent events and of the history of New Caledonian Protestantism. It stands alone among the documents preserved in the archives as an attempt to disengage important principles of mission practice from the chaos of details and clash of personalities. Unfortunately, in 1932, the Paris directors were more interested in finding a solution to the crisis than they were in rethinking its origins. They perceived Leenhardt's analysis as a partisan attack on their handling of the situation, and the text was returned to its author with a frigid warning not to meddle further in the business of the New Caledonian mission. The document provoked a minor scandal within the society. There were brief rumors of a possible attempt to oust the present leadership in favor of Leen-hardt (who had to restrain members of his family, too zealous in his defense). Although the ex-missionary had just seen a quarter-century of work undermined, he was not interested in palace revolutions. He wished to deliver himself of the truth as he saw it, to prevent Rey-Lescure's transfer, if possible, and to open a serious discussion of the issues. The directors declined to meet with him.[45]

Leenhardt had always fought any move toward diminishing the responsibilities accorded to native Christians. For this reason he re-sisted the demotion of pastors to pastor-teachers. Moreover, he looked with dismay at the rapid growth of the mission's European staff. How is it, he asked in his 1932 memorandum, that the more we intensify our effort, the worse the results? His reply: we surround the natives, and they become attached to us instead of to the spirit of God. The more numerous the missionaries, the more they feel their status se-cure and the more they lose real contact with indigenous realities. Instead of training elites to take responsibilities, the new staff will itself take on the important work. Paternalistic missionaries become just another group of whites, and the mission an "auxiliary of colonial policy."[46] In his pained memorandum, Leenhardt summarized the es-sence of the affair as he saw it. The New Caledonian church had been cut off from its tradition, a foreign structure had been imposed; the effect could only be disastrous.

"Something is spiritual only if it has fashioned its own form. Out-side this there is only the domain of human authority."[47] Leenhardt's words may stand as a distillation of the lesson he learned in Melanesia.

PART II

Do Kamo

... the person, in opposition to the individual, is capable
of enriching itself through a more or less indefinite
assimilation of exterior elements. It takes its life from
the elements it absorbs, in a wealth of communion. The
person is capable of superabundance.

—M.L.

... for biographical truth is not to be had, and even if it
were it couldn't be used.

—Freud

INTRODUCTION TO
PART TWO

Atai, warchief of Bourail, was principal leader of the New Caledonian rebellion of 1878. He never accepted French occupation of his land, protesting against repeated devastation of his people's crops by colonists' cattle. When the governor of the colony answered his complaints by advising him to erect fences, Atai is said to have retorted: "When my taro plants go eating the cattle, *then* I'll build fences." After a dispute with the authorities over land appropriated for a penitentiary, Atai became a highly effective insurrectionist. The rebel chief was finally tracked down by the army of repression. He stood his ground, along with his son and four warriors. . . .

> [The] severed heads were taken back to La Foa stuck on bayonets. [Atai's] very expressive head . . . [along with his hand] was sealed in a tin container full of alcohol. It was sent by M. Navarre, a naval doctor, to the Paris Anthropological Society, where it was presented by Dr. Broca in 1879.[1]

From the *Journal* of the Anthropological Society:

> These pieces have arrived in a perfect state of conservation. They give off no odor, and we hope that even the brains, although left in their skulls, will still be good for study.
> The magnificent head of Chief Atai attracts special attention. It is very expressive; the forehead particularly is very handsome, very high and broad. The hair is completely black. The nose is very platyrrhinian, as wide as it is long. The hand, wide and powerful, is very well shaped, except for one short finger, the result of an old wound. The palm lines are similar to our own.[2]

It is only in recent decades—largely as a result of national liberation movements—that Western scholars have been forced to confront the moral problems posed by colonial dominance. Anthropology, a science and an esthetic that functioned rather comfortably within the imperial context, can no longer ignore that its "data"—the human objects of its study and affection—have often been exploited, sometimes dying, individuals and cultures. As a response to this unhappy circumstance, a tone of elegaic regret is no longer sufficient. Neither is it enough to invoke—as in the sources above—the "expressive" power of artifacts. Atai was seen by the anthropologists not as a complex individual caught in specific historical circumstances, but rather as a choice specimen. Power relations were also beside the point. The scholarly journal did not need to mention that a standing price had been offered by the colonial government for rebel heads.

Atai's death, in an act of war, is in many ways less disturbing than his appropriation in an act of science. And if anthropological research no longer proceeds as it did in 1878, the general political, moral, and epistemological issues starkly raised by Atai's fate remain. Is it possible to study other people without asserting a power over them? How may one transmit the "expressive" power of others without immobilizing or preserving this power—in tin containers, in museums, in authoritative texts? If, on the other hand, cross-cultural research wishes to learn *from* an Atai, as well as about him, it is at least necessary to stop thinking of social science as a process of collecting and analyzing data. Anthropological "specimens"—texts and artifacts— brought back from the field should not be seen primarily as evidence of a distinct other reality or even as signs, traces to be interpreted, of the "native point of view." Rather, anthropological data must be seen as referring to the research process itself, reflecting its specific dialectics of power, of translation, of interpersonal exchange.

Such a transformation of anthropological representation remains to be accomplished in the scientific, textual practice of the Western human sciences. If there are signs that things are changing in the dynamics of ethnography, these changes cannot be conceived as independent of the continuing deployment of neo-imperial power. Westerners abroad still struggle within certain ideological roles and habits of mind constituted by colonial relationships. This is not a circumstance one may simply step out of, however enlightened or ethnological one's viewpoint. Leenhardt's experience as a professional anthropologist makes this clear.

The period from 1878 to 1954—Maurice Leenhardt's lifespan—was the heyday of unchecked European expansion throughout the world. During these years, roughly from the Congress of Berlin to the Vietnamese War, an apparently endless stream of Westerners moved out from Europe and North America in search of power, adventure, virtue, wealth, amusement, redemption, understanding. No series of terms can sum up this extraordinary desire. During these years the cultural influence of the West became fully planetary in scope. Leenhardt was an agent and a critic of this influence: as anthropologist and missionary he took part in the imperial venture while simultaneously struggling against its structures of knowledge and power.

The forms of imperial dominion have not been simple. Naked oppression of other societies has coexisted rather easily with generous esthetic appreciation of their modes of life; economic exploitation has seldom impeded the deployment of scientific understanding; European religion and medicine have been dispensed together. Western influence over the rest of the planet was—and is—inventive, protean, sometimes liberal, and to a degree dialogical. It is important to see the transactions of empire as give-and-take as well as simple oppression. A complex view of power may help account for the fact that the apparent defeat of colonialism after 1950 has not eradicated its diverse modes of influence. Such a view helps also to account for the presence, within the imperial milieu, of ambiguous roles and personalities whose activity cannot be explained by a notion of hegemonic or unreciprocal dominance.

Two such ambiguous figures, the missionary and the anthropologist, unite in the career of Maurice Leenhardt. The figure of the Christian evangelist is, of course, as old as the Pentecostal gift of languages to the Apostles. The persona of the anthropologist is newer, more narrowly identified with the modern imperial period. However, the two roles are the products of a common cultural heritage: an amalgam of Greek rationality and Christian universalism. If the evangelist goes to the ends of the earth to transform the heathen, the ethnographer goes to study them. Both participate in a restless Western desire for encountering and incorporating others, whether by conversion or comprehension.[3]

Within this informing context, the anthropologist and missionary have emerged as rivals. The social scientist, seen from the missionary's point of view, has little deep concern for the people he or she investigates. A godless person and a moral relativist, the fieldworker is usually a transient. The ethnographer has even harsher opinions of the evangelist, who appears as an enemy of science, ethnocentric, and unscrupulous in fomenting cultural chaos for the sake of questionable religious alterations. The conflicting opinions are as true as most stereotypes; they are certainly not very useful in understanding someone like Leenhardt, whose life represents at least a partial transcendence of the antinomy.

On one side, the scientific anthropologist stands for nonintervention and ultimately for a contemplative attitude toward others; on the other, the moralistic evangelist reforms, converts, exhorts. To the extent that the two positions are maintained in opposition, as an either/or choice, a whole range of political or cultural action *with* others is precluded. The outsider is condemned to write and to act *on behalf* of indigenous peoples—to represent them. Individual anthropologists and missionaries have made their peace with the two conflicting roles. Indeed some, like Leenhardt, have acted as if the opposition did not exist. But in his career we see the possibility and, simultaneously, the impossibility of stepping outside a structure of experience characteristic of evangelical-anthropological civilization. If we can see his paradoxical situation more clearly than Leenhardt did, we should be wary of assuming that the predicament is no longer our own.

CHAPTER VIII

The Making of
Ethnographic Texts

During the first fifty years of his life, Leenhardt devoted his principal energies to missions, in the last twenty-six, to ethnology. But we must avoid thinking of him as a missionary-turned-ethnologist. He never thought of separating the two callings, although he usually avoided mixing their different modes of discourse. Leenhardt's blindness to what is normally considered a contradiction of roles and purposes was not, as we shall see in this chapter, without its advantages.

As an academic social scientist, he remained active in evangelical institutions and debates. One can discern various slow changes of attitude: the attainment of a broad, ecumenical perspective and a growing willingness to challenge colonial assumptions. But there are no sharp breaks or existential crises in his life. Leenhardt would have agreed with Merleau-Ponty that "the 'healthy' man is not so much the one who has eliminated his contradictions as the one who makes use of them and drags them into his vital labors."[1]

An experience of plenitude—*do kamo*, the person in his or her authenticity—was the ideal sketched in Leenhardt's ethnology. It was also the experience he sought to realize in his own life. Thus the writing of ethnography was a process of self-reflection—a continuing evaluation of the problematic involvement with Melanesia. This aspect of Leenhardt's scientific production is hidden in his earlier books, which maintain an empirical, descriptive stance. But by the late forties, his primary concern for religious phenomenology had fully emerged. In work after work he returned, almost obsessively, to certain essential themes: myth, the person, esthetic perception. These will be discussed in detail later. Here we will survey Leenhardt's initial ethnographic effort and suggest how his position as a missionary both aided and impeded his scientific research. His research methods encourage us to rethink fieldwork as a collective mode of production, thus calling into question a number of common assumptions about ethnographic description, interpretation, and authorship.

⇒⊂

One of Leenhardt's informants was the regional chief (*grand chef*) of
the Houailou area, Mindia Néja. In 1914 the missionary wrote to his
father describing the progress of his research into local kinship:

> For the last three weeks I've been trying to get through to
> Mindia about his family, but he's hard to reach. Every Friday
> I've spent a long morning with him at the home of the Neoueo
> *nata*. The first time it was hard to get him to relax. He explains
> to me that we whites are too stupid to understand their
> kinship, and we the missionaries, too preoccupied with their
> souls to be interested in their obscure relationships of the
> flesh. I was able to lead him on with a few questions in the
> heart of the subject. On the second Friday he had prepared a
> little sheet which he brought along, after making me wait an
> hour. This last time he was waiting for me at the *nata*'s,
> having written out four large pages.[2]

The situation is familiar. We see an informant's initial resistance, the
frustrating delays, leading questions, and finally, with luck, the establishment of a measure of confidence and mutual interest. Mindia Néja
posed particular problems as a source of ethnographic information,
for Mindia's family relationships were facts of immediate political
importance.

There is, of course, a political dimension to all knowledge of native
life gained by a white in a context of colonial dominance. Thus Mindia
had *a priori* reasons for apprehension of the whites and their "stupid-
ity." The recording of a genealogy required the divulging of names
and relationships previously hidden to those—white and Melanesian
rivals—who might make political use of them. Mindia's influence as
grand chef throughout the Houailou area was based on his kinship
relations. But his position was far from secure. He had consolidated
his power only a few years before the Leenhardts' arrival in New
Caledonia, with the support of an anti-Catholic administration in
Noumea. Mindia at that time became a Protestant convert, allying
himself with a new form of Christianity lately imported by the *natas*
from the Loyalty Islands. Soon the political winds shifted; the ethnographic interviews of 1914 took place in the midst of a protracted
struggle between colonial government and Protestant mission. The
administration had just created two new "chiefs" in the region in an
attempt to undermine Mindia, the *natas*, and Leenhardt.

The *grand chef*'s relationship with his missionary was ambiguous.
The two, though allies, kept their distances. Leenhardt knew that

Mindia's "conversion" to the reformed faith was a shifting mix of sincere belief and political expediency. Mindia was the "pagano-protestant" *par excellence*. The missionary was not opposed to Mindia's legitimate traditional political roles; he defended the chief's right to authority throughout the Houailou area. Leenhardt felt that government should stay out of tribal politics as much as possible and that the Protestant Mindia was the most authentically qualified via traditional family relations to exercise power in the region. The missionary's position, like that of the chief, was a mixture of sincere belief and political expediency.

The two men needed to be able to trust one another. The establishment of mutual confidence took many years, but in the series of interviews in which Leenhardt records Mindia's genealogy we are witnessing a moment of breakthrough. The *grand chef* entrusts the missionary with the foundations of his power, facts that Leenhardt will use to defend Mindia's rights against his rivals and the administration. At the very least, it has become clear that the missionary will not turn these facts against his informant. Leenhardt, for his part, requires a secure Protestant *grand chef* in the vicinity of his harassed mission. Maurice Leenhardt's research was not always conducted in so tense a situation as that of early 1914, but it was never without immediate political consequences.

Leenhardt's relation with Mindia Néja was as openly evangelical as it was clearly political. Few anthropological researchers will remember being accused of too much concern with their informants' "souls"— and as evidence of uninvolvement, this is perhaps not altogether fortunate. Leenhardt, however, in making an ethnographic informant of Mindia, had clear ulterior motives going beyond the aims of science or politics. He was interested in the man himself, his inner morale. Inevitably, Mindia became a test case for Caledonian Protestantism in the eyes of all. In native tradition the chief was a sacred personage, "older brother," and mediator with the ancestors. His "word" (*parole*) was the unity of the clan, and thus the state of his "soul" was of far-reaching importance; it expressed the power of the group.[3] Leenhardt wanted Mindia to curb his taste for political intrigue, and he hoped that the chief would eventually bring himself to accept monogamy. We observe this moral concern as Leenhardt continues his account of collecting Mindia's genealogy:

> We got down 7 or 8 generations, and you can clearly see all the descendants who perished when the whites arrived. It's so striking that it looks like a crime. I'm going again next Friday to finish the job, but my real goal was to get closer to

Mindia. In this I haven't succeeded yet. He's opened up a bit, but [only] on exterior matters, and on things he can use to know and judge his world better. But as soon as I try to press him, I get that full and entire affirmation, those "It's true" replies, so complete that there's nothing to do but fall silent....

Leenhardt interpreted the *grand chef's* passivity when pressed on personal issues of morality and belief as a sign of demoralization. In another letter he notes that among the more savage unconverted "if you talk of religious or moral truths the traditional man may get his back up, but that's always proof that he has understood."[4] In *Notes d'ethnologie néo-calédonienne* (1930), Leenhardt published three photos of Mindia: one taken in 1872 reveals a slim young man in full traditional regalia, turban, feathers, penis sheath, ceremonial axe; the second from 1898 shows the dignified, full-fledged *grand chef*, wrapped in fine skins, spears in one hand, in the other an umbrella. But the third taken in 1912 finds him in a photographer's studio, leaning in a stylized Western pose on a false balustrade. He wears a full French military uniform, three medals, and an expression of discomfort and confusion. The

13. Grand Chef Mindia Néja in 1878, 1892, and 1912.

From M.L., Notes, plate 35; photos: Hughan, Société des Missions Evangéliques exterior changes are obvious. But what has happened within? What had been the fate of that pride so clearly manifest in the second photograph and so important to the man and his race? This was Leenhardt's concern. For Mindia there was no returning to the early snapshots. He was not going to be left in peace by encroaching cattlemen, farmers, priests, and gendarmes in Melanesia's most heavily colonized island. Native Caledonians in 1914 could no longer choose to be alone. Thus it was important to discuss seriously the old and the new, the problems of shifting moralities. Such talk, leading to self-conscious change, was the program of the liberal missionary.

We would be wrong to separate this program from his scientific ethnography. Leenhardt hoped that the very process of recording information about tradition would stimulate reflection on the part of his informants. While preserving the old in written form, they would distance themselves from it. But reflection would not entail total rejection; ethnographic attention must give value to specifically Melanesian ways of being—in the eyes of both native converts and whites.[5] If something like this process of thinking or interpreting custom could take place, then the interests of science and the mission would overlap.

>∈

It is clear that for Leenhardt Mindia Néja's "soul" came first, his kinship second. (Of course the two were not, in practice, clearly separable—a fact Leenhardt was to elaborate at considerable length in *Do Kamo* and elsewhere, and which Mindia, in his resistance to the missionary's personal questions, was perhaps trying to make clear.) But if ethnography could be a means to a broadly religious or moral end, does this invalidate it as science? Our judgment in such matters must be based on specific circumstances, not *a priori* assumptions. There is no reason here to suspect that Leenhardt's genealogies were less accurate than those that might have been collected by a supposedly neutral secular observer. Indeed, the intrusive effect of the missionary's openly religious aims may well have been less than that of a person whose motives could be less clearly understood. In any case, Mindia Néja would not, in 1914, have delivered his genealogy to any other European in New Caledonia. And the details of his lineage have been of considerable importance in writing the political anthropology of the Houailou region.[6]

Missionary ethnography is, of course, limited by the nature of its informants, a missionary tending to rely only on members of his "flock." This was true of Leenhardt to a large extent, though he was familiar with unconverted and, to a lesser degree, with Catholic groups.

Fortunately, however, many of his best informants were close to the old ways, and Leenhardt's concept of religious conversion discouraged radical rejections of the "sinful" past. One is in any event reluctant to press the objection too far, since it is always difficult to assess the representative status of anthropological informants. Ethnographies do not, typically, reveal very much on this score; few studies precisely connect individual ethnographers with specific local factions. T.N. Pandey's "Anthropologists at Zuni" is a notable exception.[7]

The most telling scientific complaints against missionary ethnography center on its amateur quality, unevenness, and the strong ambivalences toward "paganism" that tend to color its descriptions. Such criticisms are frequently justified. However, a wide qualitative spectrum exists within which individual contributions must be judged. One should recall Codrington's admission of fault—a fault shared by Leenhardt: "under the circumstances of [my] inquiries, much of the worst side of native life may be out of sight, and the view given seem more favorable than might be expected; if it be so, I shall not regret it."[8] If unevenness and prejudice (both positive and negative) are faults in participant observation, then many ethnographies, other than those written by missionaries, must be criticized. The works of a Junod, a Crazzolara, a Schärer, or a Leenhardt will probably stand the test of time, with its continually changing priorities, as well as the writings of academic anthropologists. An ethnographically inclined missionary is particularly well situated to amass information on such important topics as culture change, the content of religious beliefs, and the full semantic, grammatical complexities of native languages.

The critical test for the missionary-ethnographer is, finally, his or her ability personally to allow the two dispositions to coexist—in cooperation where possible, without interference where not. Leenhardt, whose family milieu was steeped in both piety and natural science, was able, when necessary, to hold apart the projects of evangelism and empirical research. He could do so precisely because in the final analysis, an analysis beyond his comprehension, they were a concert. He believed, like his naturalist father, that "facts are a Word of God."

This is not to suggest that science and religion were never in practical conflict. In 1915 Leenhardt wrote ruefully of an opportunity missed because of opposing loyalties. He had never been able to observe from beginning to end a full-scale *grand pilou* festival. This important ritual was being abandoned throughout the island, at least in its most elaborate forms, which included the gathering of clans from a wide region for gift exchanges, feasts, discourses, and religious dances conducted over a span of several days or even weeks. In neighboring Canala, Leenhardt finally had his chance:

It is certainly the last authentic [*pilou*] which will be performed in the region where Houailou is understood. For some time now I've been meaning to go study a *pilou* in order to understand it as a whole. Canala is pagan: no one would be scandalized if I attended; it was perfect. But what should I find [there] but a *nata* allowing his son to learn the dances along with the rest of his flock. I have to intervene and renounce my project so long in preparation. It's likely I'll never have another chance.[9]

Leenhardt had no objections to being present as an observer (if not precisely a participant-observer) of traditional rituals. He was far from the sort of missionary who attempted to forbid or forcibly disrupt the practices of the unconverted. He did, however, claim moral authority over Protestants, those who, in theory at least, had made a basic break with tradition.

In this instance Leenhardt's evangelical role impeded direct observation of an authentic *grand pilou*. But he managed to learn much about its nature indirectly, through interrogation of old people, collection of texts recording traditional rituals, observation of local "small *pilous*" and traditionally influenced Protestant ceremonies. Leenhardt came to approve the smaller celebrations more wholeheartedly than the large, multi-clan gatherings, which under colonialism tended to end in drunkenness. Moreover, the degeneration and gradual disappearance of the island's most important social ritual worried Leenhardt. He hoped the *pilou* might be preserved at the local level and "translated" into Christian ceremonial practice. In 1922 he published an extensive description of the *pilou* in *L'Anthropologie*, calling it "the rite maintaining the unifying force of the people," or, in the words of a Melanesian informant, "the movement of the needle that ties together the sections of the straw roof, to make only one roof, only one 'word' (*parole*)."[10] Leenhardt's ambivalences about the *pilou* certainly obstructed to some extent his ability to describe it ethnographically. His evocations lack something in immediacy as a result of his difficulties in attending, and he may have a tendency to play down the political importance of the *grand pilou*. But anyone reading his accounts, still the best available (either that of 1922, or those in *Notes d'ethnologie néo-calédonienne* and *Gens de la Grande Terre*), will see that no hint of disparagement creeps into the assessment.

Much of Leenhardt's ethnographic description from the 1920s and 1930s can be classified as functionalist: it portrayed the interrelatedness of custom in a more or less cohesive society, often set in the "ethnographic present." But his ethnography was never limited to this perspective. Leenhardt was on the lookout for cultural change, which he always portrayed: grimly, if it was a matter of customs being shattered by colonialism; enthusiastically, if he saw custom recreating itself in transformed conditions. For example, in the chapter on the *pilou* from *Gens de la Grande Terre*, Leenhardt is not content to show the ritual dances and speeches as reiterations and expressive reinforcements of traditional alliances, offerings to the maternal uncles, glorifications of the paternal clan, and so on. He stresses, too, the possibilities for creative expressivity in the rituals, as in one of his favorite anecdotes:

> During one of the last *grand pilous* around Ponerihouen, a Nébaye fraternity devised a totemic dance much remembered since. In it groups of dancers were coming and going gracefully, meeting, stopping, veering, forming a circle in imitation of mullet fish that come from all around to feed on algae carried by the current. Suddenly there is a rifle shot: the dancers lie still, their bellies up. The explosion and falling dancers represent a fatal explosion of dynamite in the midst of a school of fish. A mime of tragedy, it signifies the death of the mullet totem and its group in the dislocation of native society under the shock of civilization.[11]

(In another account of this dance, Leenhardt tells of its being performed for the governor of the colony.) The missionary-ethnographer's primary object of study was "living culture"[12]—culture changing, translating itself, to itself and to others. He was not tempted to confuse cultural authenticity with cultural purity.

The missionary's concern with portraying ritual life in the context of colonialism's impact and as expressive of new as well as old sentiments compares interestingly with the functionalist ethnography of Bronislaw Malinowski. Malinowski, the most famous Western interpreter of Melanesian life, missed almost entirely, as he later confessed, these historical dimensions of cultural reality.[13] If Leenhardt gave a better historical sense of culture in movement and crisis, Malinowski traced more completely the complex interrelations of the various institutions of a homeostatic culture. Although the concrete research conditions differed from New Caledonia to the Trobriand Islands, the latter suffering far less from colonial pressure, nevertheless it is fair to say that the two observers themselves diverged considerably in basic orientation. The most immediately striking divergence in the two approaches is the overwhelming role accorded to "magic" in one, to "myth" in the other. One does not have to read very far in their descriptions of native life to become aware that for much behavior Malinowski calls magical, Leenhardt would prefer the term mythical. If the difference were merely semantic, one could, with a little labor, reconstitute a unified picture. But the terminologies flow from incongruent overall strategies in the translation of alien culture. Behind Malinowski's "magic" and Leenhardt's "myth" stand, respectively, pre-science and pre-religion. The two descriptions are rooted in incompatible intellectual/spiritual gestalts. Neither description is simplistic; yet the one is generally predisposed to see native life as observable behavior and practical (a favorite Malinowskian word) activity, whereas the other tends to talk about affective perception and experience, interpreted within a landscape of lived myth (*mythe vécu*).[14]

This is not the place to embark on a full comparison of the two viewpoints. It would be interesting to reinterpret Malinowski's wealth of documentation from a Leenhardtian perspective. (Such a rereading is suggested in *Do Kamo*.)[15] Suffice it to say that Malinowski, who could be wonderfully blunt in self-criticism, indicated very well the bias in his own description of myth—something he perceived primarily as formulated stories and inadequately as manifested in everyday life.[16] Malinowski, not himself a believer, was certainly less apt than Leenhardt to identify casual, personal manifestations of "religious" experience. For its part, Leenhardt's portrayal of New Caledonian myth is certainly anomalous; few other ethnographers have shown Melanesians as so continuously engaged in mythic events and perceptions. His rather mystical *Canaque* is an exaggeration. Yet as we have seen, the missionary's instinct for religious immanence did not betray him in recognizing the feminine/totemic "side" of Melanesian life, something Malinowski glossed over.[17]

The point is not to discredit the ethnographies of either Leenhardt or Malinowski. Both men produced complex, open-ended documentations and theories available to reinterpretation. An evolving human science cannot ask for more. Marcel Mauss was fond of remarking that ethnology could be seen as a kind of ocean. "All you need is a net, any kind of net; and then if you step into the sea and swing your net about, you are sure to catch some kind of fish."[18] He went on to say, ironically, that the fieldworker unfortunate enough to spend a few years with some tribe could consume the next twenty years of his life writing up the experience.

><

Leenhardt's dynamic conception of cultural process was reflected in his manner of constituting ethnographic texts. Like Boas and Mali-

nowski, he believed that a crucial aspect of fieldwork was the collection of a large corpus of vernacular transcriptions. The advantage of
such an approach, as Helen Codere and Dell Hymes have argued, is
that it renders the ethnography open to scholarly reinterpretation
(*and* to reappropriation by native speakers). As Codere says of vernacular texts: "the ethnographer has acquired data in which he is out of
the picture, in comparison to the degree of his involvement in the
presentation or elicitation of most ethnographic data."[19] (Here Leenhardt's relations with his best informants are comparable to Boas's
with the Kwakiutl George Hunt.) Leenhardt taught Melanesians to
transcribe and interpret their own tradition: they are co-authors of
the ethnographic text. Thus the final collection is not governed by a
single interpretive authority and is relatively open to retranslation.

Leenhardt considered his entire scientific *oeuvre* as an elaborate exercise in translation. His first three volumes for the Paris Institute of
Ethnology form an exemplary cluster. The institute had been founded
in 1925 by Marcel Mauss, Paul Rivet, and Lucien Lévy-Bruhl. It became the nucleus of professional anthropology in Paris, leading in
1936 to the establishment of the Musée de l'Homme. Professional
fieldwork came relatively late to France, and the founders of the Institut d'Ethnologie felt acutely their country's backwardness. In 1925
there was an embarrassing paucity of excellent empirical work for the
new organization to publish. Thus when Leenhardt returned to Paris,
Lévy-Bruhl and Mauss immediately encouraged him to publish the
fruits of his extensive research.

Compared with Malinowski's works, bearing evocative titles like
*The Sexual Life of Savages, Argonauts of the Western Pacific, Coral Gardens and
Their Magic*, Leenhardt's first three volumes seem tentative and restrained. Their titles, *Notes d'ethnologie néo-calédonienne* (1930), *Documents
néo-calédoniennes* (1932), *Vocabulaire et grammaire de la langue Houailou* (1935),
communicate a sense of incompleteness and localism. In these works
Leenhardt makes few generalizations about "savage" or "primitive"
ways. He provides not an overall interpretation of Melanesian life
(that would come later) but rather a selected set of tools with which a
reader could work his or her way into the life of archaic New Caledonia. Leenhardt's caution reflected his feeling that French philosophical anthropology had in the past been too quick to erect its
theories of "primitive mentality" or "elementary forms" of social life,
without sufficient allowance for concrete experience seen from "the
native point of view." For Leenhardt this elusive viewpoint was not
accessible through fieldwork "rapport" or empathy, nor was it the
result of decoding "textualized" behavior.[20] What was involved was a

productive, collective work of translation that, because of its specific form, could not easily be dominated by a privileged interpretation. Leenhardt's first three works for the Paris Institute of Ethnology, while forming an ensemble, have an open quality absent from most holistically organized ethnographies. They are designed to immerse the reader in specifics never far removed from vernacular transcription; they provide twelve hundred densely packed pages of data along with the means for their translation.

The centerpiece of the trilogy is *Documents néo-calédoniennes*. Here a portion of Leenhardt's textual data is presented. On a typical page, the Houailou is given along with interlinear French equivalents; then a free rendering is attempted. Finally, footnotes, often detailed, direct attention to complexities of meaning and areas of likely confusion. This does not, however, exhaust the tools Leenhardt brings to bear on his texts. The two companion volumes play essential roles. The *Documents*—legends, orations, songs, and slices of life—are not comprehensible without some sense of their setting in New Caledonian society and ritual. This contextuality is provided in *Notes d'ethnologie néo-calédonienne*, a book its author intended not primarily as an integrated portrait of a society, but as a kind of introduction to the *Documents* and to the perplexities of translation. Nor was it sufficient to describe an institutional/ecological context for the vernacular documents. Leenhardt considered the language itself a prime source of insight. The third volume of his trilogy, *Vocabulaire et grammaire de la langue Houailou*, makes accessible much of Leenhardt's knowledge of a Melanesian tongue. As a reference in one's reading of the *Documents*, its five thousand multifaceted definitions provide a wide access to the semantic complexities and situational variations of New Caledonian discourse and ritual practice. "Dig into [Leenhardt's] dictionary," Mauss advised his students, "he transports you into another world."[21]

Leenhardt's three books together were intended to constitute "an initial, well-classified documentation for use in studying archaic mentality."[22] In according centrality to the vernacular texts, the ethnographer felt that they represented the truest available source of Melanesian expression. He based his belief on the specific manner of their "collection." *Documents néo-calédoniennes* is a group enterprise. Its table of contents gives the names of fifteen different "*transcripteurs*." What makes these texts different from most vernacular documents is that here the ethnographer was not present and actively involved in the primary moment of transcription—that process in which the transition from an oral to a literate mode is most abrupt and thus where the risk of distortion is great. Leenhardt's texts were not, as were

Malinowski's, for example, spelled out in the presence of the inquisitive ethnographer. Instead, they were composed in private by informants using a native tongue they had recently learned to read and write. Leenhardt encouraged a wide variety of people to record in school exercise books any traditional legends, ritual discourses, or songs that they knew well. When the *cahiers* were ready, the missionary discussed their contents with the authors, a long and arduous process, for the language was often archaic and the writing highly idiosyncratic. Of course "mistakes" could provide opportunities for insight beyond the codifications of the written. Sometimes, too, the texts obtained in this laisser-faire way would not fit any category of legend, song, or formal speech: for example, the personal story of "Jopaipi," an account of a trance, a slice of mythic life that Leenhardt would later subject to repeated analysis in his descriptions of the Melanesian *personnage* or "participatory" self.[23]

There are disadvantages to Leenhardt's procedure of transcription. First, the texts so obtained were divorced from immediate contexts of ritual performance. Also, informants translating oral eloquence into insufficiently mastered writing might settle for inaccurate transcriptions and short-cuts for expressions that someone more competent would be better able to capture. Writing, finally, implied a considerable degree of self-conscious distance from the customs described and thus could inject an element of abstraction and overintellectualization into the primary ethnographic evidence.

Set against these disadvantages are the considerable benefits of Leenhardt's procedure. An informant is under less immediate pressure and guidance than someone called upon to dictate into a microphone or recall a legend in the presence of a frequently rushed transcriber who ultimately cannot avoid the use of leading questions. Moreover, in Leenhardt's multistage method, the interpretation of custom could become a dialectical process of translation. A preliminary textualization, a "thick description" in Geertz and Ryle's phrase, would be initially fixed by the native speaker.[24] Then this formulated version would be discussed, extended, and cross-checked in collaboration with the anthropologist. The starting point would not be the anthropologist's interpretive descriptions, but rather those of the informant, considered here in the role of indigenous ethnographer. Leenhardt was, in any case, less interested in treating culture as an object of description than as an entity actively "thinking itself." Here scientific practice paralleled mission work. In each domain, Leenhardt tried to involve himself in Melanesians' conscious observations and reflections on their changing life.

We can see the desired process most fully in the case of his best informant, Boesoou Erijisi. Most ethnographers have relied on "privileged informants," though it has not been customary to write in detail concerning these crucial intermediaries.[25] Indeed, access to "the native point of view" depends only partially on the interpretation of described or textualized behavior. Beyond this, representatives of distinct cultures enter into some kind of interlocution concerning beliefs, a collaboration that builds on familiarity, mutual interest, and trust. The collaboration must, to some degree, invent its own language, an idiom adequate to the transmission of nuances and complex information. As a direct result of this interlocution, a text is produced, and the text is always something more than a description, however thick. It is a process of translation—of "making it new," in Pound's formula—wherein both parties may learn something about themselves by means of the other. Leenhardt's contact with Boesoou Erijisi included more than a quarter-century of mutual instruction—an extreme example of ethnographer-informant exchange, to be sure, but worth considering as an ideal type. It is condescending and false to assume that only the ethnographer derives new knowledge about custom from fieldwork collaborations or that the texts and interpretations so constituted are meaningful only to the author of the eventual ethnography.

Boesoou was, for Leenhardt's purposes, the perfect informant. He was born around 1866 into a family of chiefs much esteemed in the Houailou area. His tribal initiation, he recalled, came at the time of the great New Caledonian insurrection of 1878. Thus he came to manhood at a moment when traditional ways began to come under severe stress. (Suppression of the rebellion was followed by three decades of intense European settlement and Melanesian demographic decline.) A man of serious and reflective temperament, he was distressed by the plight of his people. When Houailou became a foothold for Loyalty Island Protestantism in the 1890s, Boesoou saw a hope—for it was known that on the Loyalty Islands there was peace and less alcoholism. Boesoou became a Protestant. Then, when the Leenhardts arrived and began a small school for pastors, Boesoou Erijisi was among the first class of sixteen. At around forty years of age, he was the oldest of the group and the first New Caledonian pastor to be consecrated. A man of great experience and tact, he was an invaluable assistant in all aspects of mission work.[26]

It was in translation and ethnography that Boesoou was indispensable. From 1912 to 1925, he composed a long series of notebooks covering a wide variety of traditional customs. Boesoou had been a fully initiated sculptor and an organizer of *pilous*. His texts were re-

markably precise and detailed, containing—as Guiart, who is still working with them, has stressed—not merely accurate records of custom
but important interpretations as well.[27] Translating them was, however, a complex task, the language being frequently elliptical and obscure. The old pastor and his missionary would spend long hours
going over the notebooks, the margins of which were soon filled with
Leenhardt's annotations. Boesoou set his own pace. His answers came
slowly, after much thought. Leenhardt often had time to write a letter
in the interval separating a question from its answer. Sometimes the
answer came later, much later.

Sometimes in his letters Leenhardt expressed impatience with Boesoou, with his archaic ways, or sometimes with his less talented and
unconverted wife. But Boesoou was such a moral person, so coura-
geous in his beliefs—once he publicly swallowed a sorcerer's bag of
deadly charms—and so original a combination of cultural ingredients,
that Leenhardt grew to love him dearly. "Good old man, he's got a
heart of gold in a head of smoke, and I certainly would like to know
all he does." Leenhardt paid a glowing tribute to his informant:
"[Boesoou's] Christianity is in no way an imitation of the white; it
is lived, and it is the Christianity of a pure *Canaque*. . . . Everything that
I have been permitted to clarify in the obscurity of native questions I
owe to Boesoou."[28] Such statements are all too rare in the annals of
ethnography.

The missionary had learned patience—how to make queries without pressing for answers—in working on his Houailou New Testament. We have seen that for him translation was a reciprocal, creative
process, indeterminate and open-ended, shaped by a collective search
for authenticity. Time was of the essence—Melanesian time, structured in rhythms of exchange. Ethnographic time is too frequently
otherwise: constrained, linear, the researcher "collecting" data instead

14. A page from Boesoou Erijisi's notebooks. Map of the village of Nindiah
at the time of one of the last large-scale traditional festivals in the
Houailou Valley, around 1900. The map shows houses (labeled with family
names and arranged according to their importance in the artist's eyes)
joined by alleyways bordered with palms and araucaria pines. At the upper
left are yam fields; on the right center the wavy lines marked by family
names are taro patches located on hillsides some distance away; and on the
lower right is the river, with fishing rights indicated by name. The map is
a spatial compression and conceptual deployment of the social landscape,
reflecting a traditional conception of socio-mythic topography

M.L., Notes, p. 18.

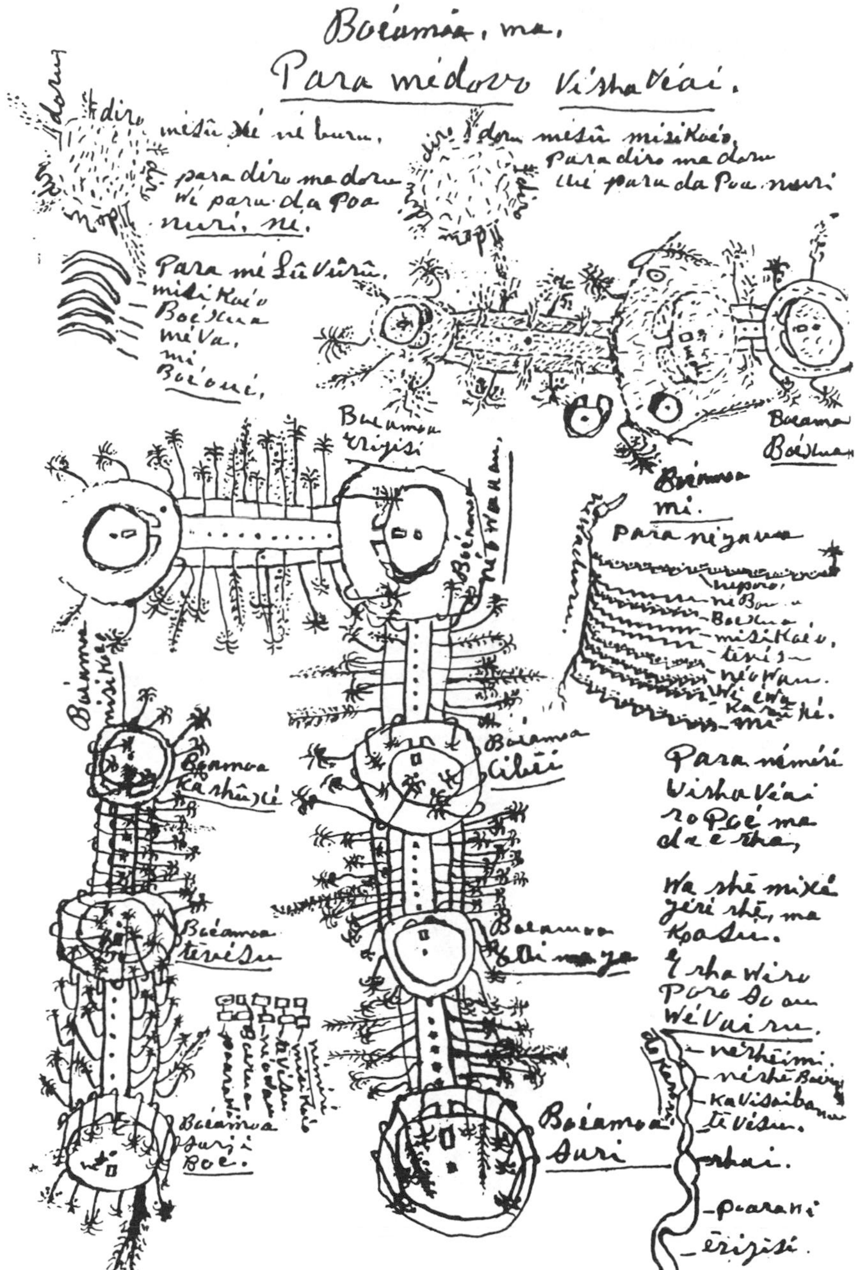

of "making" it in collaboration with informants. At the very least, fieldwork requires a certain complicity (a better term, perhaps, than rapport). But complicity is not reciprocity—though it may be part of reciprocity. A question initiates exchange; an answer confers debt. The ongoing process of gift and countergift falls into measured rhythms, a tempo that does not always synchronize with the academic calendar or with the span of research grants. A reply to a query may come decades later.[29] Naturally it is not quite appropriate to compare an experience like Leenhardt's—spanning more than three generations and involving active political and spiritual alliance with his informants—to a characteristic academic sojourn or even series of sojourns. But the comparison may encourage us to rethink the social processes by which ethnographic texts are created, returning to the word "data" its etymological root in "things *given*."

Fieldwork may best be seen not as a process of description or interpretation of a bounded other world, but as an interpersonal, cross-cultural encounter that *produces* descriptive-interpretive texts. The "authorship" of its initial written data is plural and not easily specified. Eventually these data are transformed into descriptions and explanations that are conventionally identified as the work of an individual writer. This interpretive process may run its course smoothly, resulting in an ethnography that serves as a full stop to the field experience.[30] Or it may assume the form of a lifelong encounter, an amorous struggle with an otherness that assumes the role of an alter ego. The latter was Leenhardt's ethnological fate.

CHAPTER IX

The Canaque Professor

When Leenhardt returned to Paris in 1926, it was uncertain just what he would do for a living. A life of pastoral retirement held no appeal.[1] The veteran hoped to be allowed to revitalize the training program at the Maison des Missions, but no salary was made available. He found employment nearby, expecting to teach without pay. But during the coming years the mission school began to be cut back. Leenhardt protested. Relations were already strained with the Mission Society's directors; they broke down altogether after the "Rey-Lescure Affair." From 1926 until 1935, Leenhardt worked as a pastor in the Paris Mission Populaire de la Bienvenue; and until 1938 he was secretary of the Ligue de la Moralité Publique. The family lived in an apartment at 59 rue Claude Bernard, not far from the Pantheon and the Sorbonne. If pastoral salaries were not large, they were at least regular. There was never anything left over. Not until the late 1930s did it become possible to live primarily from university teaching and research grants.

During the late 1920s and early 1930s, the Leenhardts were "urban missionaries," ministering to the indigent of the city. And although they valued this kind of social work for its human contacts, they nonetheless tried to limit it to half of the week. Ethnological scholarship and teaching occupied the remaining time, as did continuing activity in missionary contexts. Even though the Mission Society would not accord Leenhardt positions of responsibility in accordance with his experience, he continued to participate in the training of new missionaries. The veteran evangelist still gave some lessons at the reduced Mission School, sporadically in the 1930s and later more seriously as the prejudice against him abated. The focus of his teaching was ethnological. In 1928 Leenhardt was instrumental in founding the Commission Missionnaire des Jeunes (C.M.J.), where, especially in summer study camps, he maintained contact with young Protestant evangelical students. These contacts assured an audience for his ideas and were an important source of moral support.[2] For Leenhardt did not relish the role of prophet in the wilderness.

His involvement in mission questions was most actively pursued through a small journal that he founded in 1927. *Propos missionnaires* ("Missionary Talk") was designed to link isolated fields and encourage comparative discussion of methods. It contained forums on a wide variety of questions: mission responsibilities towards orphans, problems of religious education, the role of vernacular languages, translation problems, temperance, relations between mission and colonial governments, attitudes toward native dances, preventive medicine, ethnography and human geography, forced labor in the colonies, the place of the missionary beside his native pastors, ways of handling disagreements between colleagues, "le missionnaire: peut-il fumer?", etc., etc., a mixed bag of day-to-day advice plus a number of broader essays on overall purpose. (The French word *propos* can also mean intention or purpose.)

A collaborative enterprise, it bore nonetheless strong marks of its principal editor. In the very first issue, a rubric "L'Ethnologie et les Missions" announced the Leenhardtian perspective. The article presented an account of a meeting in which Lucien Lévy-Bruhl had spoken before a missionary audience, advising them of their strategic location for the collection of scientific data and urging them, in a section singled out by Leenhardt for quotation, to provide "nothing but 'observation.' Don't mix in any interpretation. We come out of Europe with ideas concerning animism, fetishism, etc., and we explain things with the aid of these notions instead of giving the facts pure and simple."[3] This was advice tailored particularly to the missionary-ethnographer. *Propos missionnaires* is sprinkled with such advice. In its first years it contained an ongoing forum on traditional African marriage practices and bride-price problems. But the focus was not primarily ethnological; it was aimed at the practical and moral problems of mission work. *Propos* is very much "missionary talk." Indeed, the reader who puts down one of Leenhardt's ethnological productions, say, *Notes d'ethnologie néo-calédonienne*, to pick up copies of *Propos missionnaires*, written at the same time, will experience a somewhat uncomfortable feeling of lurching between milieux whose basic assumptions clash.

Leenhardt writes very differently in the two contexts. In one he attempts to follow Lévy-Bruhl's advice and give "just the facts"—rough-edged, fragmentary, without drawing conclusions. In *Propos* his style is rather different. For example, in a review of Malinowski's *Sexual Life of Savages* Leenhardt explains the open sexuality of many "primitive" peoples through a dubious and condescending comparison. Primitive immorality ("cynicism" he calls it) is characteristic of "beings who do not possess the great heritage of a life in which the senses are restrained, the strength of Christian peoples. Among us the family is the ideal, for them raw sexuality reigns. . . ."[4]

Perhaps Leenhardt felt that he was taking a certain risk including *The Sexual Life of Savages* in "missionary talk." The book's detailed attention to all aspects of sexual practice was advanced for its time, in any milieu. Malinowski dwelt at great and sympathetic length on premarital promiscuity in Trobriand life, and he mounted a functionalist's defense showing sexual freedom to be subject to clear limits. This sort of argument Leenhardt could barely accept, and one senses that the liberal missionary, who usually appeared unshockable, was in fact scandalized by Malinowski's book. He criticizes its inordinate length and concentration on carnal details. This, he says, is no longer science but an appeal to prurient interest and a recommendation of libertinism. On the other hand, Leenhardt quotes approvingly Malinowski's broadening of sexuality beyond "mere physical relations between two individuals" into the foundation of love, family, social relations, and continuity—in short, into the sublimated status of a socio-mythic life-force. The missionary, he urges, must understand native sexual practices in this broadened context. In the end, however, the editor of *Propos missionnaires* manages to associate Malinowski with a subversive movement devoted to moral relaxation and based, he appears to believe, in Moscow![5]

Leenhardt's presentation of Malinowski was adapted to his audience. But if his moral background and evangelical milieu imposed constraints on his thinking, these must nonetheless be seen as the structures of his particular freedom. For Leenhardt, the life of an outsider was impossible. He was most comfortable and effective when pushing against a given context from its interior. Always the gadfly, he knew how to shock without being written off as an enemy. He liked to question, not confront.

≥⋹

Certainly the narrowness of the French Protestant "family" must sometimes have felt stifling to him, especially when conflict with his mission society's conservative directors was at its most severe. The wider horizons of ethnographic science provided a breathing space. But Leenhardt cannot be divided into compartments. The different styles of work and expression managed to coexist in the crowded family apartment at 59 rue Claude Bernard. Here at the same desk he edited *Propos missionnaires* and composed his *Notes d'ethnologie néo-calédonienne*—in the midst of chaotic family life, constant comings and goings of visitors, flocks of children, and the day-to-day demands of parish work.[6] He felt comfortable and effective in the midst of all this *va et vient*, with its opportunities for conversation, give and take, question and answer, rhythms in which his thought developed most easily.

Leenhardt was a raconteur of considerable charm. He commanded a stock of tales drawn from his African and Oceanian experiences, most of them illustrating a moral. In the years around 1930 he contributed a series to the *Dépêche coloniale et maritime*, often using the pseudonym Jean Caro. The stories fall into a number of familiar colonial styles. Caro is a veteran of the colonies, a *broussard* (back-country) type who tends to deflate pomposity (both European and native) and has a kindly appreciation of simple human nature. The tales indulge in exotic evocations of tropical landscapes and recount adventurous anecdotes of frontier life. They also portray intercultural misunderstandings and blunders, usually by whites, and draw characteristic conclusions. In one tale a thoughtful naturalist confirms experimentally certain facts about animal species that his servant, a half-breed named Tom, knows already through myth. "For millennia," the scientist exclaims, "these children of nature have been reading from the book of life; while we, looking at the page through a microscope, don't take enough note of the vibrations captured in their legends."[7] As his contributions to the *Dépêche* continue, Leenhardt tends to drop his pseudonym. And significantly, the "colonial/exotic" cast into which the tales fall is increasingly replaced by an openly ethnological emphasis, including essays on Melanesian yam culture, the esthetics of the habitat, and so on.[8] Jean Caro the colonial "character" yields to Maurice Leenhardt the social scientist. In adopting these personae—either the *broussard* or the emerging ethnologist—Leenhardt permitted himself an extra measure of freedom, expressing his love of adventure and the bizarre along with a profound cultural relativism.

In the second number of *Propos missionnaires*, Leenhardt cited as a keynote some unpublished notes from the pen of Alfred Boegner, who had been director and driving force behind the Société des Missions Evangeliques in the years around 1900. As we have seen, Leenhardt had derived important stability and inspiration from his example. Boegner's notes, published in 1927, set the tone for Leenhardt's continuing struggle to arrive at a rule within which his life could unfold freely.

> Secret of an infallible comportment: absence of all self-seeking. Preoccupation with the self falsifies everything, mixes a personal element, an awkwardness, in everything. Single preoccupation with the truth. Freedom to retreat, to change paths, to turn back.

> The criterion for using these rules is located precisely in the aid they provide in reaching the goal. If they leave me less

strong, less free, less ready to help others, then get rid of them. Better a simple life of duty and honest labor. If, on the contrary, they strengthen me, giving me more spiritual freedom in order to think of others, more strength to serve, more love of duty, more enthusiasm for work, then use them.

"Become the Rule"

It is good to have a rule, but if you do not yourself incarnate it, better not have one. . . .[9]

Leenhardt wrote a full-length biography of Boegner, based on personal papers and correspondence. The undertaking may be seen as a kind of reckoning with one of the "rules" he would have to "become," namely, the tradition of French Protestantism at its best. In 1930 Leenhardt, "*encanaqué*," the spurned liberal, might have fallen into the role of the outcast, adopting the "outsider" pose so often associated with anthropology. Instead, he embraced his "rule," not ceding to its oppressions but attaining the confidence to open and renew it.

Maurice Leenhardt's Protestant identity turned on the bond uniting him with his wife. This relationship provided an orienting source of restraint for his outgoing, multidirectional personality. Jeanne Leenhardt was much more than a supporting, background presence. She worked closely with her husband in nearly all aspects of their life together.

I have given a brief sketch of Jeanne Leenhardt at the time of her marriage—devout, intelligent, active, a young woman remarkably well educated for her time. Mme. Leenhardt retained an interest in her husband's ethnology. Houailou was frequently spoken around the Leenhardt apartment. Jeanne Leenhardt was an equal partner in the Paris social mission work that kept the family alive in the early 1930s. And when her husband began teaching at the Institut d'Ethnologie and Ecole Pratique des Hautes Etudes, she was nearly always with him, taking complete notes on what was said. She trained herself in stenography to help with correspondence and scholarship. She was her husband's co-worker on his return field trips to New Caledonia in 1938-1939 and 1947-1948, collecting important folklore from female informants.[10]

Husband and wife, in their unquestioned attachment to one another, did not always see eye to eye or react similarly to situations. Their affection was certainly, in some part, based on these differences. If Jeanne Leenhardt's religious feelings were more orthodox—or at any rate less ecumenical—than her husband's, there is no doubt that he relied on her judgments and that she responded to his need for a firm moral center. A word that sums up much of Jeanne Leenhardt's character is *pudeur*, a term that English speakers are often too quick to translate as "prudery." This sense overlaps only partially with the French. *Pudeur* means modesty, a sense of decency, qualities of discretion and reticence. The term is far from simply pejorative. It expresses a whole gamut of restraints—including sexual moralism—that, taken together, formed the characteristic reserve of Mme. Leenhardt. Her husband could be disconcertingly informal at times. As we have seen, when Maurice wrote of dangling his bare feet into the calm equatorial lake in Gabon, Jeanne—editing his letters—replaced them in the canoe.[11]

Leenhardt almost deified the Christian relationship of man and wife. It was an intenser coupling than life's other conversations. At times the constantly moving participant—ethnographer and missionary—must have felt himself to be losing perspective, merely flitting from experience to experience. "Home" was his wife and his God. Here he found a structure that, though it partook of the narrowness of a "rule," gave him the centering he needed. This structure explains, perhaps, Leenhardt's serenity in the midst of difficulties and his ability to range so freely across the field of his sympathies, a broad and contradictory landscape.

But to give a rather abstract, almost formal, interpretation of the Leenhardts' marriage is to risk falsifying its lived reality. Maurice and Jeanne Leenhardt retained for one another an almost adolescent love, a desire for a totally shared life. The spiritualized ardor of their youthful marriage never faded. And Jeanne Leenhardt, though more ironical and more of a puritan than her husband, was not a narrow or dour person. She was prepared to live in difficult situations and maintain a charitable disposition even when personally revolted—by the crude physicality of "paganism," for example. She did not hesitate to go through childbirth in the Caledonian back country, with *Canaques* and her husband her only attendants. Perhaps she is best remembered as the woman who, laughing, would tell how she had not been able to stop herself from hiding her fine, aristocratic hands behind her back while being told by an "ex-cannibal" (the *nata* Tabi) that they were the best part.[12]

⊃⊂

If Leenhardt's wife was his most intimate friend after the tragic early death of his brother Paul, he did, however, feel a strong affection for certain of his colleagues. Personal loyalties counted for a great deal with him. During the years when Leenhardt was acquiring the skills of a professional enthnologist, his most important associations were with Lucien Lévy-Bruhl and Marcel Mauss.

The two professors appealed to rather different sides of his personality. They possessed in common, however, attributes that Leenhardt respected to the point of intimidation. Both were encyclopedic scholars of immense erudition and seriousness of purpose. Both were politically involved as well, lifelong participants in the democratic socialist movement. And although Leenhardt was not precisely a socialist, he was a democrat and a reformer, and he approved wholeheartedly the brand of humanism for which Lévy-Bruhl and Mauss fought, first as supporters of Jaurès, then as advocates of the Popular Front and founders of the Musée de l'Homme.

We have seen the important role played by Lévy-Bruhl in turning the missionary toward professional ethnology. Leenhardt was not, however, a disciple, though he sometimes spoke of the philosopher as his *"maître."* The two men were, from the start, colleagues, each possessing a knowledge the other lacked and respected. Lévy-Bruhl, as author of histories of philosophy and bearer of an enormous classical culture, was deeply respected by Leenhardt. The ex-missionary, holder of his unique degree in the *"Canaque* humanities," helped the aging professor grasp beyond, as he knew he should, a knowledge of primitivism derived exclusively from reading.[13] As the philosopher

15. Paris, 1931, left to right: Paul Rivet, Maurice Leenhardt, Lucien Lévy-Bruhl.

Photo: Leenhardt

made clear in his posthumously published *Carnets* of 1938-1939, Leenhardt had helped him a great deal in recognizing and accepting the limits of Western logical categories. Lévy-Bruhl gave Leenhardt personal encouragement and also practical patronage. Employment in the centralized university system depended—then as now—on the support of certain influential figures.

But what the younger man admired most was his friend and patron's style of restrained calm, of passion tempered by politeness, and, a word that recurs in his tributes, "probity." The great man's selfless devotion to reason and science was an inspiration: Lévy-Bruhl's intellectual style always possessed something of that *pudeur* discussed above in a moral context.

Leenhardt's other important colleague and friend, Marcel Mauss, provided him with a rather different nourishment. The nephew and chief disciple of Durkheim possessed an erudition that has become legendary. "*Mauss sait tout!*" his students would whisper to each other following his lectures on ethnology, sociology, and the history of religions. Trained first in philosophy, then in Sinology and Sanskrit, by 1900 he was the principal specialist in ethnology within the tightly organized research team brought together by Durkheim around the *Année Sociologique*. Mauss was competent in half a score of languages, and his reviews of ethnographic literature for the *Année* as well as his collaborative studies of magic, sacrifice, primitive classification, and social morphology all bear witness to a mind of analytic power and insatiable curiosity.

But personally Mauss was the least intimidating of men. He loved to talk—and did so with wit and charm. Not particularly relishing the magisterial professor's role, he never completed his doctorate but remained content, for most of his career, with his research post at the Ecole Pratique. Mauss had obtained this chair, in the history of the religion of "noncivilized" peoples, in 1901 at the early age of 29. He held it until his forced retirement under the Nazi occupation in 1940. During the 1930s, however, he began to share the post with Leenhardt, who later formally succeeded him (and was in turn replaced by Claude Lévi-Strauss). Mauss's teaching at the Ecole Pratique and after 1925 at the Institut d'Ethnologie became the chief center for the encouragement and training of French ethnographic research.

Mauss's total lack of condescension towards "elementary" religions, as well as his long-standing interest in field ethnography, recommended him at once to Leenhardt.[14] Mauss was only six years his senior; there was little of the ambivalent awe that surrounded the friendship with Lévy-Bruhl. There would, perhaps, have been a momentary barrier between the two men—Mauss incarnating the Durk-heimian heritage, a sociology Leenhardt associated with aggressive secularism—but personal contact soon opened the way. The quality of Leenhardt's Melanesian documentation impressed Mauss, who had long been lamenting the absence of professional ethnography in the French colonies.[15]

The two had much in common: first and foremost an interest in religion. This was Mauss's lifelong preoccupation. Those who know his work only through the famous essay *The Gift* and through Lévi-Strauss's brilliant, though one-sided, introduction to a selection of Mauss's essays may have missed this common thread.[16] Maurice Leenhardt brings it sharply into focus in an obituary written for his friend in 1950.[17] If, as a missionary returning from the New Caledonian struggle between church and state, Leenhardt expected to find in Mauss a man exclusively concerned with the reduction of religious practice and belief to elementary and exclusively social forms, he soon realized his mistake. He found instead a man who liked to talk of his family's rabbinical background and who, though secular in general outlook, still valued his spiritual antecedents. He found also a man who had for a time specialized in the study of Indian religions. Mauss was, he discovered, actively committed to an understanding of ritual and belief from the "inside" as a phenomenologist of religion. In stressing this concern, Leenhardt probably erred, as have so many, in making an extraordinarily multifaceted scholar too much into a "precursor." Leenhardt always insisted that the "Mauss Chair" at Hautes Etudes was essentially a chair of religious phenomenology and that he was Mauss's continuer, not replacement.[18] When it came his time to retire he was thus less than enthusiastic about the candidacy of his brilliant structuralist successor.

Leenhardt and Mauss fell into the habit of breakfasting together every Thursday, and their discussions ranged widely over questions of religious ritual and belief. They shared a concern for the notion of "the person," both resisting the reduction of this category to, on the one hand, the psychologist's "individual," or on the other, the sociologist's collectivity. Mauss, in *The Gift* and throughout his later writings, stressed the existence of a person who should be seen as "total" or overdetermined. Leenhardt, as we shall see in the following chapters, championed a concept of "la personne," which he described as "a plenitude," mediating the extremes of archaic social being and rationalist individualism. Mauss's Oxford lecture of 1938, "Une Catégorie de l'esprit humain: La Notion de Personne, celle du 'moi,'" was for Leenhardt a confirmation of his notion of personal evolution.[19]

Included in the idea of personal plenitude that the two men shared was a belief that social scientific work had to be combined with *praxis*. Science was not, of course, to be subordinated to politics, but it had to be translated, made available as a concrete response to common problems. The relativist ethnological humanism shared by the two scholars contributed to their practical activities: a supple evangelism on the one hand, democratic socialism on the other. Leenhardt would later describe Mauss: "Brilliant, spontaneous, eager to see the multiple facets of things; for him study was something alive, and he pursued it as much in the actual movements of society as in books."[20] Ardent Dreyfusard, contributor to *L'Humanité*, a lecturer to working-class audiences at L'Ecole Socialiste, and a participant in the Université Populaire movement, Mauss remained politically active as a partisan of the Popular Front in the 1930s.[21] "As a true Sociologist," Leenhardt wrote, Mauss insisted on "this contact with the living world."[22]

Leenhardt found in Mauss a kindred spirit. Unlike Lévy-Bruhl, who for all his openness and generosity always retained a certain cool, formal air, Mauss was informality personified. And he was akin to Leenhardt in physical presence—in a bodily "language" of which both men were acutely conscious and which they stressed in their respective writings.[23] Mauss was a large man, an athlete, amateur boxer and practitioner of *savate*. He had big hands, a big beard, was likely to sit down and converse with a child on the living room carpet. His uncle had not succeeded in making of him a pure intellectual. Indeed, Mauss, like Leenhardt, probably never quite "fit" physically in a culture where the word for corporeal stature, *taille*, is principally associated with the modalities of cutting or pruning. In his pioneering essay on the cross-cultural varieties of "bodily technique," Mauss recalls his elementary school teacher haranguing him: "Espece d'animal, tu vas tout le temps tes grandes mains ouvertes!"[24] Leenhardt was like Mauss in that he too remained fundamentally *"non-taillé"* by the formalities of school and university.

≥€

With Mauss's help, Leenhardt was able to begin teaching at the Ecole Pratique des Hautes Etudes. The similarity of their styles helped make it easy for Leenhardt to participate actively in Mauss's courses, first as a student during 1932, and then in the following year as lecturer.[25] By the mid-1930s he was doing approximately one-third of Mauss's teaching, and by the late 1930s, one-half. Like Mauss, Leenhardt flourished in an informal pedagogical atmosphere that included questions and answers and an improvisational lecture technique.

Neither attempted to teach in the manner of Lévy-Bruhl, whose lessons were "masterpieces of order, of lucidity, of clarity."[26] Leenhardt was not as assured and loquacious as Mauss, nor did he aspire to the polymath's digressive brilliance. If Leenhardt's lectures were like Mauss's in being associative and conversational, they remained always within the world the ethnographer knew most deeply. As a teacher, according to Michel Leiris, who was his first student, Leenhardt simply tried to think aloud "like a *Canaque*." Whereas Mauss's access to culture and human nature was extensive and comparative, Leenhardt's was intensive, taking as his main order of business the dense dilemmas of a single ongoing translation project. This approach to a "primitive" culture was rare in the Paris University milieu of the early and mid-1930s.

The fieldworker would begin with a close interrogation of vocabulary and grammar, using these as threads through which he wove a variety of descriptive patterns based on his personal experience. In 1935-1936, for example, the yearbook of the Ecole des Hautes Etudes tells us that Leenhardt elaborated on a variety of vernacular locutions concerned with "blood," "wet and dry," "substitution," "exchanges," "naming," "yams," "bark," sculpture, "money," and so on. En route, this specific and painstaking inventory served as the ground for reflections on characteristic themes: Caledonian experiences of the person, the word (*parole*), myth, time, space, affectivity, participation, and totemic communion. The topics run on: notions of life-force and continuity, death and (something different) nothingness, rituals of sacrifice, relations to "gods," locutions of possessivity.

Jean Poirier recalls the "*Canaque*" professor's reaction when asked by a representative of the *Revue de Métaphysique et de Morale* to describe the "method" he employed in penetrating Melanesian mentality: "I can still see him acting astonished that such a question had been asked, shrugging his shoulders and half smiling—'My method . . . But I don't have one!'"[27] The genial professor enjoyed shocking anyone he suspected of being overly wedded to *esprit de système*. In fact, he probably suspected the entire Paris University of being rather too preoccupied with "methods."

Of course Leenhardt did possess a method, if long years of observation, experience, and controlled digression may be said to add up to such a thing. He had, more accurately, a style. As Poirier recalls:

> The teaching of Maurice Leenhardt, which could move without much adaptation from a group of young Caledonians to a lecture hall of the Sorbonne, remained perhaps above all a

form of conversation, a conversation Leenhardt pursued with himself; he let his thinking flow in a manner which, though not, certainly, very didactic, was most enriching.

His notes were only an outline, from which he took his bearings. We might here recall how assiduously he would work with Mme. Leenhardt. He would present his class to her, in its near entirety, during the hours preceding their departure for the Sorbonne or the "Museum" [the Institut d'Ethnologie]. He did everything with great conscientiousness, his scruples never quite satisfied. For many years Mme. Leenhardt was present at nearly all her husband's courses, seated discreetly to one side; she took notes on what he said, precisely because he would often improvise, and out of the presentation itself, out of the documents being discussed, might arise this or that new insight.[28]

In the first year or so of Leenhardt's teaching, the students in attendance were few. This was normal at the Ecole Pratique before a teacher had developed a reputation. Some students probably dismissed him under the stereotype *"missionnaire barbu."* He did not, indeed, bring any immediately recognizable or striking theoretical approach. He offered only his unique hermeneutical style and experience. With time this came to be appreciated, and the classroom was much fuller in later years. But in the opening sessions the hall was empty, or nearly empty. Michel Leiris, the distinguished poet and ethnologist, likes to think of himself as Leenhardt's first student. He recalls the early sessions. There were three in the room: Leiris, Leenhardt, and Mme. Leenhardt. One spoke; two took notes.

The texts survive. They are remarkably detailed, careful; the subject is Caledonian religious language. Occasionally Mme. Leenhardt's version will record a remark addressed specifically to "Monsieur Leiris . . . to whom I cannot say anything new about witchcraft" and the like. (Leiris had just returned from France's first great collective field expedition to Africa, the Griaule, Dakar-Djibouti mission of 1931-1932.) But as the lone student recalls, the class remained formal. Leenhardt, who was certainly nervous in his new role, lectured. "Lectured" is not quite the right term, however. Leiris recalls the manner as essentially "talk"—informal, containing nothing pretentious or doctrinaire, nothing of "the pastor" but having something about it that seemed strange and, as Leiris experienced it, quite extraordinary. "You had the feeling of being in the presence of an actual *Canaque*."[29] Leenhardt attempted to invest himself with the material, to speak the language and the culture from within. Thus he had a way of making unexpected connections, mixing things in curious fashion. This approach contributed, certainly, to his reputation for lack of "clarity."

Leiris saw differently; he was a poet of surrealist inclinations in search of the concrete. Recently he had published a field journal, *L'Afrique fantôme*, which castigated the abstractions of intellectualist social science. From the viewpoint of Leiris's recent contact with Africa, Leenhardt's obscure *Canaque* ramblings seemed realer than the theorizing that went on elsewhere in the university. The missionary's manner, Leiris reports, did not communicate an image of curious or mystical primitives. It gave the impression, rather, of different, but quite ordinary, people—*gens*.

CHAPTER X

Gens de la Grande Terre

New Caledonia, 1938-1940

Leenhardt's book *Gens de la Grande Terre* appeared in 1937. It offered a popular, ethnological overview of native New Caledonian life. Like most of Maurice Leenhardt's writings, the book was adapted to a specific occasion, in this case the founding of a new series by the important publishing house of Gallimard. The series was called "L'Espèce Humaine" ("The Human Kind") and was to be devoted primarily to ethnology. Leenhardt's book was the first in the new line, and its theme was the *actualité* or present relevance of the science of man. Ethnology needed popularization in France. Of the first half-dozen volumes in "L'Espèce Humaine," only two were by Frenchmen. But fieldwork-oriented research was beginning to catch on among both students and the general public. The founding of the Musée de l'Homme in 1937 contributed greatly, and *Gens de la Grand Terre* tried to encourage the growing trend.[1]

The book touches on the classic themes and divisions of ethnographic overview as conceived in the mid-1930s. It describes habitat, economics, nutrition, social and political structures, and the major ritual events. Although it appears to be lacking in its treatment of initiation, secret societies, magic and sorcery, *Gens de la Grande Terre* gives unusual emphasis to myth and esthetics. There are surprises: for example, a separate section on "spontaneity and laughter in society."

The picture is not of a completed or self-sufficient archaism, a culture functioning smoothly. The people of New Caledonia are in trouble, and Leenhardt notes this fact in nearly every chapter. However, in the 1937 edition, the book's political message is muted. We sympathize with the Melanesians and sense the beauty of their culture; we are interested in them for their "primitiveness," and we feel indignation at their exploitation. But it is not until 1952, in a new introduction and extended conclusion, that Leenhardt formulates clearly the implied criticism of white attitudes. The sharpening of his critique in the 1952 version—the notion that the colonialist needed to experience an "inverse acculturation"—certainly reflected the birth of systematic anti-imperialism in the years immediately following the Second World War. It expressed also feelings of urgency acquired by Leenhardt during two more extensive encounters with the colonial milieu.

Between 1926 and 1938, Leenhardt had been in touch with New Caledonia only through letters and visitors. After Rey-Lescure's transfer, there was no more direct news from Do Neva. Immersed in his documents and field notes, Leenhardt sorely missed the personal contacts that had been so important to him in the past. In 1931 he collaborated with Rivet, Lévy-Bruhl, and others in the organization of a Colonial Exhibition. As part of the events, Caledonians were brought to Paris to perform traditional ceremonies and dances. Leenhardt looked forward to seeing old friends; and many of the dancers, Protestants, agreed to come to Paris largely because "Missi Leenhardt" was there. But Leenhardt found himself forcibly barred from contact with the *Canaques*. The promoters of the affair had secretly—and illegally—bound the Melanesians to a traveling circus that would be showing them around Europe as "cannibal dancers." Leenhardt had to fight for their release from an exploitative contract. He took the Caledonians' case, finally, to the Ligue des Droits de l'Homme and in the end succeeded.[2] What should have been a joyous reunion had turned into another ugly—and all too familiar—colonial struggle.

The needed contact with a land and its people could not be achieved through museum exhibits and theatrical performances. Not long after the publication of *Gens de la Grande Terre*, Maurice and Jeanne Leenhardt returned to Melanesia. They arrived in Noumea on the third of July, 1938, beginning fifteen months of renewed contact with the "gens" from whom they had been so long apart.

Officially, Leenhardt returned not as an evangelist but as head of a university-funded ethnographic and linguistic research project. The aim of his trip was to compile an inventory of the languages and dialects of New Caledonia, the Loyalty Islands, and the New Hebrides—a general area Leenhardt had begun to call "Austro-Melanesia" to underline the specific mixed composition of its cultures. The ethnographer was increasingly interested in the precolonial history of the region and in particular the waves of cultural influence that he thought could be more clearly discerned through a comparative analysis of dialects. The linguistic research was designed to record in outline the grammars and vocabularies of a broad range of contiguous groups in order to trace overlays of words and expressions. These borrowings not only confused the cultural picture but, as Leenhardt stressed, also enriched the expressive life of the region's living culture.

The result of the expedition, *Langues et dialectes de l'Austro-Mélanesie*, is a massive compendium.[3] Its 650 pages contain an initial section of 242 pages in which Leenhardt sets out the structure, grammar, and phonetics peculiar to the various dialects, roughly categorized into three distinct groups: the Loyalty Islands, north and south New Caledonia. The rest of the volume contains a comparative inventory of vocabularies—words classified ethnologically according to habitat, meteorology, kinship, rituals, war, the human body, and so on, covering twenty-six dialects and twelve hundred different words. The words are arranged to facilitate ethnolinguistic and ethnohistorical comparisons.

Langues et dialectes is primarily a book for the specialist. But even the casual reader flipping through its pages will come across bits of *Canaque* "poetry" that Leenhardt included as examples of specific grammars in action. One will find a number of legends in word-for-word transcription and at least one small text included for no other reason than that the ethnographer (like the present author) could not bear to leave it out —a lullaby in the *'Aekè* language of the Koné region—

> wa poe da ma dana
> wa poe Tuaboau
> Tuaboau na le we
> na le we ko na le pala?
> na le, pala ke na pota
> na le vi na poayu
> vi na cani moa fule
> vai va demu kena
> meda ma gae vila

—for which a free version:

> Whose taro shoot is this?
> Taro Tuaboa, Tuaboa of the sea . . .
> Of the sea, but why crying?
> Uprooted crying.
> While above us the Grande Case
> Speaks in the still abode.
> And here's an old crag
> speaking
> getting up to dance.[4]

Leenhardt long maintained that language, "sonorous material," was the most subtle of all data collected by the ethnologist.[5] The compilation of *Langues et dialectes de l'Austro-Mélanésie* was not merely the fashioning of a precise document for scholarly exploitation; it was also a labor of love. Most of the thirty-six languages whose portraits he sketched in the book were in danger of oblivion. Only a few, Houailou and the Loyaltian tongues, had been fixed in any way, usually by religious translations. 'AEKÈ, the language of the little lullaby, was spoken by fewer than six hundred people in 1938.

Leenhardt made use of a questionnaire that, like one he had devised with Boesoou in 1917, was composed first in Houailou and thus reflected native associations of ideas. Acutely aware of the imprecisions built into all inquests of this sort, Leenhardt believed that a questionnaire could be safely used only when the social observer actually knew most of the answers already, and then only as a check on variation and distribution. The questions had to reflect a sophisticated prior knowledge of the culture, picked up not by direct questioning but by having acquired the usages of words and customs indirectly, "on the wing," from day-to-day usages.[6]

The assemblage of Leenhardt's linguistic inventory required long hours of transcribing and cross-checking translations. Most of this was done in the field, often in the remote mountain reservations into which native Caledonians had been pushed over the decades of colonization. Leenhardt and his wife traveled by horseback over difficult terrain, staying for the most part in dwellings provided for them by local Protestants, many of whom were old friends. Jeanne Leenhardt worried in her letters that her sixty-year-old husband would overexert himself, and she took on herself as much of the research work as she could. She recorded texts in the vernacular, administered the questionnaires, and handled most of their correspondence. This left her husband free to pursue his inquiries beyond the routine compiling of linguistic data.

It was exhilarating for Leenhardt to rediscover friends and familiar locations; and this time he enjoyed a greater freedom, for he was no longer tied to Do Neva. Not officially a missionary for the Société des Missions Evangeliques, he could take a more involved and open interest in "paganism." Nonetheless, he was still "Missi Leenhardt" in the eyes of nearly everyone he met. This was true of friend and foe alike; his influence on the island had been great, and in some quarters his reputation had grown with absence. He found, frequently, that he had become identified with a golden age of Protestantism in New Caledonia. On the other hand, those who had always mistrusted him were not particularly impressed by the label he now wore of "ethnographic scientist." They knew only that Leenhardt the *indigènophile* was back,

16. New Caledonia 1938: Maurice Leenhardt and Eleischa Nebay.

Photo: Leenhardt

circulating in the back country and up to no good. Their suspicions were not wholly misplaced, for the now venerable figure could not help becoming involved in local problems and conflicts. (Jeanne Leenhardt reports in one of her letters that upon arriving in a village the couple found that a local white cattleman had just rebuilt his fences at the legal boundary of the reservation upon which he had long been encroaching—for the sole reason that he had heard of Leenhardt's planned visit.)[7]

In fact, Leenhardt found himself in as delicate a political situation as ever. He had now to maintain an attitude of circumspection not merely vis-à-vis the government and Catholics, but also in his relations with Protestant Do Neva. After the departure of Rey-Lescure in 1933, Leenhardt's old station had diminished in importance. The mission staff had tended to content itself with defending an acquired position in the colony. The news of Leenhardt's intended return to the Grande Terre was a cause of apprehension. A circular letter from Paris preceded him, specifying that his participation in mission affairs must be minimal.[8]

Of course Leenhardt could not remain merely a marginal observer. His principal aim in returning was to see his old students. Often he would be greeted in a remote village with glad tears followed by confused and angry questions: "Why hasn't Rey-Lescure returned?" "Why won't Do Neva do something about such and such a cattleman whose animals are destroying our crops?" The ethnographer did not appear much different from the missionary. No one in New Caledonia saw anything new in "Missi Leenhardt" asking questions about languages and customs; he had always done that. And though he tried to stay out of other people's affairs and to discourage inflation of his personal prestige, this was not always possible. His main concern was still the authenticity of New Caledonia's cultural adaptation and in particular the health of its Protestant churches.

>⋲

The most interesting example of Leenhardt's continuing combination of roles stands out in the series of events that Jean Guiart has recounted in his article "The Birth and Abortion of a Messianism."[9] The brief account that follows does no more than summarize his study, completing it with the particular perspective of Jeanne Leenhardt in her letters home. It is essentially the story of the aging missionary's relationship with a pagan diviner named Pwagach.

During the 1920s, Pwagach's influence had spread throughout the northern Grande Terre and as far south as Poya, halfway down the island's west coast. He was a man of about Leenhardt's age, originating from an isolated hamlet high up in the back country above Gomen. Though nominally a Catholic, Pwagach was actually a traditional diviner, or *jau*. A *jau* was not a sorcerer, but rather a healer and prophet.[10] During the first quarter of the twentieth century, belief in sorcery had become widespread on the island. The *jau* was the traditional figure best placed to combat the new influences. In the cultural disarray produced by colonialism—the forcible separation of many clans from their ancestral lands and the crowding together of disparate groups on reduced reservations—it was natural that beliefs should develop concerning maleficent "outside" influences. The *"doki"* was such an outside threat. This dangerous "red god" could take possession of individuals and force them to cast deadly spells on their neighbors so that the "god" might be nourished. Unmasking the *doki*'s agents became a collective obsession. And since the death rate remained relatively high (though by the 1920s the disastrous demographic slide had been checked), the *doki* was held responsible for all manner of diseases and infant mortalities. Social and political stability was directly threatened—producing a wave of anomic uncertainty closely related to colonial dislocations. A man like Pwagach represented the response of tradition to the new state of affairs.[11]

Leenhardt had satisfied himself that the *doki*, though called a "god" (*bao*), was not a new incarnation of any traditional spirit. It had not been significantly appropriated by the old religious terminology, and it had no roots whatever in the deepest sacred strata—totemic life-forces and local ancestral topography.[12] By contrast, a *jau* like Pwagach, the representative of an ancient clan whose forebears were still believed to reside in the mountains of a broad region, possessed an incontestable spiritual authority. If the diviner used this authority responsibly, he might be able to disarm the *doki* beliefs and restore confidence throughout the north, where his ancestry was recognized. Pwagach was a man of integrity. He saw himself as part of a neotraditionalist movement whose aim was solely to restore in some measure the old structures and beliefs.

To most whites, however, "neopaganism" meant potential rebellion. As Pwagach's authority grew, he came to be thought of as a dangerous agitator. Leenhardt did not share this appraisal. In the past he had cultivated relationships with pagan *jaus*, whom he had come to respect as conscientious cultural healers. Pwagach's arrival in a locality usually ended quite effectively the divisive accusations. His approach was not to condemn individuals but to purify the entire clan using traditional ceremonies and a specially concocted herbal beverage guaranteed to wash away all infection from the *doki*. After they had drunk, individuals freely delivered to him the magical packets of herbs that were the signs of their participation in sorcery. Thanks to Pwagach's subtle control of collective psychology, confidence returned.

Arriving on the scene in 1938, Leenhardt was of course very interested in Pwagach. He became convinced of the *jau*'s sincerity and arranged a meeting in the northern highlands. The two men established a bond of mutual respect that resulted, rather quickly, in Pwagach's "conversion" to Protestantism. Leenhardt was under no illusions that he was making a Christian of the old seer; but it was enough for him that the man, whose earnest desire was to "save" his people, ally himself with the work of the *natas* and accept in a general way the overarching new God whom Leenhardt thought could embrace the enduring elements of tradition. For his part, Pwagach was able to escape, via "conversion," a difficult dilemma. A locally based traditional healer, he had no wide political aspirations, and least of all did he desire to act as the head of a nationalist movement of revolt. Such a rebellion would have been suppressed without much difficulty. Pwagach's repute was far from island-wide, and the military power of the colonists was overwhelming. But the old man's influence had attained so broad an extension that it was beginning to take on the features of a messianism. Pwagach was not personally ambitious. It was convenient for him to direct his movement into the broader framework that the prestige of Maurice Leenhardt could provide. In return he hoped to receive both protection and sympathy. Facing a choice between humility or rebellion, he chose the former, channeling his power into a greater and, he felt, trustworthy authority. Pwagach probably heard in the words of the ethnographer the language of religious authenticity; Leenhardt would have spoken to him using many of the *jau*'s most meaningful mythic terms.

The "conversion" of Pwagach was sealed by a series of ceremonies held at Coulna in the northern highlands. Pwagach and about twenty others—Catholics and pagans, including three diviners, one a Protestant deacon—were baptized. The "official" ceremony took place with the participation of a missionary from Do Neva. This exclusively Protestant ritual was, however, preceded by a series of traditional events, including dances and orations during which various local clan groups publicly affirmed or reaffirmed their adherence to Christianity and gave up the magical "herbs" associated with sorcery. In this way Pwagach's purification ceremonies were grafted onto the conversion rite.

A description of these ceremonies is contained in Jeanne Leenhardt's letters to her children in France. A few long passages will communicate the flavor of the occasion. Mme. Leenhardt was a sympathetic but judgmental observer, and her attitude probably differed somewhat from that of her husband. She expresses what would have been the couple's public version of the unorthodox Coulna ceremonies. Her tendency is to split the events in two: first, "savage" dances that must be tolerated in order that the people get paganism out of their systems, then the "serious" part, speeches, agreements, and Christian baptism. We do not know exactly how her husband conceived of the event, but there is every likelihood that he saw it as a more unified process in which a variety of old and new mythic expressivities were brought into play.

The meetings at Coulna began on January 28, 1939. Jeanne Leenhardt gives picturesque descriptions of the arrivals of various native groups, including ritualized welcomes and elaborate speeches in which her husband and various *natas* took part.[13] A number of long conferences followed. Mme. Leenhardt did not participate in these sessions with Pwagach and his allies, where her husband listened, negotiated, and persuaded. The *"paroles"* went on until two in the morning; finally the conversion and sequence of ceremonies were agreed upon.

Two days later the rituals began:

On Monday it had been decided that dances would be held so that once paganism had exhausted itself we could think of baptisms. Since morning we've been waiting, while working happily on the questionnaires, and finally by 3 o'clock things seem to be starting in earnest.

Planks are brought to serve as sounding boxes. Yamboetch, two old men, one other, sit beside them and begin drumming in cadence. Men gather around clapping rhythmically, beating against their thighs or one hand against the other. Every now and then they let out wild cries. They tread in place, all together. The costumes are a sad mixture; on one hat a cockade from the eleventh of November [celebration] in Noumea, and in the hand a spear—coat, trousers, but herbs too, attached to their legs. One of the chief directors of the proceedings is the deacon from Gomen. He's a sorcerer too, but it's thanks to him Gomen accepted the *natas*. He had been very zealous, but then his herbs got hold of him, and for two years things have been lamentable. But he has repented, and since then has been working on all the sorcerers of the region to get them to give up all these things. He stamps zealously in place, and every now and then, to renew his strength, out comes the little tin box they all carry where they keep their matches and tobacco dry. . . . But cries are heard from the direction of the path leading up the river, and we see a group arriving—hiding, then advancing, yelling savagely. Two old men are in the lead, running ahead with spears, hardly clothed, and wearing a great deal of greenery. They come as far as the group beating the rhythm, then return towards their people making them retreat; then they come back towards the stationary group; and during this time the new arrivals have a chance to move forward, but the old men return to push them back once more; this lasts a good five minutes. Finally, hiding themselves, advancing, retreating, shouting, the entire group is before us. The two elders position themselves on one side. Five men, almost naked, their faces and bodies blackened, and holding in their hands little white feathers (I'm bringing them back) squat down in front; behind, those following them do the same: about thirty handsome youths wearing leaves join the choir

17. The ceremonies at Coulna, 1939. Pwagatch stands on the left while a spokesman acts on his behalf, presenting gifts of symbolic bark-cloth streamers and traditional weapons.

Photo: Leenhardt

of drummers. And then the five in front begin their movement to right and left, their bodies streaming sweat, making a handsome black. Papa is taking quite a few photos. The movements are very like those we saw at the exposition [at Paris, 1931] with the *Canaques*.

Then the serious side of the ceremony begins. The old sorcerers come forward with Caledonian money, herbs, etc., and give great emotional speeches to which Papa and Ao reply. They surrender their herbs to Papa, renouncing everything, etc. But if Papa forbade them the use of all herbs no one would listen, for as Ao says, no doctor ever visits them, and they use herbs for all their illnesses, for purges, coughs, etc. What counts is not putting confidence in the hand which cures but rather in the herb, and not demanding exorbitant prices to supply herbs everyone needs. There have to be *natas* who will look after their people and act with good sense. Here too, there's a whole education involved in giving them the Gospel. And a lot remains to be done. Worthy Apou, having heard Papa's sermons and also those of the *natas*, has come to tell Papa that he'd better talk with the *natas* about God, for they seem not to be preaching like Papa, but are saying: there's a white man's god and a native god, instead of saying: there's only one God! Fifteen baptisms have been announced for next Sunday. But one never knows how many are counted and whether two *natas* may not have counted the same people! Papa has, nonetheless, written to Lehnbach [at Do Neva] that he should come on Sunday. With the uncertain weather I don't think he'll be able to make it. Luckily we are some distance from any colonists, since it could be said that ethnology doesn't include performing baptisms![14]

As the final sentences tell us, Leenhardt was in a delicate position with respect to Do Neva and with respect to his official ethnological role in the colony. His evangelizing—some would say syncretism—did not go unnoticed. Professor Guiart quotes at length from a letter sent by the neighboring Catholic missionary to his superiors. It is often inaccurate, the style is somewhat paranoid, but the first two paragraphs of the letter are certainly at least partially correct:

I've finally been able to talk with two witnesses of Pastor Leenhardt's talk to the Pemboas. He told them that it was permissible to conserve the old ways: round houses, pilou-pilou, *iarig*, etc. He told them that they should clean up the sites where the old people had pursued their superstitions and had set up [sacred] stones and wood, otherwise the tribe would perish.

The whites forbid them these customs because they want them to die out, so as to take their lands. The proof is that since giving up the old ways [the tribe] has greatly diminished.[15]

If this was not precisely what Leenhardt said, it is probably what a good many Caledonians heard. The Catholic's version naturally lays unique stress on his rival's neopaganism, downplaying the distinctions Leenhardt would certainly have attempted to make—for example, in the question of medicinal herbs. And the letter omits the new Christian forms he would have tried to graft onto certain of the "old ways." The notion, however, that the whites were out to grab native lands and that physical survival depended on religious authenticity were typical Leenhardtian themes.

The Catholic missionary's letter mentions Leenhardt's recommendation that the sacred sites "where the old people had pursued their superstitions" be cleaned up. These mythic sites were of great interest to Leenhardt and played an active role in the ceremonies of traditional revival surrounding Pwagach's baptism. These were the sacred places where the ancestors resided; and from these locations the clans drew their power, political and spiritual. Jeanne Leenhardt gives an account of a day trip to one of these secret sites, the visit occurring in the period between the dances just described and the official ceremonies of Protestant baptism. The site was located high in the mountains, attainable only after a difficult zig-zag trek on horseback along the sides of steep valleys.

High above Coulna, the Leenhardt party finally reached its goal, the secret home of the local ancestors. The missionary-ethnologist would certainly have felt the depth of meaning contained in the stones. Earlier, he had evoked this mythic landscape, "where each stone has a name, a history, a life, we might even say a personality, resulting from the spirit enclosed within it. Often in [remote] valleys I've asked the name for every detail of the land, each notable tree; and the landscape transposes itself into a scheme it would be impossible to transcribe on a map, in which each name is title to a chapter."[16] His wife's account is, however, merely descriptive, and it betrays a certain nervousness at being in the midst of an alien and still active religiosity:

> Farther along are some nicely arranged rocks enclosing in the rear a white stone, another sculptured slab (human figure), and at the side on some *awa* [bark cloth] Caledonian money. It's probably one of our Sunday baptismal candidates who, before asking to be baptized, felt the need to come offer a final gift to his god, to excuse himself in some way for being unfaithful! All the names of the stones we saw have reappeared constantly in the speeches of the past few days. You have to see and hear to believe how alive all of this is in their heart, closing off completely their intelligence!

The ethnographic couple are on their good behavior. They resist the temptation to take away with them a clay pot of an interesting old shape; there must be no scandals to interfere with the baptisms a few days hence. And Jeanne Leenhardt is ill at ease because she is a woman and is breaking a number of taboos. "My presence is completely contrary to everything. So I'd better stay healthy till the end, otherwise superstitions will simply grow and grow, whereas if I remain well it's an important breach, perhaps even the final act of ground-breaking."[17]

The visit, important ethnographically, was probably also essential in the broad context of the ceremonies taking place that week at Coulna. The names of these sites and stones had been continually present in the orations. Archaic myth was part of the occasion. It was perhaps important, in the general logic of the situation, that a European missionary visit the most sacred sites (there had been some resistance to the visit) and that he accept and understand the ancestral stones, something Leenhardt could do in his ethnological role. Mythic landscape had to be gathered up and protected, not replaced, by a Christian deity.

⧁⧀

This hopeful alliance between an ethnologically aware Protestantism and a self-conscious neopaganism was, unfortunately, only a local and temporary success. Leenhardt and Pwagach's initiative was undermined by a combination of old and new historical contingencies. There continued, as usual, incomprehension from Do Neva and the capital. Not long after the ethnographer's departure, Pwagach was exiled to the New Hebrides. Then came the Second World War and an unheard-of prosperity brought by 200,000 American troops to an island of 60,000 inhabitants. After the war, a promising liberalization of the regime made the status quo more tolerable for a time. Native aspirations for change were temporarily channeled into legal political organizations. Guiart sees in the complex of events I have been describing the birth and abortion of a messianic movement; the absent Maurice Leenhardt could have become its prophet.[18]

A Melanesian student of the period has recalled Leenhardt as a "young patriarch," a "grandfather," active, white-bearded, a spokesman for cultural authenticity.[19] For example, Waia Gorode reports that in his preaching the veteran evangelist criticized the island's newly built churches: they looked like supply sheds. In the old days, he said, a church had the dignity of a *grande case*, a distinct style manifesting group confidence. In Noumea, too, before a white audience, Leenhardt urged the gospel of ethnology—in the form of an ongoing cultural alliance between "old" and "young" Caledonia. "We, the colonizers, have not *seen*. . . ." We have not noticed the subtle, strong, and resourceful culture which existed here before us. This culture is still alive, although we came near to destroying it, having no eye for its art or ear for its poetry.[20]

On the eve of his departure, with war already declared in Europe, Leenhardt convened a group of native pastors for a final talk about the past and future of the New Caledonian church.[21] The last sure boat for France was about to depart. In Noumea confusion reigned. Leenhardt made a last dash up to Gondé in the mountains at the geographic center of the island. Pastors from Bourail, Poya, and Houailou were waiting. Their meeting would be held on the grass-covered hill above the old village. At Gondé the young missionary had first experienced the Grande Terre's intimate scale. Here too he had listened to the old man at the *pilou de temperance*—addressing his personal commitment to the mountains.

Leenhardt says goodbye, conversing in Houailou with the pastors of the area. He responds to their questions, complaints, brings himself up to date on their activities, sends messages to absent members of the conference. He reminds them that the Caledonian work is facing serious problems. The pastoral corps is disunited. They speak primarily as Lifouans, as Maréans, as Caledonians, not as servants of the Word. There is too much talk of "moi." In recent years, pastors and European missionaries have lost confidence in one other. The two roles have become confused. Worst, the local work of the Word has faltered. Too many pastors are seeing themselves and their religion as above the old ways. But the Son of God did not come to judge the world; he came to give it life. Many pastors are not learning the local tongues, are not composing vernacular texts. The Word cannot speak directly to Caledonians in French, or Maré, or Lifou.

The veteran retells the early years of the work, when the first *natas* brought their life-giving message into tribes dying of alcohol, exploitation, and disease—proud people refusing to have babies. At their first conference, on this same site, the early *natas* did not think of themselves and their differences, but of the work of the Word. Seated on the grass at Gondé, the old missionary invokes their names: Waina, Waibo, Mathaia, Owhan, Joané and Wakuba; Porio, Ibeto, Zikoziko and Weinith; Ipézé and Jakobo; Ninyima, Jemes, Melemele, Setine and Rosalet; and Washitine, and Setefano, and Drap. A few days later, Leenhardt was aboard the *Pierre Loti*, bound for Europe.

CHAPTER XI

Structures of the Person

Leenhardt never tired of recounting a conversation with Boesoou Erijisi in which he proposed to his oldest convert: "In short, what we've brought into your thinking is the notion of spirit" [or mind: *esprit*]. To which came the correction: "Spirit? Bah! We've always known about the spirit. What you brought was the body."[1]

The largest part of Leenhardt's ethnological theorizing was direct or indirect exegesis of this retort. His initial concern was simply to understand the different structure of experience that made such a response possible. In the process, however, he was led to rethink the culture contact situation as a whole and to reevaluate that ambiguous gift, the Western "body." It is worth adding, too, that Boesoou's statement offers a condensed example of the kind of Melanesian interpretation of custom that Leenhardt's evangelical pedagogy and ethnographic method sought to engage and validate. A dialog of interpretations is portrayed in the anecdote, an exchange that turns upon Western mind-body dualism and finally unravels it.

Leenhardt's general ethnological approach was both phenomenological and evolutionist. The former orientation drew directly on his extensive ethnographic documentation and on his teaching method, which, as we have seen, involved an attempt to "think like a *Canaque*." Here it is emphatically not a matter of "decoding" Melanesian culture to reveal underlying (or overarching) systems of belief, kinship, symbolism, and the like. The fragmentary character of *Notes d'ethnologie néo-calédonienne*, Leenhardt's lifelong stress on interpreting vernacular documents, the allusive quality of a study like *Do Kamo* (which slides without warning from the description of observed behavior to the evocation of myth)—these approaches may all be seen as strategies designed to frustrate theoretical foreclosure and too easy appropriation of the Other. Leenhardt's method of phenomenological exposition favored "a slow winding along *Canaque* pathways, through the islanders' thinking, their notions of space, time, society, the word, personage . . . ."[2] We may perceive in the form of his work a critique of those structural-functional paradigms (based loosely on Durkheim's

172

definition of "society," Boas and Malinowski's "culture," and Saussure's "language") that have dominated twentieth-century anthropology. Indeed, it is tempting though anachronistic to cast Leenhardt
as a post- rather than a pre-structuralist. What is important, however,
is that his mistrust of systematic closure, his emphasis on reciprocal
interpretation and cultural expressivity placed him at the boundary of
a science that, since Tylor, had concerned itself with the study of
whole, integrated ways of life in more or less continuous development.

Coexisting with Leenhardt's phenomenological approach—not always happily—was an evolutionist theory aiming to show the transition from "archaic" to "modern" experience. This is the dimension of
his thought that now poses the most problems for readers. Although
he tried to avoid positing two separate, mutually exclusive "mentalities," Leenhardt never entirely escaped a number of crude narrative
forms and dichotomies. His versions of the transition from archaic to
modern have a tendency, as we shall see, to assume the shape of "just
so stories," myths of the Fall, and fables of ontogenetic development.
Moreover, he has a tendency to generalize, uncritically, on the basis of
apparently homologous gender stereotypes drawn from Europe and
New Caledonia. "Feminine" is always close to nature, relational, immanent; "male" is political, instrumental, transcendent. Sometimes he
casts the relationship of feminine to masculine as a general sequence
of cultural development; elsewhere it appears as an equilibrium to be
redressed. By the end of Leenhardt's career, however, the evolutionist
cast of his thinking was much attenuated; he believed that the basic
components of human thought were present, or at least potential, at
all stages. Mental/spiritual change was a matter of shifting balances.
In this general standpoint he defended a view, later expressed by Lévi-
Strauss, that exotic modes of thought like totemism are "not outside
us, but within us."[3]

Among those people classed as "archaic," wrote Leenhardt, one may
observe two distinct styles of relating to the world: "cosmomorphism"
and "anthropomorphism."[4] In cosmomorphic experience the substances of nature actually live in the person. There is no clear separation
between self and world; the same flux of life circulates in the body, in
the sap of a plant, in the colors of a stone. A person's flesh is the same
flesh as that of a yam; the skin is the bark of a tree. Leenhardt does
not say that a man's skin is like bark, but rather that it is bark. This
experience of identity supposes the collapse of symbolic, even meta-
phoric, relations. There is no felt distance between subject and object,
no mediation of similarity in difference. Cosmomorphic experience is
the opposite of anthropomorphism, for a person does not project

human attributes onto "nature" but grasps his or her own being as a series of natural events identical to organic rhythms and substances. These do not so much "surround" as "invade" the subject. In a cosmomorphic world the human body is not clearly differentiated. A cadaver is part of the earth; the dead are nameless presences indistinct from other natural presences. There are no individualized ancestors, and thus there is no real ancestor worship. The landscape itself, its mountains, its plant and animal life, is experienced as living, as *vivant*. The basic rule of cosmomorphic perception is *vivant=vivant*. The living being enters into relations of identification with other living beings.

This participatory mode of life is not haphazard. The "personage" (Leenhardt reserves the term "person" for another stage of development) does not spill out chaotically into identification with all life. Participations are structured by myth, which in its earliest form *is* the landscape. The significant rocks, mountains, trees, and animals form a pattern within whose circuits the life of the personage flows. The forms provided by mythic landscape are not mentally formulated; they are not stories, but are merely "here." The personage—perpetually outside an "ego" or "body," as defined by Westerners—knows himself or herself as a participant in juxtaposed mythic occasions, experiencing no narrative or personal itinerary proper to an "individual" identity.

Anthropomorphic views of the world do not abolish this participatory form of experience, but they do represent a second stage in which humans are less radically mixed with the cosmos and have begun to distance themselves from objects. Religious "beings" are now set within, but distinct from, nature. The cadaver is now perceived as individual; ancestors are identified, named, their personalities grafted onto the mythic geography. People begin to project their attributes into the cosmos, enlarging their perceptual space in the process. The world begins to be named with parts of the body. The subject-object distance increases; participation gives way to symbolism and representation. But there is no rapid transformation of cosmomorphism into anthropomorphism. The two modes remain mixed together in archaic experience. According to Leenhardt, this experience is composed of two coexisting modes of apprehension: "mythic knowledge" and "rational knowledge."

Mythic knowledge is not narrated but "lived" in existential events whose overall pattern has not yet been grasped. This consciousness does not distance itself from events or search for overview. It is involved in a landscape—a world known in intimate detail but never described or mapped. Leenhardt links the emergence of a belief in

personal deities to the development of object-positing, analytic rationality. Totems, he emphasizes, are not "gods." An animal or tree that
is a source of life is endowed with mythic presence but not with
personality. The same may be said of all the earliest cosmomorphic
attachments to the land—invocations of the mountain, the cult of
stones, totemic identifications, and the like. In the most archaic religious experiences, the mountain is not associated with deities. Rather,
its power derives from its presence within an esthetic of place. Familiar topography constitutes "a microcosm where a man situates himself and feels himself in scale." There is "circulation between himself
and the world, a world of reduced dimensions, which his mind, still
limited to its land, can grasp." "The rock," says Leenhardt, "preceded
God." Once, however, the rock, mountain, or other natural location
begins to take on a distinct personality, then the more rational, anthropomorphic modes come into play and deities take shape.

The attempt of Pater Schmidt and many missionaries to find evi-
dences of a Supreme Being in archaic religions is doomed to failure,
Leenhardt argues, precisely because certain crucial mental changes
are still unaccomplished. In particular, monotheism requires that a
person be capable of conceiving "one." Archaic modes of knowledge
proceeded from conceptions of plurality, duality, symmetry, and equilibrium. As we shall see in Leenhardt's discussion of the structure of
the person in New Caledonia, the experience of plurality, especially of
doubleness, was elementary. Leenhardt suggested that the "Supreme
God" was originally plural, and he drew suggestive evidence from a
variety of religious traditions. He noted the role of a primal couple in
Hesiod, as well as the plural form of Elohim, which would only later
give way to the singular Jehovah.

Attaining the conception of a sole God thus involves a long process
of mental and cultural change. Ancestor worship is an important step.
Leenhardt terms it a "pious construction of rationality." Ancestor
worship in New Caledonia has a dominant masculine component,
whereas totemic myth is strongly generative and feminine. The dis-
engagement and worship of personal ancestors is a victory for the
rational/male principle of "power," as contrasted with the participa-
tive/female attachment to "life." In ancestor worship the cosmos comes
to be populated with deities. Early mythic consciousness has been
aware only of presences, "forms figuring various aspects of the world's
life, totems and genies, . . . hypostases of life." Now distinctness
(alterité) has solidified into otherness (autre). First, the personality of
the dead is disengaged; personal gods follow. But the conception of a
single god, an immanent but also overarching deity, would require

further changes in modes of thought and in the definition of the human person.

In the experience of "lived myth," however, the cosmomorphic equation, *vivant=vivant*, remained strong. Thus in *Do Kamo*, speaking of traditional New Caledonia, Leenhardt could write: "The human body is composed of that substance which turns green in jade, gives form to foliage, swells every living thing with sap and bursts out in shoots and in the eternal youth of new generations."[5] If Leenhardt here used the European term "body" to denote this nexus of cosmomorphic experience, he used it against the grain and to suggest the word's redefinition in conversation with Boesoou and Melanesia.

>€

For what was commonly called "totemism," Leenhardt preferred the name "totemic myth." This complex represented for him an important transitional form of religious experience.[6] As myth, it functioned within a cosmomorphic universe of perception, participating in the landscape while imposing a pattern on the flux of experience. Totemic myth was an extremely early effort at differentiating the world. One of its components was the experience of immediate participatory rhythm, divinity, or natural presence incarnate in the shapes and gestures of the environment, an esthetic of place. The other element was an emerging worship of ancestors, the cult of individual, differentiated deities, a system of belief crucial to the early development of rational faculties.

Leenhardt was concerned with correcting Lévy-Bruhl's characterization of primitive mentality as "mystical" by replacing "mystical" with "mythical."[7] The latter implied something more than mental flux and absence of the law of contradiction; it suggested an adequate mode of knowledge. Mythical knowledge was as appropriate to the nonempirical reality it attempted to grasp as science was to its own domain, the objective universe. Thus "myth," as Leenhardt used it, was not merely an evolutionary stage standing between cosmomorphism and objectivity. Although Melanesian totemism tended to dissolve on contact with the new ancestor gods, its constitutive, mythic modes of experience did not disappear.[8] Leenhardt frequently used the term "myth" or "mythic" to apply loosely to affective modes of knowledge ranging from the most archaic participatory geography to ancestor worship, including under the mythic umbrella communal relations with personal deities and later with a single God. Myth accommodates itself to the progress of rationality. Though science explains more and more, emotional realities remain that cannot be grasped by reason.

Leenhardt gave totemic myth an essentially religious content, thus setting himself apart from sociological and structural interpreters. By the late 1950s the accumulation of ethnographic data had placed the category of "totemism" in question. Lévi-Strauss would soon dismiss it as an illusive catch-all. Leenhardt tried to deal with the imprecision of the term by restricting it to a mythico-religious experience of attachment to the sources of life, thereby denying it primary significance at the level of social classification. Lévi-Strauss's famous response to the problem consisted in treating "totemism" as a privileged example from which to disengage transcendent structures of thought. In *Le Totémisme aujourd'hui* and its sequel, *La Pensée sauvage*, he described it as a form of concrete intellectuality, a homemade science (or *bricolage*) using categories that were "on hand" in the natural environment.[9]

Leenhardt would have approved Lévi-Strauss's tendency to render the process of thought concrete, and there are elements in his conception of *mythe vécu* that anticipate Lévi-Strauss's *bricolage*. But the great contrast between the two theoretical stances lies in the different weights they assign to "affect" and "intellect" in the structure of consciousness. "Impulses and emotions," Lévi-Strauss argues, "explain nothing: they are always *results*, either of the power of the body or of the importance of the mind. In both cases they are consequences, never causes. The latter can be sought only in the organism, which is the exclusive concern of biology, or in the intellect, which is the sole way offered to psychology, and to anthropology, as well."[10] Lévi-Strauss's approach affords a good example of the kind of analytic dichotomizing with which Leenhardt was uncomfortable. For Leenhardt the phenomenologist, what really mattered was the complex range of experience lying between the final "causes" evinced by Lévi-Strauss, the poles of intellect and biology. Leenhardt refused to reduce emotion to physiological impulse, nor would he assimilate its conscious expressive modes to rationality. The heart had its reasons or, perhaps, its rhythms. Its structure of articulation was not, properly speaking, a classification or logic, a metaphysic or theology, but a given experiential landscape.

One may sometimes be tempted to use the example of Leenhardt— so distinct from Lévi-Strauss in theoretical approach and research experience—as a weapon against structuralism.[11] Yet it is also possible to portray aspects of Leenhardt's work as anticipations of structuralism. For example, Guiart stresses that Leenhardt's version of New Caledonian kinship and social structure is of a social fabric composed of dual, reciprocal relationships. "To speak of relations," he notes, "rather than of individuals, is a very modern attitude, which in its implications goes well beyond Malinowski, preparing the way for Lévi-

Strauss."[12] In the long run, however, it is probably best to envisage the standpoints of Leenhardt and Lévi-Strauss not as oppositions, but as complementary articulations of an underlying, constituent epistemology—mind-body dualism in its Cartesian form. This perspective is suggested by Roger Bastide in a balanced assessment of the two approaches.[13]

Bastide recalls that Descartes's *cogito* was constructed through the process of distinguishing "clear and distinct ideas" (*pensée claire et distincte*) from "obscure and confused ideas" (*pensée obscure et confuse*). Descartes's method placed exclusive value on knowing through "ideas" rather than knowing with "the flesh." The Cartesian model of the mind was mathematical; pure ideas were kept apart from the infection of sensuous knowledge. Nonetheless, the existence of corporeal, affective modes of knowledge was not denied by Descartes. Reality was not a deduction of transcendental reason. *Pensée obscure et confuse* existed as a form of human knowledge translatable into *pensée claire et distincte* but of another basic type. The entire task of philosophy was to accomplish the transformation into clear intellectual categories. But elaboration of the pure forms of reason, unshadowed by any parallel *pensée obscure*, was only later accomplished by Kant. Lévi-Strauss, for Bastide, stands in this rationalist lineage, his goal being to strip ideas of their affectivity and materiality to reveal their existence as contentless relationships. Totemism and myth are stripped of their bodily, experiential qualities and portrayed as productions of a nonsubjective universal mind.

Leenhardt, by contrast, directs his attention to Descartes's *pensée obscure et confuse*. He attempts to render its lived modes—without reducing them to the forms of reason—by according to them a discrete structure, that of myth. Leenhardt's *cogito*, writes Bastide, is an "ensemble of *cogitationes*," mind thinking without a center, participating in a discontinuous variety of patterned occasions. Mythic thought deals in juxtapositions rather than classifications, contrasts rather than oppositions. Leenhardt is more concerned with the person's experience of the totem than he is with totemism taken as unconscious structure. Indeed, his account of the totem's connection with the classificatory positions of kinship is always sketchy, and he stops short of portraying either kinship or totemism as a complete system. He situates himself, characteristically, *between* structure and event, emphasizing cultural "speech" rather than "language," invention and process rather than rules.

Perhaps his most important gift was for conceiving religion not as a closed "system" of beliefs or symbols but as an open field of expressions in partial, *ad hoc* formulation.[14] Mythic life, as he renders it, is composed of immediate gestures and juxtaposed images. In a paragraph from *Do Kamo*, he gives us the actual totem, subject of so much ingenious theorizing:

> The Melanesian totem assumes a very humble form. It is the lizard of the forest next to the habitat, the plature snake on the ocean shore, the little black worms which swarm over the banked edges of the taro fields, or a common grass which grows near the houses. It is the quivering point showing the existence of life in the world's inert mass. None gives a stronger impression of this than the Caledonian gecko, a very old and very ungainly species. Long ago I placed one of them near my house to observe it. It makes a gutteral sound, *hroh*, which the natives say heralds rain. It licks its nose with a very coarse tongue that is pink like a human tongue. It takes on the color of the branch on which it sits and stays there for days without apparent movement and with only its eyes awake. Immobile on large immobile trunks, it is the living being most at one with the forest, and it is understandable that the *Canaque* has established a relation between it and life in nature.[15]

In *Notes d'ethnologie néo-calédonienne*, Leenhardt provides a multitude of details on this and other totems.[16] The totem is no distinct deity but a form encountered along the path. It signifies the presence of life in nature and renews the contact of the perceiver with the flux animating human being. One does not really perceive the totem; one enters its time.

Bastide contrasts this style of knowing with the abstract modes of *pensée claire et distincte*: "Leenhardt re-embodies this totemism-'idea,' this totemism-'essence,' this totemism-'pure nature,' to use the Cartesian terminology. He returns to it its odor, heat, and secret shadows."[17] Leenhardt does not show the pure forms of thought, but rather "the palpitation of these forms in matter."[18] These "vague and confused" styles of thought make use of experiences and perceptions that Westerners tend to dismiss as pathological or merely accidental. According to Eliane Métais, writing on New Caledonian sorcery and religion,

> dreams, nightmares, hallucinations in trances, crises of possession, productions of the imagination and also bodily reactions of fear, of surprise . . . [for the Melanesian] are means

of exploration, of knowledge and of creation, which give access to a convincing aspect of reality, that is just as objective and valid as that provided by other human methods of knowing.[19]

Leenhardt might have questioned the use of "objective" in the last sentence. But otherwise Métais evokes very well the variety of participatory states of consciousness that find expression through the mediation of "lived myth." This *pensée obscure* is vague only from the standpoint of a culture that has produced a Descartes. In Métais's words, Melanesian mythic reality "is 'given' with the same force that the street and houses surrounding us are, to our Western style of thinking."[20] As Leenhardt comprehended it, mythic perception was not mystical or mysterious, but concrete, constitutive of landscape and person.

For example, Leenhardt believed, with Malinowski, that archaic Melanesians had not disengaged the male's biological role in procreation. But on the mythic level, he argued, they understood quite clearly and concretely that life was a work of couples, a relationship in which the man played an essential role, not of "originator" but of "strengthener." As Leenhardt saw it, the great achievement of totemic myth was its structuring of a generative world of ordered male and female couplings. "Feminine" life-force or blood did not flow directly into the life of the person. It flowed in a zigzag path of exchange, linking exogamous patrilocal clans. Women moved from clan to clan in marriage exchanges, and at each intersection of the social fabric there stood a couple composed of "masculine" power and "feminine" life. Thus a rhythm was imposed on the members of each paternal clan: to hold the life confided to them, to reproduce and return it in the form of daughters. This rhythm of coupling and reciprocity established the earliest form of sexual and social discipline.[21]

Leenhardt's account of totemic myth should probably not be generalized beyond Southern Melanesia. And sometimes one hears in his accounts distant echoes of the Eden story—a transition from unmediated cosmomorphism (Adam and Eve in the garden, "one flesh") to distinct couplings (associated with differentiated male and female work, childbirth, agriculture). But the strength of Leenhardt's versions does not lie in his hypothetical reconstruction of early mythic development. Rather, what continues to be of value is his refusal of the dichotomy of thought and emotion and his establishment of an autonomous experiential reality for "mythic knowledge." Here, his work parallels in key respects that of the late, "post-structuralist" Lévi-Strauss of *Mythologiques*.[22]

The differential emphases remain—intellect versus affect, universal mind versus experiential localism. But the two arguments for the continuing value and specificity of mythic knowledge have important elements in common. Both succeed in blurring the thought-feeling dichotomy, proposing a kind of adequate knowledge, a *pensée*, that works with concrete, sensuous qualities rather than abstract concepts. And both, finally, reject the notion of a totalizing mythic structure or language—one of them assimilating myth to music, the other to the processes of esthetic perception. In the "Overture" to *The Raw and the Cooked*, Lévi-Strauss has recourse to the image of a nebula, endlessly composing its form in a universe of contingency. And Leenhardt writes of myth as a "condition of newness where neither stories nor rites are properly fixed and everything still vibrates with the event or emotion which gave it birth."[23] It is not important, at this level, that the mythic processes take place in a Melanesian valley or in a study at the *Collège de France*. What is significant is a break with common habits of closure and wholeness, structures of the intellect and the body. The results are paradoxical—formulations like Lévi-Strauss's "Kantianism without a transcendental subject" or Leenhardt's notion of a mode of thought that "juxtaposes but does not classify."[24]

A full comparison of Leenhardt and Lévi-Strauss would take us too far afield. Enough has been said to suggest certain affinities behind the obvious differences. In practice, both thinkers had a capacity for overflowing the boundaries of their own programmatic prescriptions. It is worth noticing, however, this affinity-in-opposition, for it may help explain the absolute disinclination of structuralism to build on Leenhardt's work. Lévi-Strauss's brilliant intellectual ground-clearing operation of the 1950s was based on a number of simplifications and repressions. The phenomenological perspective of *Do Kamo* was among its victims. Leenhardt was never subjected to systematic criticism but was lumped together with Lévy-Bruhl and dismissed along with the existential murkiness of "participation," the entire "primitive mentality" paradigm, and the "history of religions" approach of Van Der Leeuw and, later, Eliade. Leenhardt had much in common with these perspectives, but he was primarily an ethnographer; his point of view, as we shall see, transcended that of Lévy-Bruhl. And his work still stands as a shadowy alternative to Lévi-Strauss's, a parallel trajectory that could not be completely rejected and had therefore to be forgotten. The ascendant structuralism of the 1950s had no use for *pensée obscure et confuse*, though it came, finally, to practice it.[25]

>€

"Mythic thought" in Melanesia is as much corporeal as mental. Leenhardt portrays a world of unexpected and intense associations, of juxtapositions rather than maps or narrative sequences. It is a world in which "ideas" are close to what we might call "moods." Leenhardt describes these states in terms of "participation," "two-dimensionality," lack of subject-object distance; but these phrases must not, of course, be taken literally. Archaic New Caledonians were quite aware of the contours of the material world. They were accomplished technologists and not in the habit of stumbling over stones in a "non-objective" space. If the existence Leenhardt evokes in *Do Kamo* and various other essays seems sometimes to take place in a dream, we should remember that the "mythic consciousness" he emphasizes does not occupy the whole of Melanesian experience. There exists a related world of rationality and technology, a world Leenhardt takes for granted. Readers of *Do Kamo*, a study in socio-mythic phenomenology, are presumed to have some familiarity with *Gens de la Grande Terre*, a companion work in which the material mode of New Caledonian existence is given its due.

Leenhardt never evolved a very satisfactory theory of the relationship between "rational thought" and "mythic thought." He saw them as complementary and parallel but did not go much beyond that. In the Melanesian world he portrayed the two modes as distinct but extraordinarily close to one another: "Archaic man . . . seems always to be living on two levels; with a gesture of the hand he brushes away branches obstructing the path and, simultaneously, noxious emanations that he imagines and fears. His hand and [empirical] attention assure order in the concrete area of his habitat. His behavior and comportment maintain order in the other domain as well, a realm which the hand cannot attain."[26] It is the experience of this pervasive "other domain" that Leenhardt attempts to render.

"Space" is defined by Leenhardt as "a heterogeneous ensemble of places whose existence is experienced through bodily presence." Divinity in its various forms—natural presences, totems, gods—is simply "here now." Melanesians locate themselves in mythic "time-spaces" through adequate words, comportments, and ritual gestures that mark or circumscribe the event. Myth is figured in the most casual of gestures: sidestepping a tabooed spot on a path, replacing a lizard on the branch from which it has fallen. Ritual at this stage need not be particularly elaborate or even practiced collectively. The personal gestures of *mythe vécu* have immediate spatial references—natural sites (the mountain, the *Kuni* tree, and so on), personal altars, the *grande case* topped with its totemic sculptures.[27] Every mythic "event" into which

Melanesians "transport themselves" possesses its own "time," which becomes that of the subject. "These times are not added to one another as in linear series. They are juxtaposed; and the native may be in one, in another, or in several of them simultaneously."[28]

Leenhardt often referred to a particular example of this kind of mythic self-transport—the case of Jopaipi. A traditional surgeon, healer, and friend of Boesoou Erijisi, Jopaipi recounted his experience to the old Melanesian pastor, who transcribed it for the ethnographer. Neither song nor folktale nor formulated myth, the story is, rather, the kind of "document" most valued by Leenhardt—a slice of personal mythic life. Needing a certain power, Jopaipi seeks it at his personal altar in the "time" of a specific ancestor. He enters into trance, seizes the spirit when it appears, wrestles with it amicably (not as an opponent but in intense participatory vibration), and gains its power. Jopaipi becomes a healer, using the medicinal bark revealed to him by the ancestor whose "time" he has entered, *corps à corps*. Each time Jopaipi uses the bark, he relives this experience of the ancestor. Participations of this order were, to the Westerner, disconcertingly common in the life of archaic Melanesia. But a mythically patterned existence was not to be conceived as an external determinism or an obligatory social fact. Here, as elsewhere, Leenhardt chose to see myth as a means of personal construction. In the case of Jopaipi, the participatory struggle with the ancestor was not so much a loss of self (or possession by an Other) as it was an experience of "the event which made of him a man endowed with a personality."[29] Jopaipi, in effect, becomes somebody.

Melanesians, if they worried about such things, might say, with Rimbaud, "Je est un autre." According to Leenhardt such statements would be already built into their language. But these locutions would be more concrete than Rimbaud's and not phrased as a paradox. All personality is relational. This fundamental postulate of Leenhardt's thought was elaborated in his account of social life and social structure.[30] Indeed, the structure of experience in the "socio-mythic" world was fused with what we have seen in the "spatio-mythic." The principal building block in his model of social structure and of the person was the notion of *le duel*, a relationship of two "individuals" in which separate parts of the ensemble were not grasped.

In *Do Kamo* and in his more detailed article of 1942, "La Personne mélanésienne,"[31] Leenhardt analyzes these fundamental grammatical forms of duality, emphasizing their "suppleness" in treating a person nonabstractly—not as an individual quantity but as a quality inherent in specific groups. "The Melanesian," says Leenhardt, "never has a simple view of people and things, but sees them always in terms of symmetry, or as a participation." In this world, "two" is not a sum; "one" does not exist except as an experience of otherness, as a fraction of two. "All of Caledonian society is constructed on this base, according to principles of correspondence, complementarity, equilibrium, symmetry, alterity, and bilateralism. We see this in architecture, in the disposition of village alleys, in sculpture, in rhythms, in exchanges, potlatches, kinship terms, discourses to the chief, etc."[32]

In Leenhardt's portrayal of social structure, relational ensembles are not essentially social but are socio-mythic. A nephew's relation of parity with his maternal uncle is not simply a rapport between clans or social "positions"; it is also an access to the totemic source of blood or life. Thus "social structure" (the kinship system) cannot possess the privileged explanatory status that has sometimes been attributed to it.[33] In an explanatory approach whose point of departure is the multi-relational personage, "social" relations and "religious" relations are not in essence different. Both are articulations of patterned "events" in the flow of "life"—what Leenhardt called myth. Such an approach can be distinguished from Durkheim's in that Leenhardt constructed the Melanesian world out of personal, not social, facts. However, his approach did not involve him in the psychologizing that Durkheim so strenuously avoided. The Melanesian was, in Leenhardt's special vocabulary, a "personage"—in no sense an individual, but a locus of socio-mythic dualities.

The participatory personage is called by the Melanesian *kamo*—the living one, *"le qui vivant."* The term can refer to a natural, a mythic, or a human "being," and the socio-religious world is composed of pairs of *kamo*. The human *kamo* grasps its existence only through relations with others. If not clearly situated in one or more than one of these relations, the personage is *bwiri*, an individual acting freely, haphazardly. In a diagram, Leenhardt avoids the representation of any "ego" point:

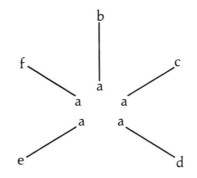

ab, ac, ad, ae, af, and so forth represent the personage and father, and uncle, and wife, and cross-cousin, and clan, and ancestor, and totem, and so on. The center of these relationships is empty. There is no experience of a defining "body." The Melanesian feels no physical envelope that separates a personal "inside" from an objective "outside." The perceptual world is "two-dimensional," the subject-object distance small. (In moments of intense participation in another's "time," the distance vanishes.) The empty space at the center of the personage cannot even be accorded a single name; the participatory experience is evoked by many names.[34] There is no essential ego, conscience, or cogito at the core of this ensemble.

So ex-centric a portrayal of experience cannot fail to place in question the modern organization of what Burridge has called "institutionalized and generalized individuality."[35] And in this connection it is worth mentioning the influence of Leenhardt's portrayal of the personage on Jacques Lacan's reformulation of the psychoanalytic subject. Leenhardt's image of a self endlessly engaged in otherness, as well as his emphasis on a broadened conception of "speech," or the Word, as constitutive of subjectivity, was taken up in Lacan's famous *Discours de Rome* of 1953. The psychoanalyst had found *Do Kamo* to be "somewhat confused, but how very suggestive. . . ."[36]

Lacan, Lévi-Strauss, and the early structuralists in effect generalized and reformulated Leenhardt's "archaic" model, thereby dissolving the person in the signifying processes of language and language-like cultural relations. The separate individual was declared to be a fiction and an ideological construct. Leenhardt, though he did not live to see an adequate deployment of structuralist arguments, would probably have agreed with much of the attack on "individualism." But his own concern was to rescue an authentic conception of the person, and he would have been uneasy with any tendency to reduce the self to a mere function of linguistic or cultural processes. Abstractions like "language" and "culture" could not replace the concrete, enveloping environment of mythic geography and kinship that had made the archaic "personage" a viable model of existence.

A personage without concrete participatory supports was adrift, according to Leenhardt, alienated and closed to *communitas*. Thus in modern life a certain "body" was necessary—if not a closed physical envelope, then at least some stable phenomenological base from which the subject could enter into communal exchanges with environment, kin, and divinity. The precise constitution of this authentic body remained indeterminate in Leenhardt's work. Perhaps "body"—to follow Roland Barthes—functioned as a "mana-word," the name of a powerful, open, unstable but persistent locus on which life itself, now organized as "personality," depended.[37] Boesoou Erijisi's notion of "body" thus corresponded—more or less comfortably—to the ethnologist's concept of a centered, *and* relational, "person":

> Could it be that the person—the human being living in respiratory exchange with the atmosphere—cannot exist, cannot live, except by communal exchange? Might it be that the person cannot find himself except through a transport, and that he can only exist, live his own time, by confusing it with the time of another? . . .[38]

≫∈

Questions. Leenhardt tended to cast his most important points in the form of questions. These were posed in 1937, at the end of a period of intense intellectual engagement with Melanesian archaism. In the preceding years Leenhardt had published his three volumes for the Institut d'Ethnologie, had become a regular teacher at Hautes Etudes, and had finished *Gens de la Grande Terre*. In his teaching and writing he had interpreted, with obvious fascination and sympathy, various experiences of lived myth, *mythe vécu*. Much of what he discovered attracted him—the fullness of engagement with others, the fervor of religious attachments, the concreteness of language, the authenticity of rapports with the natural environment. Leenhardt delighted in revealing the nuances of languages that had not yet hardened into tenses, that excelled in expressing subtle modulations of the present. He fully appreciated modes of speech that made relativism and plurality obligatory in the perception of "persons" and "things." Finally, the entire Caledonian esthetic, based on equilibrium and complementarity, confirmed and influenced his own values.

Such sympathies placed him in apparent conflict with evangelism, with its commitments to monotheism, individualism, literacy, and nationality. But Leenhardt believed that these innovations were inevitable and finally desirable. How then could the participatory essence of mythic life be preserved in the new conditions dictated by European global expansion? In *Gens de la Grande Terre* and in his articles of 1937, he raised this issue without developing it. His prime emphasis during this period was on a relativist comprehension of archaic custom. But after his return to the Grande Terre in 1938-1939, he turned his theoretical attention directly to the problem of "individuation." Perhaps the renewed, immediate contact with his ex-students, the pastors of New Caledonia, had sharpened his awareness of the need for a guide to the dilemmas of acculturation. It was time to attempt a synthesis of missionary and ethnological wisdom. His theory of the "authentic" person was the result. In it he addressed himself to what he believed to be the most crucial question facing both Melanesians *and* Europeans. The emphasis on authenticity is, of course, reminiscent of Heidegger. Indeed, Leenhardt's late work, *Do Kamo* in particular, may be seen as an ethnological, Christian-syncretist reworking of Heideggerian issues.[39]

In his article of 1942, "La Personne Mélanésienne," he refined ideas he had previously only sketched out. He extended the analysis in *Do Kamo*. From Mauss he had derived the distinction between *personnage* and *personne*, to which he added a third category, *individu*. The development traced by Mauss from personage to *"moi"* (individual self) had, in the West, required millennia. In lands like New Caledonia, the evolution was apparently being accomplished in a few generations. Mauss, like Leenhardt, saw the development of a "self" as valuable. But he too seemed to harbor doubts concerning the universal applicability of the European prototype. Mauss tended to portray this particular *moi* as an eccentric and rather fragile historical experiment.[40]

Leenhardt hoped that Melanesians might avoid a path of change in which their affective life would slide towards the spiritual impoverishment of magical rationalism. Once the *mythe vécu* of the Melanesian personage became no longer sufficient, a dangerous disintegration might follow, leaving only separate "individuals" cut off from occasions of intense affective communion and capable only of quasi-rational modes of controlling the world.[41] The historical principle of "power" would have largely obliterated the regenerative attachment to "life." Acculturation could mean sacrificing the essence of personhood, which Leenhardt thought was the capacity for communally sharing the time of others, mythic and human. *La Personne*, his ideal, was a norm mediating the two extremes, archaic personage and modern individual.[42]

According to Leenhardt's schema, it was necessary for Melanesians to enter the world of clear and distinct bodies to experience new mythic modes of interaction based not on diffuse "participation" but on "communion." Leenhardt did not always distinguish clearly between these two basic affective modes. When he did, he specified that "communion" was participation structured as the interaction of "persons," mythic or human. In archaic participation, the personage had deduced itself from the ensemble of landscape, habitat, and altar. This ensemble was the only concrete locus for "mind" or "spirit"—in Boesoou's sense of the term *esprit*, knowledge as mythic influx. Leenhardt thought that the modern world, with its physical dislocations and vastly enlarged geographical space, had exploded this small-scale existence. A mind no longer anchored in a densely familiar landscape would be *bwiri*, adrift, unless it located itself materially in a body. A body was, in effect, something to get around with in a drastically expanded existential space.

But what if the personage, by situating itself "inside" an objectified body, should rupture all participative ties without translating them into communal ones? "J'ai un corps," announced the Protestant convert, expressing joy at having discovered a new, mobile support for his or her personality. But this new body, unless tutored in the modes of mythic communion, might become a prison. This individualistic confinement was Leenhardt's diagnosis of the European condition.

One notices a hesitant evolution in the ethnologist's thinking from the 1942 article on the Melanesian person to *Do Kamo*, published five years later. In the former, Leenhardt talks unhesitatingly of the "disappearance" of "mythic thought" in the process of personal emergence. But in *Do Kamo*, mythic thought is presented as a permanent structure of human consciousness, complementary to rationality. In 1942, Leenhardt leaves his readers with the "true person," *do kamo*, at the point of "escape from" the "socio-mythic domain" as it abandons the use of dual substantives and begins to have recourse to "one" and "*je*." But in *Do Kamo* he describes a "return to myth," the need for a renewal of mythic modes of knowledge. Here he distinguishes unambiguously the secular "individual" from that plentitude of mythic communions that he saw as the foundation of a "person."[43]

During the last decade of his life, Leenhardt would continue to investigate the nonrational bases of personal authenticity, the enduring mythic forms of *pensée obscure et confuse*. In doing so, he continued to reflect on the troubling exchange with Boesoou Erijisi. For if the "body" named by the old man was not a closed, objective form but was open to otherness in the form of emotional, spiritual communions, then it could not be seen as something *brought* by the Western evangelist to Melanesia. The idea—or better, the utopia—of this body was an invention of the ethnographic-evangelical exchange. It was a commonly constructed utopia that the ethnologist would endlessly interpret. In Chapter 13 we will sketch some of these elaborations: Leenhardt's analysis of "participation" (in response to Lévy-Bruhl), his adoption of Melanesian ideas of the Word, and his ongoing concern with the phenomenology of esthetic perception.

But we must follow the ethnologist, one more time, to the Grande Terre.

CHAPTER XII

The Colonial World

Leenhardt's theories cannot safely be separated from his continuing research. The imprecisions, uncertainties, and repetitions so evident in his writings reflect their basic condition of involvement. The value of such a standpoint is, of course, its nearness to experience, a continual conversation with the "material." In the present chapter, we will observe some of the weaknesses inherent in these same qualities, notably a general inability to step back from specific personal and historical circumstances to identify underlying structures and limiting ideologies. In this sense, Leenhardt was true to his conception of authenticity. He was very much a person of his time—or times, since he participated in a range of discontinuous milieux.

His attempts at theoretical overview in books like *Do Kamo* remain tied to specific occasions. Leenhardt's work in comparative ethnology was limited, for he really trusted only knowledge he had gained first-hand.[1] His books do not posit sharp theoretical contrasts; they avoid polemics. Often he does not so much argue as seem to tell a story; and he is frequently evocative, throwing out hints and questions. *Do Kamo*, for example, is at once a fascinating and a frustrating work. Its examples are startling, cryptic, and supercharged with sense. Leenhardt's esthetic approach characteristically presents the general in the particular—a heightened detail of daily life, a word's unexpected meaning, a fragment of a myth. In its organizational rhythm, *Do Kamo* frequently communicates a sense of unrecognized ambivalence. Dense sections that sympathetically render mythic patterns of life tend to be framed by summary statements cast in the language of an apparently unexamined evolutionism. Its stress on the insufficiencies of archaic mentality and on the necessity for personal development in a religious context suggests a rather obvious attempt to justify liberal missionary priorities. At times Leenhardt relapses into a "primitive mentality" paradigm characteristic of the early Lévy-Bruhl. The archaic mind is held at a distance from rationality, characterized by what it is not, by the logical operations it does not perform, rather than by what it *is*. But *Do Kamo* grew out of a series of lectures whose major intent was to question this very paradigm. Leenhardt wanted to demonstrate that myth was not simply a relaxation or hiatus of the rational mind, as Lévy-Bruhl had tended to portray it, but was rather an independent and adequate mode of knowledge.[2] That he should so often have succumbed to the negative definitions he set out to challenge is ironic. It is also characteristic.

Leenhardt always criticized his friend loyally, and in doing so he adopted much of Lévy-Bruhl's terminology. Leenhardt was continually trying—in all domains of his life—to make old forms adapt to new contents. If he felt ill at ease with the philosopher's general perspective, he nonetheless respected and needed it. The author of Do Kamo was not a builder of broad theories. In the 1940s there were few models to which he could attach his thinking. Malinowskian functionalism did not provide much more than a framework for full description. In both England and France, the general influence of Durkheim was dominant, and ethnology was primarily the study of social structures. A phenomenological approach found little support in existing ethnological theories. Only Lévy-Bruhl's philosophical approach to "mentalities" even began to raise the relevant questions. In fact, Leenhardt was never able to carve for himself a recognized theoretical domain, and by the 1950s his perspective was lost in the wave of enthusiasm for structuralism. Indeed, his habit of looking at culture primarily from the point of view of the "person" is still rare in ethnological literature.

A Protestant viewpoint, to be sure, but Leenhardt's stance need not be dismissed as merely that. The dilemmas of personal authenticity in acculturation, the need for concrete mediations between individual and social, rational and mythic, secular and religious, are universally important problems. In this sense, Leenhardt's utopia of the authentic person, do kamo, is more than a simple advocacy of modernization by religious means. If it is a justification of a missionary practice, it is perhaps the most attractive utopia to emerge from the missionary-colonial age, an age coming to an end during the final years of Leenhardt's life.[3] The do kamo ideal struggles to reach beyond the historical period in which it was developed. But Leenhardt's loyal critiques of evangelism, colonialism, and the mentalité primitive paradigm were frequently implicit, overly involved in the very structures they struggled to transform. His final theories are best understood as the attempts of an individual born in 1878 to find expression for a life led in the midst of rapid cultural and historical change. His thinking was never that of an old man retiring late in the day to put his life in order. It remained an involved thought grappling with the compromises of actuality. Thus in 1947-1948 the Paris professor is again in New Caledonia.

≥∈

The war and its aftermath had brought considerable changes to the archipelago. The Grande Terre was a staging ground for United States campaigns in the South Pacific. Hundreds of thousands of Yankees, along with their wealth and liberal attitudes, made a sharp impression on the life of the island. Change was in the air. In September 1946, the first Melanesian priests were ordained in the cathedral at Noumea. In the same year the interdiction on free native travel was finally lifted. Citizenship rights in the French Empire—now to be called the Union Française—were significantly extended. Two mission groups, Catholic and Protestant, worked in concert to prepare the way for the islanders' assumption of full citizenship, decreed in 1951. In the first election held under the democratized regime, a "pro-native" representative was elected to the French Chamber of Deputies—M.-H. Lenormand, who had studied ethnology in Paris with Leenhardt.[4] Perhaps the missionary's earlier dream of a small-scale, biracial democracy would finally become fact.

Leenhardt was optimistic about the new turn of events. After 1947, Do Neva was in the hands of a young missionary who was receptive to his advice and who shared many of his ideas on native independence.[5] Leenhardt had the satisfaction of seeing a number of young reformers he had trained in ethnology become active in the life of the Grande Terre. He had wanted scientific research to be a liberalizing force in the local cultural scene. He therefore took considerable interest in plans for a government research center in Noumea, the Institut Française d'Océanie (I.F.O.). He wanted to be sure that the new institution began in the right spirit—and at the start it was not at all obvious that this would be the case. In 1948 the seventy-year-old veteran returned to New Caledonia as first director of the I.F.O.

Leenhardt walked into the middle of a nasty political squabble. The American military had constructed its headquarters in an idyllic location on the outskirts of Noumea. What was to become of this installation and the considerable quantities of equipment left behind by the departing fleet? There were two competing proposals. One, propounded by an influential administrator in the all-powerful commercial society, "Le Nickel," envisaged the construction of elaborate tourist facilities, casino, and the like. The other urged that the land be given to the French Government for the establishment of a research institute. After much maneuvering, the supporters of the latter proposal won the day, thanks largely to the efforts of René Catala, an enterprising amateur naturalist who had good connections with the American Navy. Those who favored the hotel idea had not given up, however. They still hoped to obtain, through political machinations, at least part of the land. Catala, for his part, felt that he deserved the directorship of the institute. The I.F.O. was potentially a luxurious establishment for the genteel support of scientific amateurs. The idea of a modern research body controlled and staffed from Paris did not appeal.[6]

Thus in early 1947, when Leenhardt arrived to take charge of the I.F.O., his presence in Noumea threatened a variety of interests. Catala and his associates on the spot—some of whom enjoyed rather unsavory reputations—feared that Leenhardt would consolidate control of the institute by the Paris Overseas Research Office (O.R.S.T.O.M.). "Le Nickel" and elements on the Conseil Général suspected the ex-missionary, knowing that he would not bend to their continuing pressure for a share in the American bounty. It was also generally believed, in the older colonial milieux, that Leenhardt was a dangerous character, "pro-native," and likely to cause trouble among a native population more than ever inclined to demand its rights. Swayed by local pressures, the governor wrote to the head of overseas research in Paris, suggesting that Leenhardt would be a risky choice as director. But the ethnologist's scholarly reputation was secure. The governor was overridden and Leenhardt departed for Noumea.[7]

Earlier, Leenhardt had written to the authorities, in support of the I.F.O.: "Beyond the scientific interest it presents, this Institute is the first creation in the French Pacific which can show the large French population of these islands that colonialism is something other than a money-grubbing enterprise for the benefit of metropolitans, and that its dignity resides in its extension of culture."[8] In his letter, Leenhardt warned of the power of big mining and commercial companies, which "exploit the country without leaving her any other benefit than that of making her people into a proletariat." Colonial governors, he added, have a bad habit of assuming that these powerful companies represent the real interests of New Caledonia.

In his private letters of the period, Leenhardt did not mince words concerning colonial realities. But upon his arrival in Noumea, he was publicly the soul of restraint. He tried to calm the governor's anxieties about his presence; he paid social calls on hostile members of the Conseil Général; he assured everyone that the I.F.O. researchers would stay out of politics. Meanwhile, a campaign of personal slander was being mounted against "le Pasteur"—who before long was writing to friends in Paris: "I've become a communist, an agitator of natives, dangerous, undesirable, etc." Once more the old hostilities surfaced. The Leenhardts awoke one morning to find a swastika painted on the wall of their bungalow. The campaign was extended to Paris; he was denounced to the Colonial Office. Official inquiries were set in motion. Leenhardt wrote to his scientific friends in Paris who had political connections.[9]

In the end he was vindicated. Governor Parisot cabled that Leenhardt was indeed the victim of malicious slander and that "the chief complaint against him—and the only one explicitly advanced—is that of having been too great an *indigènophile* when a missionary here over twenty years ago." Parisot continued: ". . . it was essential, without further delay, that the I.F.O. be presided over by a director who was competent, energetic, and above all, independent. These qualities were wholly lacking in those previously on the spot."[10] Those in prior control of the institute were, according to a reliable witness, "un trio très tropicale." Their activities comprised "luxurious living, grand-style diplomatic relations with local financial and political authorities, preliminary oceanographic research as fantastic as it was spectacular. . . ." There was also a shady side: extensive stores of equipment and supplies left by the Americans were being disposed of privately. Calm tropical nights at the institute were punctuated with revolver shots, theatrical pursuits of imaginary robbers, and so on.[11]

Leenhardt walked into a mess, the kind of colonial intrigue he knew all too well, with all the usual suspicions, rumors, recriminations, and indirect political maneuvers. He had brought along a team of researchers from Paris, and his young colleagues immediately urged him to "clean house." But the veteran of colonial politics preferred slower, safer methods of diplomacy and indirection. His enemies commanded considerable influence, which could be harmful to the I.F.O. in its future work. From his long experience he knew how to prevail in a conflict while seeming to be uninvolved. In the face of youthful impatience, "he listened, pleaded calmly, and almost always ended with his deep laugh, that laugh which was for him a way of temporizing. . . ." Leenhardt waited for the slander campaign to discredit itself. The image he presented to his colleagues was one of serenity, calm, and complete devotion to the scientific work at hand. But he felt the strain. His wife wrote in some distress to Raymond Leenhardt in Paris, urging his to do what he could in the ministries. It was essential that they get down to work without the distraction of always having to defend themselves. She added: "Papa may leave his health here."[12]

As the tension gradually diminished, Leenhardt was able to concentrate on his primary goals: organizing the institute's various branches and renewing his personal contact with the land and its people. He presided over a staff of dedicated young social and natural scientists, and he enthusiastically supported their research. Leenhardt was the sort of person who was capable of showing interest in just about anything. And he knew how to pose his criticisms in the form of simple questions. He was, by all accounts, a skillful questioner. His urge was to participate. (Indeed, more self-conscious and reserved individuals could feel invaded by the pastor's overflowing enthusiasm.) Leenhardt's perpetual questions could seem casual, even naive; later, perhaps, their method became apparent.[13] He is remembered by students from this period as a never-quite-venerable figure: white-bearded, energetic, handsome, with active blue-grey eyes. The words *bonhomie* and *génial* recur in their descriptions.

Leenhardt was basically a man at peace with himself and capable of forgiving. And if there was much to forgive in New Caledonia, especially in the capital, there was much to love in the interior of the island. The seventy-year-old director made frequent trips into the highlands to familiar locales. Many of his beloved *natas* and pastors were gone—Boesoou Erijisi, Joané Nigoth—but some old-timers like Eleisha Nebaye and Apou Hmae were still active and eager to greet their "Missi." And there were children and grandchildren whose families he knew intimately, whose births he had witnessed; some were homonyms of his own offspring, Raymond, Renée, Stella. *En brousse*, for him, meant *en famille*. And yet the period of his active evangelism was distant, and personal ties were becoming attenuated. Perhaps Leenhardt felt a little like a *bao*—in traditional usage, an old man on the way to becoming an ancestor, about to return to the land. The New Caledonian landscape still vibrated with the traces of an intelligible mythic life.[14]

The missionary-ethnologist was now more than ever a spokesman for tradition. When he conversed with young Melanesians on religious matters, he turned their attention to "the ways of their grandfathers." He still described the "Kingdom of God" in terms of the *maciri* or traditional "peaceful abode." One of those who listened reported surprise when, expecting to be told about a Christian heaven, he found instead that "Our Patriarch . . . turned us back on our tracks, back toward the religion of our *Canaque* ancestors. I must confess that I had some difficulty getting in tune with my very old and dear missionary."[15] The culture was evolving rapidly. Much of the rich religious language preserved in Leenhardt's New Testament and in his Houailou dictionary was incomprehensible to the new generation.

Ethnography would give new value to the past. The I.F.O. would be more than a center for the collection of information by European science. Leenhardt outlined his plan in an address to the Académie des Sciences Coloniales on the occasion of his election shortly after his return from the Pacific.[16] The I.F.O., he says, will stimulate an increase in knowledge of the land; and this knowledge will pass among the various Caledonian races, binding them together. The institute's young researchers are a surprise to the colonist. They spur him to reveal what he knows of the region. And the Melanesian, overjoyed at finding himself consulted, revives his knowledge of his habitat. "Culture," says Leenhardt in a characteristic phrase, "creates a circulation of life. . . ." His eloquence owes much to the generative imagery of totemic myth:

> Culture is that ensemble of activities which loosen the earth and sow it, make it flower and give grain. It is a collective activity of long duration. It creates in the land an abundance of sap and a circulation of life. Culture, for man, is that body of social riches that help him in situating himself, finding his own reasons for action, opening out, bearing fruit. In humans it creates an affluence of pith and vigor, a circulation of thought. It is the foundation of humanity.
>
> The glory of a country cannot reside in her economic wealth. Her supreme glory is always her culture.[17]

Caledonians, Leenhardt suggested, both white and black, needed this kind of vibrant local culture. If the I.F.O. could make people more aware of shared attachments, it could enrich their experience in a host of small but essential ways. The school teachers, for example, would begin to relate their lessons more directly to their immediate surroundings, bringing their students to know the secrets of their region and to love their island for its true virtues.

⋗⋖

Leenhardt's utopia had always been small in scale, "Melanesian" in its commitment to localism. Though he sometimes extended his vision of cultural circulation to include international cooperation and the Union Française, he placed his deepest faith in small producers, living in harmony close to the land. In New Caledonia, unfortunately, his idealistic program has not been borne out. Leenhardt seems to have

underestimated the stubborn racism separating small *colons* from Melanesians. And during the 1950s, those forces of large commerce and
industry that he warned against came to play an ever greater part in
the island's destiny. An unprecedented boom in nickel mining would
bring thousands of new foreigners to the Grande Terre, people whose
aim was to extract resources and make money, rather than to live in
healthy equilibrium with land and neighbors. If Leenhardt's utopia
seems naive, it ought perhaps to be remembered that, in New Caledonia around 1950, little was to be gained by cynicism or by political
radicalism. Here, unlike other less colonized nations of the Union
Française, there was no immediate prospect of national independence.
Leenhardt was not unaware of colonial realities. But he chose benevolence—to be optimistic about human nature. Jean Guiart, one of the
first contingent at the I.F.O., recalls moments of disillusionment. The
ex-missionary and his student are walking along the Anse Vata beach
at sunset. "What have we really brought to these people?" Leenhardt
asks, shaking his head sadly.[18]

Worth it or not, the colonial enterprise was a "given" for Leenhardt;
his role was to bring out its most positive aspects. It is interesting to
compare his public attitudes with those of his early student, Michel
Leiris. Leiris may have been the first European ethnologist to identify
colonialism as a passing episode, thus marking it off as a specific
context of anthropological research. In 1950, he spoke out systematically on the dilemmas faced by human sciences practicing in colonial
milieux.[19] But Leenhardt—all too familiar with the dilemmas analyzed
by Leiris—never isolated "colonialism" as the source of the obstacles
confronting his dreams. He continued, for example, to write praises of
the civilizing value of French presence in the Pacific and to advocate
the "rayonnement de la culture française." A year before he died, the
centennial of French sovereignty in New Caledonia was celebrated.
Leenhardt was on the organizing committee. He would never have
considered not participating in such a celebration. But he would use
the occasion to promote his own view of colonial evolution, finding
ways to remind the celebrants of the terrible errors of colonial history.[20] For him these were always errors, diversions from the true
and noble goal of colonization, which was the free extension of culture, the establishment of reciprocities leading to progress, democracy, citizenship, and Christianization. He had already expressed his
admiration for the American experience in Hawaii. In the 1940s he
liked to say that soon there would be qualified Melanesian doctors in
the Union Française—a prophecy greeted by white Caledonians with
amused disbelief.[21]

In the early 1950s, Leenhardt did not openly denounce colonialism. As liberal critic, he was an integral part of its evolving ideology. In 1950 a more radical form of criticism could be initiated only by outsiders. It will be recalled that Leiris was linked with radical Third World intellectuals; he was an early sponsor of the *négritude* movement and was a close friend of Aimé Césaire. But it would be anachronistic to make too sharp a distinction here between "liberal" and "radical," "colonial" and "anticolonial." During the last years of Leenhardt's life, it was difficult for anyone to step back from a changing and ambiguous historical moment. The "colonial era" came to an end—in theory at least, for it has still not disappeared in fact—with unexpected rapidity. No one could have predicted that within a decade France would give political independence to nearly all of her colonies.

Leiris's classic *prise de position*, "L'Ethnographe devant le Colonialisme," published in *Les Temps Modernes* (1950), analyzes the colonial context in terms of capitalism and political oppression, denouncing recent French activities in Vietnam and Madagascar. The stance is radical. However, when Leiris deals with specific positions to be taken by ethnologists working in colonized countries, he is often very Leenhardtian in his emphases. For example, Leiris urges ethnographers to act as committed advocates for subject groups, defending their aspirations against colonial interests. He distinguishes clearly between "safeguarding" small cultures and "preserving" them—as objects of study and esthetic appreciation. He criticizes the tendency of ethnologists to focus on the "pure" savage, as opposed to the "contaminated" *évolué*. He argues with great force that the real essence of culture is change and adaptation ("living culture" as opposed to "folklore"). Leiris urges that all opportunities for education at all levels be open to those kept dependent and inferior. He adds, however, that this education must be offered, not imposed; and it must be conducted as much as possible within a localized historical and natural context. It should strive to be bilingual and bicultural. Leiris cites Leopold Senghor. He could as well have referred to Leenhardt.[22]

The first director of the Institut Français d'Océanie summed up his own position on colonialism two years after Leiris. The occasion was the publication of a revised edition of *Gens de la Grande Terre*, to which he added a new preface and concluding chapter. The 1937 version had left the New Caledonians either "opening themselves to the present" or remaining in the constricting grip of "totemic and ancestral determinisms." In the 1952 edition, Leenhardt brings the island's whites into the picture, sketching an overview of the colonial encounter. He outlines historically the Melanesian "effort" toward acculturation and citizenship, which has shown them worthy of the vote extended to them in 1951. He warns against current political machinations to blunt the power of the new electorate. He shows also the inadequacies of official educational efforts in New Caledonia. But if the Melanesian acculturative effort is to bear fruit, it will require, says Leenhardt, a commensurate effort on the part of whites, an "inverse acculturation."[23]

European colonization has been dominated by l'esprit positif—an abstract, detached mode of thought that judges others by its own standards only. Leenhardt opposes to this a mode of apprehension taught by "ethnology" and characterized by "simplicity of observation and a certain lightness of touch"—l'esprit concret. This mode of knowledge accepts the Other in its own terms and sees it concretely as a complex of virtualities, a characteristic past, present, and future. If colonial Europeans are able to recover this concrete mind, they will be able to see themselves simply as co-occupants of a land with others whose skills and aspirations they need to preserve and respect. L'esprit positif, says Leenhardt, has been the creation of nineteenth-century Europe; the twentieth century must rediscover l'esprit concret.[24]

Acculturation should proceed intelligently in two directions. Leenhardt praises the Melanesians of New Caledonia for not having rushed headlong into the world of the whites, for having opened their culture to new influences without "falling into servile imitation." Europeans have much to learn from their culture, which has preserved its basic elements of "reserve, community, and solidity."

> For if [Melanesian culture] has preserved so much of its past in its very acts of progress, this is because it holds in itself certain elements which, very ancient, are essential to mankind. To grasp these elements is to recover, perhaps, those categories, indeed values, which we have allowed to diminish or disappear in ourselves. . . . Through them, we rediscover elements of the affective life, the esthetic life, and the mythic life, which we had forgotten, and which were lacking in the balance of our thought.[25]

Thus the evils of colonialism were ultimately rooted in the West's mental-spiritual imbalance. To redress the situation, Europeans would have to recover lost habits of communion—with others, with the land, and with divinity.

Leenhardt's hopes for change in New Caledonia have, at best, been only partially fulfilled. Countervening forces of economic domination and cultural incompatibility have prevailed. Let us accept that the do kamo ideal is a utopia—without, however, dismissing it. Like any guid-

ing ideal emerging from real dilemmas, a utopia is a source of orientation and knowledge. Individuals, at least, may gain strength from its
proposals; the project of "inverse acculturation" still confronts Western sensibilities. To understand better how Leenhardt conceived this
project, we must now pursue his late analyses of myth.

CHAPTER XIII

Participation and Myth

In attempting to isolate some of Leenhardt's characteristic ways of conceiving myth, seen now as a repertoire of styles available anywhere to human emotional knowledge, one cannot draw on a sharply etched theory. The ideas formulated in this chapter are scattered through his late writings, fragments addressed to particular occasions. One such occasion—crucial in determining the overall shape of Leenhardt's theory—was his loyal critique of Lévy-Bruhl.

We have already encountered this relationship. It continued even after the older man's death in 1939, for Lévy-Bruhl had left something of himself to Leenhardt:

> Thin, cheap notebooks, in black oilcloth, thirty small pages of crosshatched, poor quality paper. The philosopher habitually kept one in his pocket, and when walking, if an idea in the line of his current thinking occurred to him, he would sit and write. The surviving notebooks cover the final months of his life. Their pages are filled with fine handwriting, regular, and without a correction. The conclusion is always at the foot of the page, as if the space of the wording had been measured out beforehand. The place and date appear below, so that we can follow Lévy-Bruhl on his outings in the Bois de Boulogne, at Bagatelle, along the coasts of Normandy or Brittany. Inside the cover, his name and address and . . . a table of contents. For he re-read his notes, discussed them with himself; the true title of their collection should perhaps be: The Soliloquies of Lévy-Bruhl.[1]

Leenhardt gives us the essence of the man. We see the philosophical *promeneur solitaire*, the steady pen, a mind proceeding with scrupulous care in its daily self-interrogation. But there is also a hint of ambivalence in the picture—a certain distance taken. For the philosopher's style is domesticated, like the parks and vacation spots in which it takes shape—almost too orderly.

Leenhardt termed these notebooks, Lévy-Bruhl's *Carnets*, "soliloquies." They contained primarily a rigorous questioning of their author's previous ideas on primitive mentality. But as the notebooks' editor well knew—and was too modest to underline—they contained an important element of dialog. The one proper name regularly cited in these pages is Leenhardt's. The central themes of the *Carnets* had previously been discussed by the two men. It must have been gratifying for Leenhardt to read these final manuscripts, for they showed his friend moving carefully in a direction earlier proposed by the ethnographer. There was a developing area of agreement. But it was not complete. Thus Leenhardt wrote something more than a preface to the *Carnets*; he wrote a reply.

It is impossible here to enter into the details of Lévy-Bruhl's "soliloquy"—the long development of his thinking, beginning at the turn of the century with *La morale et la science des moeurs*, the work that turned his attention to the differential analysis of "mentalities." This exemplary intellectual experiment has, in any event, been treated recently with sympathy and sophistication.[2] In the context of Leenhardt's biography, it is primarily the "conversation" taking place in the *Carnets* that commands attention. The two men's theories were closely related. If either of the two was in "advance" of the other it was Leenhardt; Lévy-Bruhl acknowledges his influence handsomely in the *Carnets*. But Leenhardt's thought was less systematic, and in the end there can be no simple determination of who was influencing whom.[3] The two methods of research were widely divergent. At the very time the philosopher was carefully thinking about primitive mentality on his walks in the *Bois de Boulogne*, his colleague was in the New Caledonian highlands, engaged in *"paroles"* with Pwagach.

For the younger man, such a relationship of mutual influence could not exist without ambivalences. In 1953, the year before his own death, Leenhardt jotted down some of his personal feelings for the man he had met on the Normandy beach in 1921: "I found a great elder, the best of friends, most deferential of teachers. I felt small in his presence, knowing only my theology and my *Canaques*. But he knew how to maintain one's confidence with simple questions corresponding to deep preoccupations. Bit by bit I became more bold, asking two things of him to which he would not agree." Leenhardt's first objection concerned the "affective category of the supernatural." Lévy-Bruhl had suggested that primitive man possessed a category of feeling specifically manifested in relations with the supernatural. Leenhardt, however, had proposed in his analysis of *mythe vécu* that the archaic supernatural was merely the mythic aspect of ordinary nature. Thus, a Melanesian's relations with the supernatural (gods, totems, spirits) need not be fundamentally different from his relations with nature (objects, landscape, animals). These relations, when not instrumental, were participative. Lévy-Bruhl had kept this general "fluidity" of participatory thought analytically separate from the special "category" of feelings appropriate to the "supernatural." Leenhardt questioned the separation and suggested to his friend—after reading *Primitives and the Supernatural* (1932)—that "the affective category was merely a logical interpretation by which another name is given to participation."[4]

Leenhardt's second objection followed the publication of Lévy-Bruhl's *Mythologie primitive* in 1935. Lévy-Bruhl had for some time ceased using the term "prelogical" to characterize primitive mentality. He adopted "mystical," a word he defined as "belief in forces, influences, actions, which are imperceptible to the senses but nevertheless real." Leenhardt found this formula overly negative and unsuitable for characterizing the invisible but concretely experienced and structured socio-mythic relations he knew from Melanesia. Like Ernst Cassirer, Leenhardt thought that Lévy-Bruhl's *mystique* should be replaced by *mythique*. But myth for Lévy-Bruhl figured only as a story or else as a fund of examples for demonstrating the "fluidity" of the mystical mentality.[5]

Leenhardt advanced his two objections in the years preceding his return to New Caledonia in 1938. The philosopher was not convinced. Leenhardt recalled that the only response was a calm, thin smile. However, Lévy-Bruhl pondered his friend's points. When the fieldworker returned from the Pacific, the octogenarian had already passed away. In the ensuing years, Leenhardt wrote admiringly of Lévy-Bruhl, his criticisms muted or oblique. It was only in the last year of his own life that he privately recorded the disillusionment he had earlier felt as he became aware of the great scholar's limitations. These hesitations are important, for in certain respects Leenhardt's thinking was held back by Lévy-Bruhl's formidable influence. It has already been suggested that Lévy-Bruhl replaced Franz Leenhardt as patron and judge of the younger man's intellectual development. Overawed at first, Leenhardt was inevitably disappointed. "For me [he wrote in 1953] the decisive moment was when his *Mythologie primitive* appeared; this was when I understood that my *Canaque* culture could not go all the way with the high culture of the philosopher, whose language was so clear and classically shaped."[6]

Leenhardt had urged upon his friend that archaic myths were not, fundamentally, stories but rather ways of circumscribing immediate emotional experiences that discursive language could not express. He then suggested his own interpretation of a folktale Lévy-Bruhl had included in his volume. When he had finished, "The philosopher leaned back and said softly: 'I'd never have thought that.' Seated before him, I was surprised and saddened. How could a philosopher of this stature, of this value, not imagine the meaning of these simple tales. . . . I asked myself whether I might have been wrong to provoke such a reply. I was pained by it, and I've never recounted this before today, because my admiration and affection for this teacher never allowed me to imagine that a detail might escape him."[7] Why did Leenhardt finally need to unburden himself of such a story? That Lévy-Bruhl was something more than just another university colleague is certain. He represented, perhaps, an ambivalent paternal heritage that had become identified with positive science, rationalist philosophy, logic, and those "clear and distinct ideas" against which Leenhardt would urge the expressivities of myth, accesses to *la pensée obscure et confuse*.

Let us return to the theoretical issues involved in Leenhardt's disagreement with Lévy-Bruhl. The folktale in question—quoted in *La Mythologie primitive*—had been published in 1917 by Gunnar Landtman in a remarkable collection of Kiwi-Papuan folklore. It concerns, in bare outline, a young man who is unloved because his body is covered with ulcerated sores. A girl takes pity on him and gives him bits of food, for she sees past his skin into his eyes, which are those of a healthy boy. With her help, the youth makes a bow and arrow. Then secretly he kills a heron, puts on the feathers of the bird, and soars in the air. He keeps his new condition secret, continuing to masquerade as a diseased pariah. But the girl still suspects a healthy person beneath the sores. Wanting him for her own, she hides at his house, burns his ulcerated skin when he removes it for that of the bird, and when the boy returns she confronts him in his own body, taking the bird skin from his hand and placing it under her grass skirt. The youth is confounded: "She find me out now."[8]

Lévy-Bruhl quotes this portion of the story as an example of mental "fluidity."[9] The boy/bird is what he calls a "duality-unity." The story —which Lévy-Bruhl had classified as a folktale, perhaps because it was more a slice of life than a heroic precedent or charter—is translated by Leenhardt into an experience of *mythe vécu*. From his preface to the *Carnets*:

[What Lévy-Bruhl has classified as stories] are still, in the eyes of primitives, living myths, revealers of reality. Like the New Guinean whose skin is covered with ulcers. . . . This ensemble outlines moments through which a man passes who is unhappy, thus ulcerated, or full of hope and growing wings,

victorious at last and experiencing fluttering hours of passionate excitement. Primitive men do not have abstract terms
relating the psychology of love. Stories like this one circumscribe the event, and by way of its details the Papuans obtain
knowledge of its nature.[10]

Lévy-Bruhl had found only mental fluidity in his example. But Leenhardt asks, in another version of the analysis, "can we not see also, in
this fluidity so apparent to our eyes, the rapid projection of events
which take place beyond our vision? Each event corresponds to a time
lived by the hero, where he feels himself to exist."[11]

Mythic consciousness, according to Leenhardt, grasps complex emotional states through juxtaposed images. Leenhardt has, in effect, "de-
narrated" the story. (In Lévy-Bruhl's text it is much longer, and in
Landtman's, longer still.) He has translated it into an emotional "event"
that is a cluster of participations. The ambivalences and ecstasies of
passionate love are a bundle of feelings experienced as mythic times.
Such ensembles form a language of emotions. "When, a victim of
emotional confusion, the New Guinean has transported himself into
this domain of passionate powers, his own being, by way of a figure or
an other, is revealed to him. Similar moments, translated into discursive language, appear as confusion; but revealed through juxtaposed
images, they order themselves in an epic fabric where myth is the
warp and reality the weft."[12]

Leenhardt had written in the same article, which is frequently referred to in the Carnets, "the primitive does not classify, he juxtaposes. . . ."[13] Lévy-Bruhl was struck by this formula:

> It is to this that my present reflections once again lead me.
> Since this thinking does not classify, there are no—or very
> few—inclusions and exclusions, and as a consequence the
> incompatibilities and contradictions which are intolerable to
> us do not exist for them. One should thus not say that they
> tolerate them. They have neither to tolerate nor reject them:
> they do not exist for them. Leenhardt shows very well how
> from this point of view the fluidity of the mythical is
> explained.

In thinking through Leenhardt's article, Lévy-Bruhl sees again the
need to transcend negative definitions. Thus, he adds, we must not
speak of "mystical" thought as a state of confusion. "Confusion implies distinction; clear distinction, again, implies concept. Accordingly
let us not say confusion, but let us recognize participation here."[14]

Participation is the positive, affective experience that the philosopher now sets about to make intelligible, or rather—since he explicitly rejects any denaturing through conceptual rendering—it is the experience that he attempts to circumscribe more adequately.

Leenhardt's material shows Lévy-Bruhl "the essential difference between concept and participation." Participation is a personal experience, occurring *hic et nunc*, in its own space and time. "Whence it follows, as again says Leenhardt, that in the mythical world there are no contradictions, but only contrasts; events either come to terms with each other or disagree more or less strongly with each other; in so far as they are felt in their own space and time they clearly cannot exclude one another." Participation is nonconceptual in the sense that "concepts are not events."[15]

Lévy-Bruhl's essential problem is to give an account of participation as an initial synthetic experience. To do so, he has to find a language that can talk about "duality-unities" without seeing them as fusions of previously distinguished entities. He returns repeatedly to this problem. How is it possible, he asks, to grasp a relation without assuming its constituent parts? Leenhardt's analysis of dual-substantives and parities in New Caledonian socio-mythic life would attempt to systematize this problematic experience. The centerless personage described in Chapter 11 rendered for Melanesia what Lévy-Bruhl summarized, in considering the Australian Aranda:

> A participation is not only a mysterious and inexplicable fusion of things (*êtres*) that lose and preserve their identity simultaneously. Participation enters into the very constitution of these things. Without participation, they would not be *given* in experience: they would not exist. This will become clearer through some examples the full meaning of which is illuminated by a remark of Leenhardt quoted above: the primitive mentality does not know what an individuality subsisting on its own is: individuals, human or others, only exist in so far as they participate in their group and with their ancestors. Participation is thus *immanent* in the individual. For it is to it that it owes being what it is. It is a *condition of its existence*, perhaps the most important, the most essential. One might say: for this mentality, to exist is to participate in a mystical force, essence, and reality.[16]

Lévy-Bruhl does not specify whether "this mentality" is limited to primitives or to some extent constitutes all "direct apprehension," "feeling," "experience-belief." Leenhardt is less cautious. According to the ethnographer, the "primitive" analyzed by Lévy-Bruhl probably exists nowhere in pure form. But the philosopher has nonetheless isolated a mental type "in such a way that whites and blacks, archaic and civilized people, have always recognized there something of their own mind. This victorious effort [Leenhardt continues] has permitted him to overflow the logic he employed with such discipline, to show that there are functions active in the mind which logic itself cannot contain."[17]

Lévy-Bruhl recognized the necessity of doing something beyond thinking rationally about feelings, but he could not, finally, do more than circle around the unreasonable fact of participation. He clung to his notion of a "mystical" mentality, a formulation that remained largely a negative definition. ("Mystical," as Leenhardt pointed out, had a tendency to serve as a vague catch-all, embracing whatever experiences could not be reduced to clear and distinct ideas.)[18] The philosopher chose not to go all the way with his friend in calling participatory experience "mythical"—a term of a more positive, but ultimately religious, content. Moreover, Lévy-Bruhl was not, in any ordinary sense, a believer. A true intellectual, he was not predisposed to "live" the experience of the Other. This limitation was what disappointed Leenhardt when he perceived the philosopher's disinclination to put himself in the skin of the boy-with-sores-who-was-a-bird. And yet Leenhardt knew that for Lévy-Bruhl philosophy was no mere intellectual exercise. One senses even today a submerged passion in the cool but unrelenting prose of the *Carnets*—the workings of a spirit almost obsessively thinking and rethinking the logical scandal of participation. Occasionally a word or phrase gives us a glimpse of the personal need underlying the writing. It was a need to gain access to an experience of reality for which, as he recorded two weeks before his death, "our philosophical and psychological terminology is cruelly inadequate."[19]

≷

Leenhardt, too, lacked an adequate vocabulary for rendering in positive terms the various experiences of participation. But he plunged ahead and like Lévy-Bruhl made use of ethnological material to demonstrate certain characteristic forms through which the Cartesian *pensée obscure et confuse* expressed itself. Leenhardt became aware of "lived myth" in the small-scale valleys of New Caledonia. But he wrote relatively little concerning just how this mode of knowledge might be experienced in the landscapes and cities of modern Europe. Myth's concrete inscription in the environment was basic to Leenhardt's notion of experiential authenticity. Thus, he rarely involved himself in the Jungian project of cataloging trans-cultural mythic archetypes. When he did attempt something of this order, as in his tentative discussions of stories like "Beauty and the Beast" and "Prometheus," he was not as convincing as when he wrote of localized mythic presences or events.[20]

In his own life, as in the Romantic tradition generally, Leenhardt primarily sought feelings of mythic immanence in natural settings. He wrote of the Grande Terre, the land that "spoke" to him most directly: "Nature is harmonious and full of grace, man is poised (*posé*). Nothing moves, and all vibrates. If you don't perceive the vibration, everything is extinguished. As soon as you grasp it, all is life and form."[21] Or, traveling on the waterways of Equatorial Africa, he recorded in a letter:

> The rain comes unexpectedly in the midst of our navigation, and though we're soaked, it's an improvement on the leaden sun. In our canoe, we are almost level with the water, and the drops of rain rebound from the liquid surface. We normally view this landscape of rain on waves by looking over it, from above; but at water-level the gaze moves horizontally, and the ricochets from drops striking the river seem larger, firmer. You could say, a dance, on a mirror. And this makes the rain into something living and beautiful, as the canoe slides beneath the shower.[22]

This mode of mythic perception is "down close" to the world, an idea Leenhardt would express in the somewhat misleading formula of "two-dimensionality"—misleading because it could too easily suggest a lack rather than a positive mode of apprehension. Leenhardt's participation in the "event" of the downpour on the Ogoowé river, with his recognition of a proximate, gesturing *vivant*, is almost myth. (It lacks, perhaps, a permanent, familiar landscape and a relational name for "rain.") However fragmentary, mythic experiences have the essential characteristic of entering the time of another, which can be either a clearly named god or person, or a less definite totem or natural event such as the rain shower. Mythic experiences do not occur when the perceiver locates his or her consciousness "outside" the event, merely representing it. Nor can it be seized from above, from the mapmaker's viewpoint so fundamental to modern experiences of space.

But how, precisely, are the proximities and rhythms of participation to be grasped? What are its modes of expression? Going against the grain of much recent psychological and ethnological thinking, Leenhardt does not believe that the flow of participatory emotions must be structured in the same way as verbal language in order to be communicated. He avoids the phrase *"langage mythique,"* speaking instead of *formes mythiques*—an informal, "given" landscape of expressions, events, juxtaposed emotional states and clusters of images. Leenhardt does not argue systematically against the use of linguistic analogies in the comprehension of myth and culture. But he clearly suggests their insufficiency in the course of his fragmentary analyses of two basic mythic modes of affective expression, which he calls *"esthetique"* (esthetics) and *"parole"* (the word). These were Leenhardt's two chief accesses to *la pensée obscure et confuse.* They were his solutions to the problem posed by Lévy-Bruhl: how to circumscribe the "experience-belief" of participation in terms that were not those of discursive reason.

Leenhardt never brought together his thinking on esthetics, as he did his ideas on myth.[23] Yet the topic preoccupied him in the final years of his life. *Esthétique,* as he defined it, was not the study of beauty as usually conceived. It was, rather, to be taken "in its original sense, which includes all sensations and feelings arising from contact with the life of forms." Form, here, is defined "in its broadest sense," presumably to mean not exclusively visual forms but also acoustic and rhythmic shapes.[24] Esthetic perceptions were the earliest styles of human thought still extremely close to nature and prior to myth.[25] But as a mode of immediate, affective perception, esthetics coexisted with myth and later with rationality and discursive language. At the beginning, however, Leenhardt imagined that "ideas" were composed of natural forms juxtaposed in concrete works of art. These ensembles were attempts to comprehend and express the felt rhythms and relationships of cosmomorphic life. Through esthetic perception, Leenhardt addressed himself to the problem that had preoccupied Lévy-Bruhl in his thinking about participation and "duality-unity." How could one conceive of a felt whole or relationship as something preceding its empirical parts, and indeed, as the very condition of their separate existence? For nature is composed not of discrete objects but of processes, events, relationships.

In his analysis of Melanesian languages, Leenhardt had found them to be peculiarly apt at expressing relational ensembles. We can see this in his exegesis of *xa,* a Houailou term meaning "a few," "some," or "ensemble." *Xa,* in the expression *xara,* is "difficult for the European," because, Leenhardt explains, it evokes, prior to number, the image of a group.

boe xara osari xie, woman ensemble child she,
> a woman with her child.

kuru xara pei, lying ensemble his illness.

ne tani xara e, he waits ensemble it (his herb,
> the magician waiting, holding
> his magical herb).

Xa implies that the *Canaque* circumscribes his vision and grasps it as an ensemble or group. He acts a little like the artist who fixes his vision by mentally describing a circle around the characteristic people or objects he has perceived. Our analytical mind abandons the group or ensemble; it sees connected unities, a woman with her child, a man lying with his disease, a magician with his herb; *xara,* whose sense, as ensemble or group, is so full, turns into the preposition "with." But "with" is not a translation of *xara,* nor is it a transposition; it is a distant, schematic, interpretation of a concrete reality, an ensemble. The distance separating these two expressions marks the difference of the *Canaque's* thought from our own concerning the plural: we see a quantity, or unities in relation with each other; he sees an image.[26]

In old Caledonian usages, Leenhardt discerned an archaic style of thought in which numeration played no part whatsoever. Plurality was grasped through the mediation of concrete ensembles.

The ethnographer could penetrate to the most archaic level of perception by carefully determining the earliest forms of language. But more directly, he could investigate the forms of esthetics, a permanent mode of human knowledge and an expression of the affective imagination. Leenhardt took as an example a New Guinean prow-board—an ancestor portrayed as a crocodile's head with human features and wings. This was a participatory grouping of man/reptile/bird, a formation, Leenhardt says, that makes perfect sense esthetically but becomes a logical problem when translated into discursive language. Moreover, if a Melanesian wanted to express or "explain" this ensemble verbally, he would tell a story. But in Leenhardt's schema any inclination towards the narration and textualization of myths was considered a relatively late development. *Mythe vécu* in its early stages dealt primarily with esthetic forms. Thus, as we have seen, Leenhardt had translated Landtman's Papuan folktale into an event or synchronous experience. He transformed the narrative into, as it were, a sculpture, or ensemble of concretely juxtaposed forms—ulcerated skin/normal boy/bird. The contrast between Leenhardt's "reading" of the tale and Lévy-Bruhl's is instructive. Leenhardt grasped it immediately as the single expression of a felt complex. His friend began with separate elements joined in a narrative. Then he addressed himself to the problem of how they could be logically joined, how different "bodies" could be thought to be equivalent or to flow into one another. From the standpoint of Leenhardt's style of "thinking" in juxtaposed images, Lévy-Bruhl's problem did not exist.[27]

Esthetic perception of this sort, and "art" generally, were not set apart in everyday Melanesian life as they tend to be in Modern Europe. Leenhardt's *Les Arts de l'Océanie* aimed to demonstrate this and argue for what he termed "the primacy of esthetics" in lived Oceanian experience. Esthetic form and intention could be found in the smallest details, and these forms were not merely decorations, emblems, or representations of beings or powers from the nonempirical world. They were vibrant presences contributing to a plenitude of states, moods, and comportments, all of which served to bring the person into meaningful emotional relations with socio-mythic others as well as with the processes of the natural world.[28]

Esthetic perception, as Leenhardt portrayed it, was a nascent *logos*, recalling Gaston Bachelard's notion of the "poetic image" situated phenomenologically at the "origin of language," the "onset" of thought.[29] But something additional would be required for the formation of an effective expressivity that could stand not simply as a precursor or embellishment of rationality but as its permanent counterpart. Esthetic modes could generate an immediate grasp of emotional ensembles, but they were not communal. Esthetic perception did not institute dialog between subjects, and thus, by itself, could not attain a fully cultural articulation. If *esthétique* was the general form of mythic perception, *la parole* (the word, speech) was the mode of mythic expression.

>€

Leenhardt's vision of personal authenticity proposed a reunification of intellect and emotion, of concept and act. His conception of *parole* embodied this vision but by means of a cross-cultural detour. In a Melanesian expression, the Houailou *nô* (and its near synonym in Lifou, *ewekë*), the ethnologist glimpsed the concrete possibility of such a reunion. In *Do Kamo* he devoted two chapters to the ramified usages of these terms. Their importance lay not merely in the fact that Caledonians employed them with disconcerting frequency and in a number of—at first sight—contradictory senses. Their ultimate significance lay in the Melanesians' own translation of the terms into French.

18. Esthetics and *mythe vécu*: repairing a net, Houailou 1907. "In this social ensemble the work of art finds its true meaning. Sculpture of the habitat, prowboard of the canoe, earring, diadem, noise-maker or song, are a person's gesture manifesting some myth from which he draws his life" (M.L., *Arts de l'Océanie*, p. 138).

Photo: Leenhardt, from Notes, *plate 12*

They had chosen the term *parole*: the spoken word, speech, tone of voice, word of honor. This translation, in effect, broadened and enriched the French by combining the constitutive, cosmological implications of "Word" (*Verbe*) with the concrete immediacy of personal "speech" (*parole*).[30]

This new *parole* welded together "speech" and "language"—the one personal and tied to immediate events, the other formal and socially constraining. The sense of *parole* recovered by Leenhardt in Melanesia was something akin to older European usages in which an individual "gives his word." In the process, a self manifests itself in thoughts and deeds, simultaneously engaging the general socio-religious traditions, values, and meanings that provide any speech-act with substance and durability. Melanesians are not wrong, Leenhardt argues, to choose *parole* as a translation of *nô* and *ewekë*, for they see what we have forgotten—that speech and language are properly "manifestations of being." In a revealing passage from *Do Kamo*, he summarizes what is at stake—a possible authenticity of being, neither individual nor cultural, given neither to event nor to system. Leenhardt's search, by way of Melanesia, is for a way to *name* this way of being:

> It is sad that in our French tongue no term has emerged to absorb the deep meaning that speech (*la parole*) or the Word (*le Verbe*) possessed originally, a term that could have preserved the expression of a reality no longer rendered by speech, which has deteriorated into chatter, or by the Word, which meanders through grammar and theology.[31]

In this passage Leenhardt delivers his judgment on the condition of Western expression: *la parole* has become artificially dissociated. On the one hand, it has suffered a deliquescence into mere colloquialism, talk. And it is precisely in this domain of "ordinary language" and "language games" that much modern philosophy has conducted its search for the grounds of meaning. Such truth lacks substance for Leenhardt; it dissolves "being" in circumstantiality. On the other hand, the new "grammarians" and "theologians" of the human sciences have concentrated on disengaging transcendent language-like structures from the cultural immediacies of speech, gesture, and act. The resulting structures are ill suited as guides for personal experience. "Being does not recognize itself in what is formal."[32]

Nô and *ewekë* do not distinguish thought from expression and concrete action. An idea is already a *parole*, and saying is doing. Leenhardt stresses that *parole*, in this sense, is not primarily tied to elocution; it is located more concretely in the substance and object of gestures. In

New Caledonian gift exchange, for example, *parole* does not reside primarily in the words spoken, though these are important. It exists in the actual food given or in the body and fibres of the bark cloth used to wrap the offerings. Speech has substance in the act and in its objects. Making and doing are *parole*. In technology, "what" is made is a *parole*. (And one is reminded in this of Valéry's insistence that the essence of poetry resides in concretely executed *acts*.)[33]

Parole is also inseparable from thinking. But "thought" here is conceived as a kind of solidified emotion—*pensée obscure et confuse*, not intellect. This affective knowledge begins in "the vibratory movements of the entrails," according to Leenhardt:

> it is the impulse springing out of emotional shock; it brings forth behavior. Behavior—gesture, action, or spontaneous remarks—reveals thought. But as a movement it is ephemeral. It has no stability until it is held, fixed, formulated, circumscribed, and gathered into the form the *Canaque* designated as *nö*. Here the word is a kind of intermediary (*truchement*) necessary to begin the objectification of affective thought. Thought rises from the intestines like a flood; the idea becomes specific. The idea is the projection of a reality against a background, the image, the representation, the beginning of awareness. And for the *Canaque* all this is *parole*.

The expressive fixing of emotional flux is *parole*. The Melanesian often says *parole* when a Westerner would say "thing." It is whatever manifests the person: "his eloquence, the object he fashions, what he creates, what he possesses in his own right, his work, his word, his goods, his garden, his wife, his psychic property, his sexual organ."[34]

In the Melanesian world, *la parole* is many living *things*. But being and object are not sharply distinguished. Figured in sculpture, a large tongue extends downward in front of the chin. Nothing rude or grotesque, says Leenhardt, merely a calm face, serious look, and—displayed in its full dignity—the divine muscle: *parole*, strong, active, and mobile, manifestation of inner being. *Parole* could also take the shape of the immense conical roof of the *Grande Case*, embodying the unity of the clan, something woven out of many fibers. Women, who carry the totemic life-force from group to group, are *paroles*, as are all manner of exchanged objects. Elders are called "baskets of *parole*," "maintainers of *parole*," for their thought is deemed consistent; it manifests what Westerners call "tradition." The chief is spokesman for the paternal clan. His *parole*, which gathers up the ancestors and habitat, is an eloquence constituting the solidity of socio-mythic relations.[35]

Leenhardt argues strenuously against any translation of sociality and tradition into formal or juridical terms. In Melanesian experience, *parole*, personal expressivity, adheres so closely to any "law" that it is a distortion to disengage a formal structure. If, inevitably, the ethnographer speaks of property, signatures, exchanges, seals (of agreements), contracts, debts, adultery, and so on, he must make a constant effort not to conceive of these phenomena juridically. For a Melanesian, each of these is *parole*, a manifestation of being not properly existing outside a concretely experienced event. Leenhardt does not deny the constituent importance of collective patterns, classifications, reciprocities. But he will not permit such forms to be called "laws." They are thought of merely as *"paroles* that endure." Moreover, important openings are built into the social repertoire of expressivities: "free-word" relationships, for example, or *bwiri* expressions, where "anything goes."[36] Here, Leenhardt's phenomenological perspective counterbalances, though it does not refute, a more common approach to the analysis of cultural life, an approach that centers attention on obligatory social facts. Much of Leenhardt's theoretical writing is, in effect, a critique of the Durkheimian paradigm. But the polemical element in his work is submerged. Leenhardt attempted less to disprove the Ecole Sociologique than simply to provide a positive and different account.

Similarly, Leenhardt's work is a counterweight to those in the structuralist tradition who have chosen to analyze cultural forms as analogous to "language," the system of signs marked off by Saussure. Rather, Leenhardt used the modalities of "speech" as his general model, thus keeping mental competence tied to actual performance. The Melanesian *parole* is expressivity, not structure; it is a "gushing *(jaillissement)* of conceptual force."[37] It is always something more than discourse. It is acts, considered and spontaneous, action itself, psychic comportment. Elocution is but one of its modalities. Discourse is here associated with technological competence and tied to the world available to the senses. Discourse for Leenhardt tends toward conceptualization and formality; it provides the central structure for developing reason. It works in the opposite direction from nature, "whose vitality is in superabundance and waste. . . . Language plays the role of an excellent technical instrument, but to the extent that it does, it no longer participates in *parole*."[38]

Parole is primarily expressive of emotional events. As articulate myth, as an experiential "landscape," it gives a certain solidity and recurring form to the participatory impulsions that surge into expression from the entrails. *Parole* does not classify but rather juxtaposes, occupying an indeterminate, projective field. When reduced to "language," it becomes formal, abstract, incapable of superabundance. Leenhardt saw this narrowing take place in the lives of the young Melanesians who had been sent to government schools, where they were encouraged to think in exclusively rational, nonreligious ways. As an old *Canaque* had told him, in words the missionary liked to quote: "Ever since they've chucked 'em into schools, they don't know anything any more."[39] A threatened *parole*—concrete expressivity of the obscure "thought" of heart and entrails—was what Leenhardt's converts seemed to recover in the "Word made flesh" of First John. And the vernacular "Word," *nô*, that they brought to the Scriptures returned to *Verbe* its original immediacy.

In principio erat verbum. But Goethe would add: *Am Anfang war die Tat*. Leenhardt mistrusted mere words. *Verba volent*. He believed, finally, in acts and energies—concrete gestures. *Nô* and *ewekë*—thought, speech, act, thing—helped him transcend the gulf between conception, word, and deed. Through his broadened concept of the word, he advocated a return of immediacy and substance to a language that had become formal and emotionally hollow. Personal authenticity could find renewal in mythically expressive *paroles*—events, movements. "For in the Western world today movement is dead. Theology has forgotten it. But in the Bible, movement is everything; there is no manifestation of God without it: a column of fire in the desert, a prophet convulsing the people, the Son descending to the world, His spirit flowing out; the creation is movement; God is love, which moves."[40]

CHAPTER XIV

Plenitude

Let us be wary of conclusions. We feel an almost irresistible temptation to understand a life at its end as adding up to something, as manifesting a direction, a plot structure, or as composed of systematic contradictions, inversions, symmetries. Biography as a genre partakes of that myth of personal identity that Leenhardt did so much to question and open out. However some lives, perhaps most, are best conceived not as wholes but as plenitudes. The latter view allows for the experiential complementarity of differences that in the former would appear as conflicts. We must think of personality as openings into otherness. In a passage from *Do Kamo*, Leenhardt proposes that ". . . the person, in opposition to the individual, is capable of enriching itself through a more or less indefinite assimilation of exterior elements. It takes its life from the elements it absorbs, in a wealth of communion. The person is capable of superabundance."[1]

One is sometimes inclined to comprehend Maurice Leenhardt as a bundle of contradictions, his life a pattern of oscillations: between ethnology and evangelism, science and religion, between Christian monotheism and archaic myth, the orientations of "power" and "life." One might expect to find a man torn by feelings of ambivalence. But there is little evidence that Leenhardt actually did feel divided between the various contexts of which he was made. Perhaps the notion of personal identity follows from the experience of crisis, and not vice versa. We must follow Lévy-Bruhl and soften our concept of contradiction.

Leenhardt "lived" the dilemmas of his age. If the surface of his existence was often troubled by struggle and disappointment, he nonetheless enjoyed real serenity, an extraordinary openness of spirit. His life might well have assumed the shape of a series of alienations: first as "problem" student, then as colonial subversive, later as evangelical renegade and university misfit. He might have learned to value the outsider's oppositional stance; he could easily have become bitter. But he did not. He was composed of others: Boesoou Erijisi and Lucien Lévy-Bruhl, Mauss, the mission "family," Pwagach, his students—

Melanesian converts, ethnographers, missionaries, surrealists, colonial administrators. Leenhardt somehow engaged all on their own terms, giving and receiving loyalty. All of these, along with his most intimate relationships—with wife and father, with his brother Paul, with his dissimilar children, and with the orienting landscapes (the Midi, the Grande Terre)—all were resumed and reconciled not in a "self" but in a "person."

This person, too, was an other—a relation. Communion with a human-divine Christ, immanent and transcendent, made Leenhardt someone who could not be dispersed. But if the structure of his personality was Christian, we should avoid thinking of the encounter with Divinity as a core or center. In moments of adversity Leenhardt did not, characteristically, retreat inwards to Christ. He sought meaning in participation, interlocution, renewed effort—God encountered in external events. To "map" this experience, to narrate it as a linear development or as a structure of oppositions, is to sacrifice plenitude to form. What is essential to a personality is the expressivity or *parole* that overflows, alters, gives newness to the rules.

⤜⤛

Death overtakes Leenhardt in his seventy-sixth year, in the midst of his usual activism. A glance at his written production near the end shows the broad range of contexts in which he continues to find nourishment. In the glossy pages of *L'Amour de l'Art*, he writes piquant essays on modes of personal expressivity: "Carve your mask," "Why wear clothes?" In a survey of linguistics he presents a scholarly overview of Melanesian languages. He composes an important discussion of archaic forms for a collective *History of Religions*. In *Tropiques*, "Review of the Colonial Troops," we find his graceful appreciation of Melanesian dances. His revision of *Gens de la Grande Terre* provides an opportunity for critical reassessment of colonialism. He is busy with official plans for the Caledonian Centennial. He prepares, at this time, a detailed ethnographic questionnaire for use in French West Africa. In his journal, *Le Monde Non-Chrétien*, he contributes a long series on "The Missionary Condition." He publishes, with commentaries, a "diary" composed in the 1890s by Kapéa, one of the Grande Terre's first Protestants.[2]

Most of the themes of this late production are familiar to us. The contents of *Le Monde Non-Chrétien* are characteristic. Like *Propos missionnaires*, it bore the mark of its founder's personality. Unlike *Propos*, however, *Le Monde Non-Chrétien* was not primarily "missionary talk" but served as a forum of encounter between the evangelical and eth-

19. Maurice Leenhardt
in 1953.

Photo: J. Dardel

nological worlds. A few sample issues will show its scope. Number 2 begins with an overview, "Missions 1946," partly authored by Leenhardt; it is followed by Gerardus Van der Leeuw's study of anthropomorphism, then by two articles on "rural construction" in India and French Equatorial Africa. There is a full account of a conference sponsored by the South Pacific Commission, followed by a commentary from Dakar by Théodore Monod, centered on the translation of a long "Sudanese mystical poem." Number 26, of 1953, includes an article on "The Rise and Fall of the Shakers," followed by one of Leenhardt's series on "La Condition Missionnaire," juxtaposed with Edmond Ortigues's meditation on Jung and myth, followed by a report from the Institut Français d'Afrique Noire on "Traditional Religion in West Africa," followed by a debate on Bultmann's theology of kerygma; then by first-hand documents concerning Congolese Christian sectarianism, and so on. A broad and eclectic field of encounter. The editing of a review always entails a large time commitment, and Leenhardt worked hard on *Le Monde Non-Chrétien*. It was a manifestation of his existence—a forum for the juxtaposition, circulation, and exchange of ideas drawn from an unclassifiable variety of sources.

It would be hard to sum up these final years; they were in no sense years of retirement or synthesis. Leenhardt moved from editorial correspondence to organizational duties at the Society of Oceanists, to study groups at the Ecole des Langues Orientales, to the writing of articles, to meetings on the New Caledonian Centennial, to participation in the varied life of his large family. There were long talks on the philosophy of religion with his son-in-law Henry Corbin, discussions with kindred intellectual spirits like Gaston Bachelard, work with his scientific assistants, Jean Poirier, Pierre Métais, Jean Guiart, correspondence with ethnographers in the field.[3]

Leenhardt also maintained his involvement in evangelical circles. If one is overly inclined to see his life as a movement away from the preoccupations of a missionary towards those of a scientist and scholar, one should leaf through his writings in the *Monde Non-Chrétien* (whose very title reveals a significant attitude). And one should note, too, that from 1952 to 1954 Leenhardt served as president of the Alliance Evangelique Universelle, a venerable organization with a rather conservative reputation. He would seek to widen the group's perspectives, recalling it to its early ecumenical goals.[4] Leenhardt continued to believe in missions—that they constituted the most open, living element of the church. He thought that the formalism, sectarianism, and hierarchy plaguing European religion could give way, in mission life, to cooperation and openness.[5] Evangelists, as Leenhardt saw them, spoke for Christ; thus they must be on their guard lest they become merely agents of Western civilization. During the early 1950s, the missionary movement came under widespread attack. And in response, many evangelical societies became more supple in their practice, generally more willing to recognize national autonomies. This was what Leenhardt had called for in his thesis on Ethiopianism fifty years previously. If in his final years Leenhardt did not evolve as rapidly as the times, it is because, in important respects, the times were catching up with him.

One cannot imagine him ever breaking with the missionary movement—as one can imagine him openly marking himself off from colonialism (had he lived a decade longer). It would be too strong to say that Leenhardt believed Christianity to be the one true religion. But he did believe it to be the truest religion for the modern world. Through all his investigation and valorization of alternative mythic systems, Christianity remained the mythology within which his personal belief and experience found expression. However, Leenhardt cast his analyses of the mythic life in forms that could be accessible to a wide variety of believers. The conclusion of *Do Kamo*, for example, makes no apology for Christianity but merely defends the existence of myth as a permanent structure of human consciousness. Leenhardt steered clear of theology. His ultimate goal was to discover, through comparative analysis, the essential forms of the religious experience, whenever and wherever they occurred. The important theoretical statements of his final years addressed themselves to the ethnological study of religion as such.

We glimpse Leenhardt's general attitude in a letter to a colleague at the Ecole Pratique des Hautes Etudes, Jacques Soustelle. Leenhardt urges Soustelle, an authority on Pre-Columbian cultures, not to give up his teaching and scholarship for politics: "I believe that in your meditations outside the fray you will find many subjects for wise reflection. In the religions called primitive (which they all are), and in the religion of your [Native] Americans, you will discover the constant fund of humanity. You do not suffer from the skepticism which closes to others the fertile path in this study."[6] And in a tribute to Gerardus Van Der Leeuw, Leenhardt salutes the scholar's "interrogation of man's commerce with divinity, in that undifferentiated domain where one doesn't know any longer what is esthetics and what religion."[7] The two citations may serve to mark off Leenhardt's broadly based approach.

As he defines it, religion is a fund of experiences that have been elemental to humanity from the beginning and which must continue to inspire man's modes of affective, esthetic expression. In concluding his analysis of the "Common Elements of the Inferior Forms of Religion," Leenhardt stresses that the term "inferior" refers only to "an older stage, not a lesser quality."[8] In a few rapid comparisons, he suggests that the basic modes of religious experience do not change. Whether one feels the presence of powerful "otherness" or of a "god," whether moral restraint is organized personally or via participation in totemic myth, whether an offering is made to an elder or to a deity, the fundamental experiences of transcendence are comparable. There exists an overall contrast between archaic and modern religions, the one more emotional, the other more conceptual, but the differing elements are permanent and essential at all stages.

In this late essay Leenhardt proposes more clearly than ever before the dichotomy between female "life" principles and the male virtues of "power." He had discovered these categories in the structure of New Caledonian culture and had made them his own. Archaic Melanesians grasped the world about them according to two general principles. One was the element of "universal fecundity," figured in totemic myth, the other, the element of "power" that found affirmation somewhat later in the discrimination and worship of deified ancestors. "But man was unable to control his rational thought, and made use of it to shatter the equilibrium and augment his power. He created his gods, and these have crushed the totems."[9] Nevertheless, the female element of the religious life persists, reduced to secondary cults and still the most basic spiritual attachment. Finally, according to Leenhardt's parable of religious history, the two principles are reunited. As an old man he argues—and it is more of a testimony than an argument—that reunion is attained through a revealed God in whom feeling and understanding are again one flesh. This final recognition of Christ's androgyny allows Leenhardt to circumscribe religious evolution, uniting its two poles, archaic and modern. These are also the terms of his own life. Reason and myth can, in the modern world, be returned to their lost complementarity through a deity with whom it is possible to enter into communion. God's all-embracing qualities become those of the human person.

It may be appropriate here to pose a few skeptical questions. How adequately, one wonders, is the Christian (and especially the Protestant) "God the Father" suited to adopt a "maternal" role? How inextricably is monotheism tied to rationalist individualism? Do the New Caledonian categories of male "power" and female "life" make sense in a modern context? What is the universal status of these kinds of gender essences? Are not many of the permanent mythic aspects of the religious life as perceived by Leenhardt dependent on inscription in a local, restricted landscape? Finally, is there not a fundamental contradiction betwen a single, transcendent God and the plenitude of relations—esthetic, social, religious, ecological—that Leenhardt recognized as elemental?

The list of questions could be extended. Leenhardt did not usually feel it necessary to wrestle with these dilemmas explicitly. Perhaps they did not exist for him. His basic attitude toward religion remained one of confident research, of openness to new forms. "Facts" were still "a Word of God." Specifically Christian conclusions, such as the one just discussed, were not prominent in his work.

⋙⋘

The most interesting publication of Leenhardt's last year is a curious text entitled "Religious Sociology. Questionnaire with a view to establishing a religious map of French West Africa." It appears in Théodore Monod's *Bulletin* of the Institut Français d'Afrique Noire and is largely a list of questions designed for the use of fieldworkers studying religious phenomena. The questionnaire, an important document in the development of Leenhardt's thinking, sketches a kind of *ad hoc* charter for a field of inquiry that would treat religious phenomena as facts *sui generis*. "Religious sociology," as Leenhardt sketched it, would resist a common theoretical tendency to explain religions as systems of symbols or beliefs, as semantic fields, as collective representations, adaptive mechanisms, and so on.

The most critical questions facing "religious sociology" in 1953 involved simple definitions. There existed no established vocabulary for denoting the basic experiences in question, no consensus on what phenomena were, properly speaking, religious. There is still no firm agreement on these matters.[10] Leenhardt prefaced his 1953 "Questionnaire" with a series of spare definitions, the purest distillation of his general approach:

Participation

A felt relation between the self and an interior or exterior object, immanent or transcendent. It determines a comportment peculiar to that being, accompanied by various sentiments, fervor, fear, loss of self, fidelity.

To a certain extent, it contributes to the structure of myth, of belief, and of faith.

Religious

We qualify as religious all manner of a being's participation with a transcendence . . . which can be in the form of a person or not.

Religion

All systems tending toward an explication and an organization of participation with a transcendent or immanent object.[11]

So run Leenhardt's first three definitions. We notice at once the progression from a basic mode of feeling to its formulation into "systems." As a guide to research on religious experience, these definitions counsel the ethnographer not to begin with preconceived ideas about what specific sorts of systems—dogmas, institutions, rituals, cosmologies—constitute religion. The researcher studies what is "religious" by first observing any and all feelings of personal transcendence.[12] As always, Leenhardt begins with personal experience and moves from there to its various expressive formulations, the most important of which is *mythe vécu*: "Myth— All manner of gesture or speech which, by circumscribing a reality that cannot be realized in rational language, imposes on man a comportment in relation with that reality."[13]

Religion, as Leenhardt defines it, pervades human experience.[14] It is present in all affective relations with others or otherness; in the form of mythic words and acts it adopts the shape of a "language" of feelings, counterbalancing cognitive, empirical language. Religion coexists with various forms of thought, ritual, technique—forms that are not themselves religious. In drafting his questionnaire, Leenhardt casts his net widely. (I have cited only his most basic definitions.) It was precisely because the field was so broad and the observed behavior so overdetermined that he held closely to a definition of the religious based on personal experience. Religion as he conceived it must not be permitted to lose specificity in its overlappings with technology, with magic, with cosmological speculation, and with thought itself. Leenhardt's definitions do not exclude other approaches to religion—those that shed light on it from the outside, for example, portrayals of religion *as* a cultural or semiotic system. But his approach resists the tendency of such explanations to substitute themselves for the religious phenomenon itself. The isolation of "religion" is notoriously difficult.[15] Let us simply observe, finally, that the very spareness of Leenhardt's definitions is a precondition for openness. There is no Christian or monotheistic bias in his viewpoint.[16] The twenty-two dense pages of questions that follow his definitions make clear that Leenhardt was prepared to consider the broadest range of human experience.

The questionnaire is his most open series of propositions on the religious experience, and it stands as an appropriate final image, though in no sense a summation, of his life's research. It is worth noting that, according to these late definitions, esthetic experiences of participation—such as Leenhardt's own encounters with the rhythms of place in New Caledonia, Africa, and the Midi—are unambiguously qualified as religious. Minimal definitions—presented, characteristically, in the company of hundreds of questions: we see again the fieldworker's empirical thoroughness as well as his constitutional reluctance to conclude. Over and over, Leenhardt advises against premature theoretical closure. The forms of religion must be scrupulously mapped, with local names, sites, qualities recorded. Moreover, the best process of research is improvisational; it must "overhear" its answers rather than elicit them. The questionnaire is an initial point of reference; it is helpful, its author warns, "on the sole condition that you don't use it."

⇒∈

In his seventy-fifth year, Maurice Leenhardt was preparing for another visit to the Grande Terre. This would be the last—his health was failing. One wonders whether he harbored a half-conscious desire to end his days among the mountains and pines of the Houailou Valley. But during the late summer of 1953 his health gave way altogether; the final illness lasted six months. In its early stages he attempted to work, dictating reminiscences and reflections on myth. Soon even this reduced activity was no longer possible; the diagnosis was cancer of the lung and throat. During the final three months Leenhardt was mute but lucid, communicating by gesture. Family and friends believed him to be preoccupied with the experience of beauty.

His death, apparently, was a peaceful one—in the family apartment at 59 Rue Claude Bernard, Paris, January 26, 1954.

Afterword

Testimony of the *grand chef* Mus, Moméa, June 1978:[1] "From what I know, the old pastor worked for [us] natives, especially in religion, customs and all. So much so that nowadays, for example, if we old ones know pretty well what custom, as they call it, is all about it's because he sought out custom and inquired from old people who were knowledgeable; he searched deep, deep down. Me, I've read his work and that's how I know. And so I rediscover what our elders used to say, the ones who didn't tell, and who forgot to tell. That's where I find this kind of knowledge—such as on the clan, on the family, on customs. . . . All the work of the old people, that's been lost; well, me, I get it back because when I used to be with my father and grandfather I'd hear all about this; but I forgot; but when I look again at his book, there I remember. Now I can tell you things because I know Leenhardt's book where you find out about customs before the whites arrived here in Caledonia; it's the ancient art; it's old, ancient, and pure too; it's pure.

"Yes those of us who are old are like rocks. You can't know what's in a rock unless you ask it, you see, that's how you find out what's inside. Us old ones are like that; because if you lose an old one you've lost a whole history, something you'll never get back.

"Now I'm going to tell you in our language the story of the fish: One day here in the neighborhood there was a mother fish, and also some little fish, her children. One day the mother fish says to her young: when the river rises, when the river overflows you must always stay close to the rock by the bank: don't go far away out there with the others, because the river that rises falls fast, and you won't have any way to get back to the rock; and the water on the plain only lasts for a little while, just an instant; and when there's no more water it's dry you see. Well, you'll get eaten by the buzzard like this . . . like this . . . like this . . . and there won't be any more fish. I'm telling you not to leave the rock, because underneath the rock there's always something to eat; and in the roots beside the river we can stay forever."

225

⇒⇐

In August 1978 the centennial of Leenhardt's birth was celebrated
at Do Neva—a secondary school for Loyalty Islanders. Alongside the
road that crosses the central chain at mid-island, a monument now
commemorates Leenhardt's work. Beside the missionary's stele—by
decision of the local centennial committee—has been placed the memo-
rial he erected to the Melanesian dead of the First World War. The
two markers form an ensemble symbolic of the most noble and—in a
changing milieu—the most ambiguous aspects of the island's colonial
past. This past is in the process of being reunderstood and transcended
by New Caledonia's Melanesians and whites. Thus Leenhardt's name
is remembered by some with reverence, by others with suspicion. It is
a complex symbol. His centennial coincided with that of the island's
most important anticolonial uprising. This other anniversary was celebrated privately, without university or government subventions. The
name of the rebellion's leader, Atai, killed in the year of Leenhardt's
birth, was significantly juxtaposed with that of the great reformer.

The juxtaposition symbolizes less the island's colonial past, in which
neither figure played a typical or dominant role, than it does the
present struggle for the island's future. Colonialism in New Caledonia, deeply rooted, liberalized, economically profitable, will probably
not yield to violent rebellion and direct confrontation. It is, however,
being steadily undermined by Melanesians using a combination of
tactics, cultural and political, liberal and radical—new tactics inspired
by the traditions of both Atai and Leenhardt. It seems unlikely—
perhaps un-Melanesian—that either tradition will definitively triumph
over the other.

Leenhardt's monument is a white cement column about seven feet
high, tapering to a point. It was designed by a committee composed of
prominent Melanesians from the Houailou-speaking area: a Catholic
grand chef, the mayor of Houailou and his secretary, pastors from various Protestant factions, concerned citizens. On the stele the missionary's profile, military in bearing, has been modeled in bronze by a
noted Paris artist. An engraved plaque has been supplied by the powerful mining conglomerate, "Le Nickel." At the narrow summit of the
monument the local committee has placed an ordinary-looking smooth
stone. The colonial press in its accounts of the Centennial tended to
dwell on the many inspirational speeches and on long lists of governmental, tribal, ecclesiastical, and diplomatic dignitaries (including
Maurice Leenhardt's *"biographe américain").* The stone was ignored.

Rocks are forms of local history, mythic "words." Traditionally, the spirit of an ancestor could be seized and solidified in the form of a rock gathered from a riverbed. The stone atop Leenhardt's monument is taken from a stream in the home valley of one of the missionary's original pastoral students. It solidifies, gathers, symbolizes the presence of the ancestors, of Leenhardt, and of the Melanesians who made his work possible. It gathers the landscape's past. Rocks are crucial in New Caledonia—a land where mountains are called "*cailloux*," pebbles. They stake out the habitat, providing permanent markers around and over which flow the ongoing currents of social, historical, and natural life.

Perhaps, by means of a smooth stone, Leenhardt's tradition has been appropriately, discreetly, coopted. The missionary and ethnographer would surely have wished for this kind of comprehension.

Abbreviations

JOURNALS

J.M.E.   *Journal des Missions Évangéliques*, Paris.

M.N.C.   *Le Monde Non-Chrétien*, Paris.

Propos   *Propos missionnaires*, Paris.

DOCUMENTS

M.L.—P., 21.6.05.   Letter, M.L. to his parents, 21 June 1905.
                          (Dates have been kept in French form.)

M.L.—Je.   Letter, M.L. to Jeanne Leenhardt.

Jnl.   M.L.'s journal entry, cited with date.

(R.H.L.)   Document in the possession of M. R.H.
                          Leenhardt, 59 Rue Claude Bernard, Paris
                          5e. All of M.L.'s letters and journals cited
                          by date alone are located here.

(R.D.-L.)   Document in the possession of Mme. Rose-
                          lène Dousset-Leenhardt. Citations are to
                          her two-volume published selection, "Cor-
                          respondance inédite de Maurice Leen-
                          hardt," Paris, C.N.R.S., 1969, 1970.

S.M.E.   Archives of the Société des Missions Évan-
                          géliques de Paris (presently D.E.F.A.P.,
                          Bld. Arago, Paris^{14e}).

FREQUENTLY CITED WORKS
OF MAURICE LEENHARDT:

Documents   *Documents néo-calédoniens*. Paris, 1932.

Do Kamo   *Do Kamo, la personne et le mythe dans le monde
                          mélanésien*. Paris, 1947, 1960; references to
                          1960 French edition and in parentheses to
                          English translation, Chicago, 1979.

Gens	*Gens de la Grande Terre.* Paris, 1937; citations to revised ed., 1952.
Langues et dialectes	*Langues et dialectes de l'Austro-Mélanésie.* Paris, 1946.
Notes	*Notes d'ethnologie néo-calédonienne.* Paris, 1930.
"La Personne"	"La Personne mélanésienne," *Annuaire,* École Pratique des Hautes Études, section des sciences religieuses, 1941-1942, Melun, 1942, pp. 5-36; citations here to *Structure,* pp. 92-120.
"Quelques éléments"	"Quelques éléments communs aux formes inférieures de la religion," in M. Brillant and R. Aigrain, eds., *Histoire des religions,* Paris, 1953, I:83-110.
"La Religion"	"La Religion des peuples archaïques actuels" (1937), in *Histoire générale des religions,* a collection by Quillet editions, Paris, 1948, 1960, pp. 48-80 (1960 ed.)
"Sociologie"	"Sociologie religieuse. Questionnaire en vue de l'établissement d'une carte religieuse de l'A.O.F.," *Bulletin de l'Institut français d'Afrique noire* (Dakar), 15, no. 2, April 1953, 768-97.
Structure	*La Structure de la personne en Mélanésie.* Milan, 1970, selected essays.
"Le Temps"	"Le Temps et la personnalité chez les canaques de la Nouvelle-Calédonie," *Revue Philosophique* (Paris), Sept.-Oct. 1937, pp. 43-58; citations here to *Structure,* pp. 75-91.
"Traduction"	"Notes sur la traduction du Nouveau Testament en langue primitive," *Revue d'histoire et de philosophie religieuse* (Strasbourg), May-June 1922, pp. 193-218.
Vocabulaire	*Vocabulaire et grammaire de la langue houaïlou.* Paris, 1935.

Notes

INTRODUCTION

1. M.L., *Do Kamo: Person and Myth in the Melanesian World* (Chicago, 1979), translated by Basia Miller Gulati, Introduction by Vincent Crapanzano; originally published in French (Paris, 1937, 1960).

2. Jean Duvignaud, *Le langage perdu* (Paris, 1973), p. 30.

3. See James Clifford, "'Hanging Up Looking Glasses at Odd Corners': Ethnobiographical Prospects," *Harvard English Studies*, 8 (Cambridge, Mass., 1978), 41-56.

4. From the French translation of A. Wabaelo and Jean Guiart; complete text in Guiart, *Structure de la chefferie en Mélanésie du Sud* (Paris, 1963), pp. 165-69.

CHAPTER I

1. André Siegfried, "Le Groupe Protestant Cévenol sous la IIIᵉ République," Alfred Boegner and Siegfried, eds., *Protestantisme français* (Paris, 1945), pp. 387-88.

2. L. Perrier, *Franz Leenhardt, naturaliste et théologien* (Paris, 1924).

3. E. Léonard, *Le Protestant français* (Paris, 1953), ch. 1.

4. A. Sardinoux, *Mémoire sur la Faculté de Théologie Protestante et le Séminaire de Montauban, 1808-1878* (Paris, 1888), pp. 342-44.

5. Perrier, *Franz Leenhardt, passim*; and various oral testimonies, especially that of J. Cadier.

6. Perrier, "L'Expérience religieuse d'après le Professeur Franz Leenhardt," *Cahiers de foi et vie*, 1 Nov. 1923, cahier B, p. 342.

7. F. Leenhardt, "L'Evolution," *Séance publique de rentrée* (Montauban, 1899), p. 45; see also his *L'Evolution doctrine de liberté* (Saint-Blaise and Roubaix, 1910). For a photo of the "Musée Leenhardt," *Souvenirs de fêtes universitaires* (Montauban, 1903), p. 120

8. F. Leenhardt, "Quelques mots à des étudiants chrétiens," *Bulletin des Associations Chrétiennes d'Etudiants* (Paris, n.d. [1903?]), pp. 129-42.

9. M.L.—P., 5.1.17; M.L.—P., n.d. [1918?].

10. M.L.—Membres du Comité des Missions Évangéliques de Paris, 21 Nov. 1896, S.M.E. Archives.

11. "Consacration de Maurice Leenhardt, Montpellier, 1902," typescript p. 2 (R.H.L.).

12. M.L.—Membres du Comité.

13. E. Goblot, *La Barrière et le niveau, étude sociologique de la bourgeoisie française moderne* (Paris, 1925), ch. 6; J. Piobetta, *Le Baccalauréat* (Paris, 1937).

14. M.L.—P., April 1896.

15. J. Clifford, "Le Paysage néo-calédonien et Maurice Leenhardt," *Objets et mondes*, 17, no. 2 (summer 1977), 69-74.

16. F. Leenhardt—Boegner, 14.9.96, 21.9.96, S.M.E. Archives.

17. F. Leenhardt—Boegner, 28.9.96, *ibid.*

18. M.L.—P., 2.10.97, 22.4.98, 20.6.98.

19. M.L.—P., 7.12.97, 3.97, 2.10.97.

20. "Consacration," p. 3.

21. M.L.—P., 7.2.97.

22. M.L.—Paul Leenhardt, March 1898 (R.H.L.).

23. *Ibid.*

24. M.L.—P., 15 Oct. 1899 (R.H.L.).

25. M.L.—P., 2 Oct. 1897 (R.H.L.).

26. *Ibid.*

27. M.L. wrote a full-length biography of Boegner: *Alfred Boegner, d'après son journal intime et sa correspondance* (Paris, 1938).

28. For the history and character of the society: J. Bianquis, *Les Origines de la Société des Missions Evangéliques* (Paris, 1930-1935); M.L., "Missions protestantes françaises," André Siegfried and Alfred Boegner, eds., *Protestantisme français*, pp. 372-405.

29. M.L., "Jacques Liénard," *Almanach des missions* (Montauban, 1902), p. 31.

30. M.L., "Missions protestantes françaises"; and "Methode Missionnaire (Cours donnés à l'Ecole de la Maison des Missions)," S.M.E. Archives.

31. M.L., "Savoir Regarder," *Propos*, 15 April 1928, p. 19.

32. M.L.—Boegner, 1 Sept. 1900, S.M.E. Archives, pre-1902 file.

33. M.L., "Jacques Liénard," p. 33.

34. M.L., *Le Mouvement éthiopien au sud de l'afrique de 1896 à 1899* (Cahors, 1902).

35. B.G.M. Sundkler, *Bantu Prophets in South Africa* (London, 1948); in Sundkler's select bibliography, Leenhardt's is the earliest source listed. It has been republished by the Académie des Sciences d'Outre-Mer (Paris, 1976), Introductions by R. Delavignette and R. Cornevin.

36. M.L.—Boegner, 17 Nov. 1901, 31 Oct. 1901, S.M.E. Archives.

37. "Jeanne André-Michel, veuve Maurice Leenhardt, 25 June 1881-15 Nov. 1970, Extraits du Service Religieux," p. 2, typescript; oral testimonies and letters (R.H.L.).

38. M.L., *Propos*, April 1931, p. 78.

39. Robert (unidentified)—M.L., 26 Sept. 1901 (R.H.L.).

40. "Jeanne André-Michel," p. 2.

41. Paul Leenhardt-Suzelly Boudet (his fiancée), 1 Sept. 1902 (R.H.L.).

42. "Consacration," p. 2.

43. Paul Leenhardt—Suzelly Boudet, 5 Oct. 1902, 6 Oct. 1902 (R.H.L.).

CHAPTER II

1. The narrative contained in this chapter is drawn primarily from published letters in the *Journal des Missions Evangéliques* (*J.M.E.*) by Philadelphe Delord (1899-1901) and especially Maurice and Jeanne Leenhardt: 1903 (I), pp. 130-34, 278-84, letters of 12 and 19 Nov. 1902, and 9 March 1903. I have also used M.L.'s unpublished letters to his parents (M.L.—P.) 22 Nov. 1902, and 4 Feb. 1903. For contemporary atmosphere and the portrait of Noumea, I have relied on the indispensable documentary collections of Father Patrick O'Reilly, *Calédoniens, répertoire bio-bibliographique de la Nouvelle Calédonie* (Paris, 1953), and especially *La Nouvelle Calédonie au temps des cartes postales* (Paris, 1973). I have not altered the actual sequence or location of events, and the Leenhardts' reactions are normally given as recorded in their letters. In a few instances I have taken the liberty of assuming or extrapolating what M.L. must have seen or felt, based on later evidence and on my general understanding of his personality. The narrative draws also from: M.L., "Kapéa," *M.N.C.* no. 25, 1953, pp. 52-70 and *Gens de la Grande Terre* (Paris, 1937); R.-H. Leenhardt, "Trois Pasteurs Lifou à Houailou" (Paris, 1977), 36 pp.

2. G. Malignac, *Rapport démographique sur la Nouvelle-Calédonie* (Paris, 1957), for the Institut d'Etudes Démographiques.

3. M.L.'s working, from *Gens*, pp. 20-21; also *Documents*, pp. 500-01.

4. See below, Chapter 11. For New Caledonian ethnographic background: J.P. Doumenge, *Paysans mélanésiens en pays Canala, Nouvelle Calédonie* (Bordeaux, 1974); J. Guiart, *Structure de la chefferie en Mélanésie du Sud* (Paris, 1963); R.P. Lambert, *Moeurs et superstitions des Néo-Calédoniens* (Noumea, 1900); M. Leenhardt, *Gens* (1937, 1952), *Notes* (1930), *Documents* (1932), *Do Kamo* (1947, 1971, 1980), *Langues et dialectes* (1946), *Structure de la personne* (1970); J.-P. Faivre, J. Poirier, P. Routhier, *Géographie de la Nouvelle-Calédonie* (Paris, 1955); E. Métais, *La Sorcellerie canaque actuelle* (Bordeaux, 1967); P. Métais, "Nouvelle Calédonie," *Ethnologie générale*, Pleaide, vol. 1 (Paris, 1972); P. Métais, *Mariage et équilibre social dans les sociétés primitives* (Paris, 1956), publications de l'Institut d'Ethnologie, vol. 59; E. Rau, *Institutions et coutumes canaques* (Paris, 1944); J.C. Roux, "Crise de la réserve autochtone et passage des mélanésiens dans l'économie de la Nouvelle-Calédonie, essai de géographie sociale," O.R.S.T.O.M. (Noumea, 1974); J.M. Tjibaou, "Recherche d'identité mélanésienne et société traditionelle," *Journal de la Société des Océanistes*, 53 (Dec. 1976), 280-92.

5. M.L., *Gens*, pp. 18-19.

6. Guiart, "Maurice Leenhardt," *M.N.C.*, Jan.-Mar. 1955, pp. 53-55; R.H. Leenhardt, *Au Vent de la Grande Terre, histoire des Iles Loyalty* (Paris, 1957); K.R. Howe, *The Loyalty Islands: A History of Culture Contacts 1840-1900* (Honolulu, 1977).

7. Guiart, "Maurice Leenhardt," p. 58.

8. *J.M.E.*, 1903 (II), p. 355.

CHAPTER III

1. M.L.—P., 13.1.06.

2. Roux, "Crise de la réserve," p. 6 (estimate based on B. Brou, *Histoire de la Nouvelle Calédonie* (Noumea, 1973), 2 vols.); Malignac, *Rapport démographique*, p. 9.

3. Guiart, "Naissance et avortement d'un méssianisme," *Archives de sociologie des religions*, Jan.-June 1959, pp. 12-13.

4. M.L., Jnl., 26.3.14.

5. M.L.—P., 2.6.03.

6. Historical background: Richard Adloff and Virginia Thompson, *The French Pacific Islands* (Berkeley and London, 1971); Brou, *Histoire de la Nouvelle Calédonie*; W. Burchett, *Pacific Treasure Island, New Caledonia* (Melbourne, 1941); R. Dousset-Leenhardt, *Colonialisme et contradictions, étude sur les causes socio-historiques de l'insurrection en Nouvelle Calédonie* (Paris, 1970); Dousset-Leenhardt, *Terre natale, terre d'exil* (Paris, 1977); J. Guiart, *Destin d'une église et d'un peuple, étude monographique d'une oeuvre missionnaire protestante* (Paris, 1959); Guiart, "Naissance et avortement d'un messianisme," *Archives de sociologies des religions*, Jan.-June 1959, pp. 3-44; Guiart, "Maurice Leenhardt, missionnaire et sociologue," *M.N.C.*, Jan.-March 1955, pp. 52-71; K.R. Howe, *The Loyalty Islands* (Honolulu, 1977); L. Latham, "Revolt Reexamined: the 1878 Insurrection in New Caledonia," *Journal of Pacific History*, fall 1976, pp. 48-63; R.-H. Leenhardt, *Au vent de la Grande Terre, les Iles Loyalty de 1840 à 1895* (Paris, 1957); G. Malignac, "Rapport démographique sur la Nouvelle Calédonie," Paris, 1957, Institut National d'Etudes Démographiques; R.P. O'Reilly, *Bibliographie de la Nouvelle Calédonie* (Paris, 1955); O'Reilly, *La Nouvelle Calédonie au temps des cartes postales* (Paris, 1973); O'Reilly, *Calédoniens, repertoire biobibliographique de la Nouvelle Calédonie* (Paris, 1953); O'Reilly, *Pèlerin du ciel* (Paris, 1952), esp. ch. 10.

7. Between 1848 and 1865, accurate ethnological information was recorded by R.P. Gagnère: *Etude ethnologique sur la religion des Néo-Calédoniens* (St. Louis, New Caledonia, 1905); also R.P. Lambert's valuable treatise, *Moeurs et superstitions des Néo-Calédoniens* (Noumea, 1900).

8. On Guillain, see O'Reilly, *Calédoniens*.

9. L. Michel, *Légendes et chants de gestes canaques* (Paris, 1885).

10. The official number of rebel dead was given as 1,000 to 1,200, a figure that Guiart does not believe exaggerated; see Guiart, "Le cadre social traditionnel et la rébellion de 1878 dans le Pays de La Foa, Nouvelle Calédonie," *Journal de la Société des Océanistes*, 24, no. 24, Dec. 1968, 117. For a lower estimate see Latham, "Revolt Re-examined," p. 57.

11. *La Nouvelle Calédonie*, 23 Oct. 1879, as quoted by Burchett, *Pacific Treasure Island*, pp. 129-30.

12. Dousset-Leenhardt, *Colonialisme*; Guiart, "Le cadre social traditionnel"; for a revisionist version see Latham, "Revolt Re-examined." Latham stresses the native Caledonians' accommodationism toward whites, the unevenness of colonial pressures; and she sees the 1878 war as primarily one in a series of tribal conflicts, for certain groups at least. The analysis is not complete enough, however, to serve as more than a partial corrective to prevailing interpretations.

13. On Feillet, see O'Reilly, *Calédoniens*. See also M.L.'s favorable opinion of Feillet: Académie des Sciences Coloniales. "Réception de M. le Pasteur Maurice Leenhardt," *Contes rendus des séances*, 17 Dec. 1948, pp. 789-90.

14. "Notes sur le régime de l'engagement des indigènes en Nouvelle-Calédonie," March 1914, typescript (R.H.L.); published (with an introduction by J. Clifford) in *Journal de la Société des Océanistes*, 34, no. 58-59, March-June 1978, 9-18.

15. M.L.—P., 31.10.03.

16. M.L.—P., 1.10.03; 18.10.03; personal communication, J. Guiart; also his "Naissance et avortement," pp. 3-5.

17. M.L.—P., 1905, no month or day. In a recent assessment of M.L.'s evangelical practice, P. Teisserenc presents this unwillingness to separate religious conversion from political engagement as an anticipation of "liberation theology"; "Maurice Leenhardt en Nouvelle Calédonie: sciences sociales, politique coloniale, stratégies missionnaires," *Recherches de science religieuse* (Paris, 1977), pp. 1-56. See also J. Massé, "Maurice Leenhardt, une pédagogie libératrice," *Revue d'Histoire et de Philosophie religieuse*, no. 1 (1980), 67-80.

18. M.L.—P., 11.12.14.

19. *Ibid.* (The initials stand for Leenhardt and Paul Laffay, who was schoolmaster at Do Neva from 1912 to 1914.)

20. M.L.,"La Réquisition des indigènes en Nouvelle Calédonie," 1918, typescript (R.H.L.). Published in *Objets et mondes*, 17, no. 2 (summer 1977), 85-88. On labor policies, see Guiart, *Destin*, pp. 7-8. For a typical dispute involving the head tax and native labor, see "Commission d'Enquête nommé à l'occasion des troubles de Wagap, Ina, et Tieti, dossier complet" (Noumea, 1900).

21. M.L.—P., 13.10.12; 17.12.12; 21.12.12; 22.8.13; 3.10.13; 5.12.13; *France australe*, 4 Dec. 1913.

22. M.L.—P., 20.6.14; Brunet, "Discours d'Ouverture du Conseil Général," *Océanie française*, Feb. 1913, pp. 49-50; also, August 1912, pp. 186-87.

23. Brunet, speech to the Conseil Général, *Océanie française*, Feb. 1914, pp. 48,49.

24. M.L.—P., 1.9.13.

25. *Ibid.*

26. M.L.—P., 23.11.13.

27. M.L.—P., 31.10.03.

28. Letters to his superiors by Father Hily, 7 Jan. 1902 (two letters), 4 March 1909, 28 March 1913; and by Father Busson, 26 Feb. 1924; also "Rapport de visite," Father Marion, 1925, p. 6; Archives Pères Maristes (Rome), Océanie, Nouvelle-Calédonie, 208.

29. Father Provincial, "Rapport de visite," 16 Oct. 1913, pp. 21-22; Archives Pères Maristes, Océanie, Nouvelle-Calédonie, 208.

30. *Ibid.*, p. 25.

31. M.L.—Je., 13.6.19.

32. M.L.—Je., 11.8.19.

33. M.L.—Boegner, 28.1.05, S.M.E. Archives, 1905.

34. M.L., "Rencontre du missionnaire avec l'administration," 1927, manuscript and typed notes (R.H.L.).

35. *Ibid.*

36. *J.M.E.*, 1906 (I), p. 40.

CHAPTER IV

1. M.L., "Kapèa," *M.N.C.*, March 1953, pp. 78-79, 84.

2. Guiart, "Maurice Leenhardt," p. 62.

3. Precise figures are difficult to obtain, since official censuses do not record religious affiliation, and church statistics are contradictory. I have relied, for the present period, on provisional figures kindly provided by J.M. Kohler of O.R.S.T.O.M., Noumea, in 1979, which indicate that the Melanesian population of the Grande Terre is about 11,000 Protestant, 23,000 Catholic. (The situation is reversed—almost three to one Protestant—on the Loyalty Islands.) By the 1930s there were only a very few "unconverted" tribes in New Caledonia; competition between the two missions diminished, each respecting the other's territories.

4. Guiart, "Maurice Leenhardt," p. 63.

5. *J.M.E.*, 1904 (I), pp. 426-28.

6. *Ibid.*; M.L., "Contes rendus des conférences pastorales," January 1904, Houailou, manuscript notebook (R.H.L.); M.L.—Boegner, 2.5.04, S.M.E. Archives (1904).

7. *J.M.E.*, 1904 (I), p. 430.

8. R. Needham, "Introduction," Durkheim and Mauss, *Primitive Classification* (New York, 1963), p. vii, fn.

9. M.L., *Gens*, p. 221.

10. M.L., "Ethnologie," three-page typescript, undated (R.H.L.); notes for a lecture given before prospective missionaries. On issues of authority and understanding in mission work, see also: M.L., *Propos*, April 1930, pp. 53-54.

11. For a description of a Protestant temperance "pilou," see below, Chapter 6, pp. 100-102. M.L.'s increasingly *laisser faire* attitude appears in M.L., Jnl., 10.10.11. Guiart summarizes M.L.'s mature policy in "Maurice Leenhardt," pp. 66-67.

12. R.-H. Leenhardt, "Un Sociologue canaque: le pasteur Boesoou Erijisi, 1866-1947," *Cahiers du Pacifique*, no. 4, 1976, pp. 19-53.

13. *J.M.E.*, 1903 (II), p. 358.

14. R.-H. Leenhardt, *Le pasteur Joané Nigoth, 1866(?)-1919* (Paris, 1976), 43 pp.

15. This was the general policy of French Protestant missions in opposition to Third Republic secular schooling (which insisted on the French language alone). The issue was hotly debated around 1903, particularly with reference to native education in Madagascar. See an eloquent defense of a position similar to Leenhardt's by Raoul Allier, *Cahiers de la quinzaine*, 4th cahier, 6th series, 1905, pp. 96-97. For a later view see M.L., "Lingua franca et langues de base," *M.N.C.*, April-June 1952, pp. 222-26.

16. M.L., "Lettre aux pasteurs de Nouvelle Calédonie," 10 Oct. 1939, origi-

nal text in Houailou, translated by R.-H. Leenhardt, *M.N.C.*, Oct.-Dec. 1963; also, *Langues et dialectes*, p. xiv.

17. M.L.—P., 1905, no day or month.

18. M.L.—Je., 18.5.19; the text under discussion is First Corinthians, 1, 18-31. See A.N. Whitehead, "Space, Time and Relativity," 1917; in *The Aims of Education and Other Essays* (New York, 1967), p. 165. Note in this context W.V. Quine's analysis of the difficulties of grasping patterns of meaning outside "our object-positing kind of culture"; in R. Brower *et al.*, *On Translation* (New York, 1959), p. 155.

19. M.L., Jnl., 23.1.11.

20. See the 36-page circular letter with responses by the New Caledonian missionaries and a summary of debate by J. Bianquis, S.M.E. Archives, 1911.

21. M.L.—P., 27.8.03.

22. M.L.—P., 15.3.03; my account of Do Neva station life is drawn generally from the letters and also from conversations with Leenhardt children who remember these years.

23. M.L.—P., 29.1.14.

24. M.L.—P., 13.12.13.

25. M.L., "Rencontre du missionnaire avec l'administration," 1927, mss. (R.H.L.).

CHAPTER V

1. M.L., *La Grande Terre* (Paris, 1909).

2. Franz Leenhardt—President S.M.E., 2 Mar. 1907, copy (R.H.L.).

3. The classical formulations for these ideas, which were in the air in 1909, were Lévy-Bruhl's *Les Fonctions mentales dans les sociétés inférieures* (1910) and Durkheim's *Les Formes élémentaires de la vie religieuse* (1912). For Leenhardt's early objections to Lévy-Bruhl see M.L.—P., 21.9.11, 4.6.12, 24.5.14, containing comments such as the following: ". . . they [the Melanesians] place their causes in the mystery of the spirits, and effects result from powers delegated by these spirits. And so they reason, by intuitions, by juxtaposed representations, by deduction or induction, but in a domain which is beyond positive knowledge. . . . For the moment I still see in everything which is magic or properly religious, associations of ideas, correspondences, links of cause and effect. . . ."

4. M.L.—P., undated fragment, probably 1905.

5. See E. Christen, *Philadelphe Delord, au secours des lépreux* (Geneva, n.d.), Collection "Les Vainqueurs," 23.

6. M.L.—P., 2.6.03.

7. Leenhardt's thinking on conversion appears to anticipate recent "intellectualist" views of the process. See primarily Robin Horton, "African Conversion," *Africa*, April 1971, esp. pp. 93-101. Horton distinguishes between (a) traditional religious doctrines that combine the experience of "communion" with "explanation-prediction-control" of the world's "space-time events" and (b) Christianity, which tends to abandon day-to-day control func-

tions and concentrates on communion with a personal God. In Leenhardt's view, as in Horton's, full Christianization entails a profound general revolution in the ways a person communes with and manipulates the world.

8. M.L.—P., 10.10.03, 20.11.03.

9. M.L.—P., 22.3.05.

10. M.L.—P., 31.8.11.

11. M.L.—P., 6.2.04.

12. M.L.—Boegner, 13.2.04, S.M.E. Archives.

13. See below, Chapter 7, pp. 110-111, for M.L.'s critique of Coillard's much publicized mission in Barotseland; see also M.L., "La Place du missionnaire dans la mission," *Propos*, April 1931.

14. M.L.—P., 13.9.04.

15. M.L., *Le cathéchumène canaque*, Cahiers Missionnaires, no. 1 (Paris, 1921); "Expériences sociales en terre canaque," *Revue du Christianisme social*, Oct.-Nov. 1922, reprinted *M.N.C.*, no. 66, April-June 1963, pp. 2-20; *La Grande Terre*, expanded edition (Paris 1922); "Aurores d'âmes primitives," *M.N.C.*, O.S. no. 2, 1931, pp. 29-52; *Do Kamo*, chs. 11 and 12.

16. M.L., "Expériences," *M.N.C.*, no. 66, April-June 1963, p. 18.

17. "Cahier d'Eleisha Nebay, 1911," translated from the Houailou by R.-H. Leenhardt (R.H.L.).

18. M.L.—P., 1905, no month or day.

19. Franz Leenhardt—Maurice, 24.12.02 (R.H.L.).

20. M.L.—P., 1905, no month or day.

21. *J.M.E.*, 1913 (II), pp. 309-13.

22. *Ibid.*; M.L., "Traduction," *passim*; for a full, later version of the underlying theory of religious evolution see M.L., "Quelques éléments."

23. M.L.—P., 25.10.13.

24. "La notion de dieu chez les mélanésiens," typescript (R.H.L.), no date. (Lecture notes for a class at the S.M.E. school, probably late 1930s.) On the "dieu long" see M.L., *Notes*, pp. 187, 233-34.

25. M.L.—P., 25.10.13.

26. M.L., *Gens*, "Deuxième Avant-Propos," 1952.

27. M.L., "Ethnologie," typescript (R.H.L.), no date. (Lecture notes for a class at the S.M.E. school.)

28. M.L.—P., 19.3.15.

29. M.L., "Traduction," pp. 216-17.

30. *Ibid.*, pp. 216-17. A fuller discussion of translating "redemption" appears in *Propos*, August 1931, pp. 15-18.

31. *Ibid.*, p. 212.

32. M.L.'P., 4.6.12; see below, chapter 13, pp. 208-209.

33. On Houailou duals and plurals, see esp. M.L., "La Personne," pp. 5-17; *Langues et dialectes*, Introduction, pp. xxxiii-xxxix.

34. See, particularly, E.A. Nida and C.R. Taber, *The Theory and Practice of Translation* (Leiden, 1969), pp. 22-32, which sets out principles developed by Nida in a distinguished career as linguist and Bible translation theorist. "Dynamic equivalence" translating looks for verification to the response of recep-

tors: ". . . a translation of the Bible must not only provide information which people can understand but must present the message in such a way that people can feel its relevance (the expressive element in communication) and can then respond to it in action (the imperative function)" (p. 24). Nida was a reader of Leenhardt's *Do Kamo*; see his *Customs and Cultures: Anthropology for Christian Missions* (New York, 1954), *passim*; and as editor of *The Bible Translator* he published a—rather mangled—translation of M.L.'s article of 1922 on the Houailou New Testament: vol. 2, no. 3, July 1951, and no. 4, Oct. 1951. Many of Leenhardt's general ideas may be found in recent pages of *Practical Anthropology* (now *Missiology, an International Review*). For an extension of "dynamic equivalence" principles to the structure of indigenous churches (a very "Leenhardtian" perspective), see C.H. Kraft, "Dynamic Equivalence Churches: An Ethnotheological Approach to Indigeneity," *Missiology*, 1, no. 1 (Jan. 1973), 39-58.

35. M.L., "Traduction," p. 196.

36. M.L., "La Bible en mission," *Evangile et liberté*, 21 Oct. 1934.

37. M.L., "Traduction," p. 218.

38. M.L., *Notes*, p. 234. For an account of discovering that *bao* = cadaver, *Do Kamo*, p. 80 (30).

39. M.L., "Modes d'expression en sociologie et en ethnologie," *Synthèse*, vol. 10, Proceedings of the 6th International Significal Summer Conference (n.d. [1951?]), p. 262.

40. For M.L.'s later dealings with the *doki*, see below, Chapter 10; see also *Notes*, p. 239.

41. See the very beautiful ritual discourses to and by the *kanya* in M.L., *Documents*, pp. 341-51.

42. See M.L., *Notes*, pp. 179-212; M.L.—P., 24.5.14.

43. M.L., *Notes*, pp. 77-79, and 98 fn., where he traces the development of his thinking beyond evolutionism to the recognition of a reciprocal system. See also, M.L., "Observation de la pensée religieuse d'un peuple océanien et d'un peuple bantou," *Histoire générale des religions* (Paris, 1948), 1:53; for the system of social exchanges see *Notes*, ch. 5. (The kinship system, for M.L., was not separate from myth.)

44. C. Lévi-Strauss, *La pensée sauvage* (Paris, 1962), p. 285.

45. See below, Chapter 6, p. 101.

46. M.L., "Traduction," pp. 210-11.

47. M.L., *Notes*, pp. 233-34.

48. See the list of terms drawn from totemism provided by Pierre Métais in his valuable analysis of M.L.'s translation: "Sociologue parce que linguiste," *Journal de la Société des Océanistes*, 10, no. 10, Dec. 1954, 42, 44. On Christian appropriation of totemic terms, see also M.L.'s report in *Annuaire*, Ecole Pratique des Hautes Etudes, 5ᵉ section, 1949-1950, p. 31.

49. M.L.—P., 1904, no day or month.

50. On the Christian God (Christ) as unity of male "power" and feminine "life," see M.L., "Quelques éléments," p. 109.

51. See below, Chapter 10, p. 168.

CHAPTER VI

1. M.L.—P., 10.3.14.

2. M.L., Notebook No. 2, 1918, R. Dousset-Leenhardt, ed., *Correspondance inédite*; quoted in R. Dousset-Leenhardt, *Colonialisme et contradictions* (Paris, 1970), p. 18.

3. M.L.—P., 17.11.14.

4. M.L.—P., 31.10.14, 22.6.15; *J.M.E.*, letter of June 1916; *Notes*, p. 38.

5. See Mindia Néja's recruitment speech, cast in the style of traditional oratory, M.L., *Documents*, pp. 313-18; see also M.L., "Les Chefferies océaniennes," Académie des Sciences Coloniales, *Comptes rendus des séances*, 5 Dec. 1941, pp. 359-76.

6. M.L.—P., 31.1.16, 9.6.16; in total, 1,037 native New Caledonians served in Europe; about 350 of them perished; *Océanie française*, Jan.-Mar. 1920, p. 17.

7. J. Guiart, personal communication; *Destin d'une église*, pp. 29-30.

8. M.L.—Je., 5.8.17.

9. M.L.—P., 15.1.17.

10. M.L.—P., 13.7.17.

11. J. Guiart, "Les événements de 1917 en Nouvelle Calédonie," *Journal de la Société des Océanistes*, 26, no. 29, Dec. 1970, 265-82. My account relies largely on this preliminary study, as well as on Leenhardt's letters and reports. A full history remains to be written. Government archives in Noumea are only recently becoming accessible; D. Bourret has published certain documents in *Centenaire Leenhardt* (Noumea, 1978), and A. Bensa and J.-C. Rivièrre have been collecting oral tradition in the Hienghène, Koné areas. See the summary, map, and vernacular text prepared by Bensa in *Le Courrier du Musée de l'Homme*, no. 2, Jan. 1978.

12. Thompson and Adloff, *French Pacific Islands*, pp. 249-50. Guiart seems to limit the number of white victims to eight; "Les événements," p. 273.

13. M.L.—Je., 13.4.17.

14. M.L.—Je., 29.4.17.

15. M.L.—Je., 19.6.17.

16. M.L.—Je., 20.6.17, 25.6.17.

17. M.L.—P., 27.7.17.

18. M.L.—Je., 5.8.17, 11.12.17; see also O'Reilly, *Pèlerin du ciel* (Paris, 1952), p. 165.

19. J. Guiart, "Les événements," p. 267; M.L.—Governor, 14.9.17 (R.H.L.); M.L.—Je., 13.9.17, in Dousset-Leenhardt, *Correspondance*.

20. *Océanie française*, Sept.-Dec. 1919, pp. 84-85.

21. Guiart, "Les événements," pp. 274-75; Bensa, map in *Courrier*.

22. M.L.—Je., 15.7.18.

23. M.L.—Je., 17.8.18.

24. M.L., "Quelques éléments," p. 95.

25. M.L.'s report, *J.M.E.*, 1920 (II), p. 349; see also M.L., *Do Kamo*, pp. 238-39 (146), for the important testimony against Bwaxat by one of his "free-speaking" relations. On the trial see D. Bourret, "Introduction," *Centenaire*

Leenhardt (Noumea, 1978); and in the same volume, various documents concerning M.L.'s role and a newspaper account of his testimony, pp. 67-91.
26. M.L.—P., 5.9.19. The suicides were taken as confessions. But Melanesian suicide was not necessarily an act of despair. It could be an act of righteous vengeance by an aggrieved party. See *Do Kamo*, pp. 88-94 (36-40).
27. M.L.—Bianquis, 27.2.18, 11.1.19, 11.5.19, S.M.E. Archives.

CHAPTER VII

1. Franz Leenhardt, *L'Activité créatrice, évolution, rédemption* (Paris, 1922).
2. M.L.—P., 4.6.12, 24.5.14; Jnl., 21.9.11.
3. M.L., "Témoignage," *Revue philosophique*, Centenaire de Lucien Lévy-Bruhl, no. 4, 1957, p. 414. See also M.L.'s Introduction to Lévy-Bruhl's *Carnets* (Paris, 1949).
4. M.L., "Témoignage."
5. Recounted by R. Delavignette, "Réception de M. le Pastuer Maurice Leenhardt," *Académie des Sciences Coloniales, compte rendus des séances*, 17 Dec. 1948, p. 782.
6. M.L., "La fête du pilou en Nouvelle-Calédonie," *L'Anthropologie*, 32 (1922), 221-63.
7. M.L.—Je., 1.11.22, Ngomo, Gabon.
8. M.L.—Je., 1.11.22, Gabon, mss., p. 95 reverse (R.H.L.).
9. M.L., *Etapes lumineuses, visite aux chantiers missionnaires* (Paris, 1928), p. 34.
10. M.L.—Je., 5.4.23 (R.D.-L.).
11. M.L.'s original text has apparently not survived. Its contents may be deduced from "Réponse aux notes de Maurice Leenhardt," typescript, 6 pp., by a Gabon missionary, probably Hermann or Cadier (S.M.E., Gabon, 1923). See also M.L.—Couve, 15.12.22 (S.M.E., N.Cal., 1923).
12. C. Hermann—Couve, 3.11.22 (S.M.E., Gabon, 1922).
13. H. Perrier—Couve, 30.11.22, *ibid.*
14. M.L.—Couve, 19.1.23, 15.12.22 (S.M.E., N. Cal., 1923); M.L.—Bianquis, 28.12.24 (S.M.E., N. Cal., 1924).
15. Letter from Pastor J.P. Burger to the author, 23 June 1977. (Burger was active in the Zambeze field from 1927-1960, serving as its president for a quarter-century. His detailed letter has been of great help in constructing the present all-too-superficial sketch.) M.L.'s official report is found in S.M.E. Archives, Zambeze, 1923.
16. Burger—Clifford, 23 June 1977; J. Bouchet—Directors, 15.4.23 (S.M.E., Zambeze, 1923); Couve—M.L., 23.2.24 (R.H.L.); *J.M.E.*, 1923 (II), pp. 299-300, 304.
17. "Rapport de Maurice Leenhardt sur la Mission du Zambèze, et la Question de sa Cession" (S.M.E., Zambeze, 1923).
18. See esp. M.L.—Couve, 7.10.23 (S.M.E., Zambeze, 1923); and M.L.—Couve, 23.6.25 (S.M.E., N. Cal., 1925).
19. Burger—Clifford; see M.L., "Sur une plage des Nouvelles Hébrides," *Propos*, Feb. 1940, which Burger states was for many years the best analysis of the field.

20. See a very strained letter, Couve—M.L., 23.2.24 (R.H.L.).

21. M.L.—Je., 10.4.23 (R.D.-L.).

22. Rusillon—Couve, 4.8.23 (R.H.L.).

23. M.L.—Je., 20.12.23, 21.12.23 (R.D.-L.).

24. M.L.—Je., 6.1.24.

25. P. Pasteur, "Rapport 1922" (S.M.E., N. Cal., 1922) describes his problems with the Do Neva schools; also M.L.—Bianquis, 18.2.23, 15.6.23 (S.M.E., N. Cal., 1923); M.L.—Je., 5.2.24 (R.D.-L.).

26. M.L.—Je., 5.1.24 (R.D.-L.).

27. H. Capt—Directors, no date, J.M.E., 1923 (II), pp. 259.

28. M.L.—Je., 14.1.24 (R.D.-L.).

29. M.L.—Je., Gabon.

30. See below, Chapter 13.

31. M.L.—Je., 17.2.24 (R.D.-L.).

32. M.L.—Je., 11.5.24 (R.D.-L.).

33. M.L.—Je., 15.3.24 (R.D.-L.); see also, M.L.—Allegret, 27.8.24 (S.M.E., N. Cal., 1924).

34. See above, Chapter 1, pp. 23-25; for M.L.'s developing views on the relation of the missionary to the native church, see *Propos*, April 1931, and further debate, June 1931; see also his series of articles on "La Condition missionnaire," *M.N.C.*, no. 24, 1952-53, pp. 448-63, no. 25, pp. 52-70, no. 26, pp. 160-72, and no. 65, 1963, pp. 9-38, on native pastors, *Propos*, Feb. 1940, pp. 6-10.

35. See above, Chapter 4, p. 68.

36. M.L.—"President de la Société des Missions Evangéliques," typescript, 52 pp., Dec. 1932, pp. 11, 12 (S.M.E., M.L. file, 1932); numerous letters on the "scandals," esp. M.L.—Bianquis, 28.12.24, H. Capt—Bianquis, n.d., Bergeret —Allegret, 10.6.24 (S.M.E., N. Cal., 1924), Bergeret—Couve, 29.8.27 (S.M.E., N. Cal., 1927).

37. Official report of the annual conference, N. Cal. and Loyalty, 1925 (S.M.E., N. Cal., 1925).

38. M.L.—"President. . . ," pp. 21-22; M.L.—Allegret, 8.9.26, 9.9.27, copies (R.H.L.).

39. M.L.'s ambition is asserted in Couve's marginalia, M.L.—Couve, 28.5.32 (S.M.E., M.L. file, 1932); intense defensiveness toward M.L. is manifested in the various reactions (letters and marginalia) by the directors to his protests of that year. The "family squabble" aspect of the affair, attested to by much current oral testimony, does not appear to have become dominant until 1932. On M.L.'s teaching plans see M.L.—Couve, 27.5.32 (S.M.E., M.L. file 1932); on the W. Africa (Togo) assignment see M.L.—Boegner and Mounier, 15.11.29, copy (R.H.L.).

40. Official report of the annual conference, N. Cal. Loyalty, 31 Oct. 1927 (S.M.E., N. Cal. 1927); *Rapport de M. Allegret sur son voyage en Océanie, juillet 1926-février 1928*, S.M.E. monograph, n.d.; M.L.—"President. . . ," pp. 21-25.

41. The clearest statements in the complex "pastor-teacher" debate are M.L.—"President. . ."; Rey-Lescure—Couve, 1.10.30 and a reply, Bergeret—

Couve, 2.12.30, E. Bergeret, "Note au sujet de la question des pasteurs-moniteurs," Rey-Lescure—Couve, 23.1.31, 25.2.31 (S.M.E., N. Cal., 1930, 1931).

42. M. Anker—Allegret, 19.1.32 (S.M.E., N. Cal., 1932), a restrained and informative report, admits to Loyalty suspicion of "the spirit of Do Neva." Rey-Lescure complains of this prejudice in R.-L.—Couve, 25.2.31; he is himself frequently accused of separatism in various letters, esp. by Bergeret and Seigneur.

43. From 1930 to 1933 the correspondence in the S.M.E. Archives becomes voluminous and personal. The most informative sources are the letters cited in note 41, above, the annual reports for the Missionary Conference, minutes of the Commission d'Océanie Française, 2.11.31, Bergeret—Allegret (letters from August to December 1932).

44. On the condition of Do Neva after the departure of Rey-Lescure, see Guiart, *Destin d'une église et d'un peuple, Nouvelle-Calédonie 1900-1959* (Paris, 1959), pp. 27-28; Guiart, "Naissance et avortement d'un messianisme," *Archives de sociologie des religions*, Jan.-June 1959, p. 23; M.L.—Marc Boegner, 24.9.38 (R.H.L.).

45. M.L.—"President. . ."; reactions may be seen in marginalia and Directors—President, 14.12.32; M.L.'s intentions, M.L.—President, 19.12.32 (S.M.E., M.L. file 1932); on scandal and family factions, "Notes rapportées de la conférence consultative de Paris, Jan. 23 1933, sur la situation générale de la direction," informal minutes of an acrimonious meeting with Couve and Allegret, by Messrs. Luidi, Lathure, Loux, H. Rey-Lescure, Perrier, H. Leenhardt (R.H.L.).

46. M.L.—"President. . . ," p. 48; Guiart, *Destin*, p. 18.

47. M.L.—"President. . . ," p. 25.

INTRODUCTION TO PART TWO

1. R.P. O'Reilly, *Calédoniens, répertoire bio-bibliographique de la Nouvelle-Calédonie* (Paris, 1953), pp. 6-7.

2. *Bulletin de la Société d'Anthropologie de Paris*, séance du 23 oct., 1879, p. 616.

3. For a sophisticated discussion of these issues, see K.O.L. Burridge, *Encountering Aborigines* (New York, 1973), ch. 1.

CHAPTER VIII

1. Maurice Merleau-Ponty, "Everywhere and and Nowhere," *Signs* (Evanston, Ill., 1964), p. 131.

2. M.L.—P., 29.1.14.

3. On Mindia's "word," see M.L., *Do Kamo*, pp. 195-200, 227 (114-18, 137).

4. M.L.—P., 31.10.03.

5. This attitude pervades the letters; see also, M.L., "La vieille Calédonie et le Musée de l'Homme," *Études mélanésiennes*, no. 1, Dec. 1938, pp. 11-16.

6. See J. Guiart, *Structure de la chefferie*, pp. 19-77. The lineage of the Néja clan collected by M.L. (and verified by Guiart) is printed on p. 25.

7. T.N. Pandey, "Anthropologists at Zuni," *Proceedings of the American Philosophical Society*, 116 (1972), 321-37.

8. R.H. Codrington, *The Melanesians* (New York, 1972), p. vii.

9. M.L.—P., 6.11.15.

10. M.L., "La Fête du pilou en Nouvelle-Calédonie," *L'Anthropologie*, 32 (1922), 263.

11. M.L., *Gens*, p. 170. Leenhardt's most complete description of the *pilou* is in *Notes*, pp. 143-78.

12. Michel Leiris, "Folklore et culture vivante," in R. Jaulin, ed., *Le livre blanc de l'ethnocide en Amerique* (Paris, 1973), pp. 357-75; see above, Chapter 5, pp. 86-87.

13. B. Malinowski, "Confessions of Ignorance and Failure," Appendix II, *Coral Gardens and Their Magic* (London, 1935), esp. pp. 479-81.

14. Malinowski's basic definitions are set out in *Magic Science and Religion and Other Essays*. On his pragmatic epistemology, see E.R. Leach in Firth, ed., *Man and Culture*; see also M. and R. Wax, "The Notion of Magic," *Current Anthropology*, 4 (Dec. 1963), 500, where Malinowski's distinctions are portrayed as products of Western rationalism. His over-assimilation of magic to instrumental proto-science is noted by S.J. Tambiah in a recent reassessment of the Trobriand data, "The Magical Power of Words," *Man*, 3, no. 2 (June 1968), 176; in a similar vein the "boundary problem" of separating "magic" from "religion" is discussed by Nadel, "Malinowski on Magic and Religion," *Man and Culture*, esp. pp. 199-205. Leenhardt's clearest statement on the overlap between magic and religion is found in "Sociologie religieuse," esp. pp. 770-71. On myth see esp. *Do Kamo*, p. 301 (189-90). His final, nuanced definition is found in "Sociologie religieuse," p. 772: "Tout ordre de geste ou de parole qui, en circonscrivant une réalité dont le langage rationnel ne peut rendre compte, impose à l'homme un comportement en rapport avec cette realité." Leenhardt was influenced by G. Van der Leeuw, "L'Homme primitif et la religion (Paris, 1940), p. 131: "Le mythe n'est donc pas une spéculation, si même la spéculation s'exprimait souvent sous forme mythique; il n'est pas un poème, si même il est souvent un poème aussi. Il est encore moins un produit de la fantaisie libre. Le mythe est une parole qui circonscrit et fixe un événement, et qui devient active ensuite par le fait qu'elle se répète et décide du présent. Un mythe sans activité ne vit plus; il peut être un récit charmant, il peut avoir un sens profond, mais comme mythe il est mort." For Leenhardt's views on Caledonian magic, see "La Religion des peuples archaïques actuels" (1937), Quillet, ed., *Histoire générale des religions* (Paris, 1948, 1960), pp. 53-56. See also *Notes*, pp. 259-60. Chapter 10, entitled "Magic," includes much that is properly religion. (In the late 1920s, when *Notes* was composed, M.L. was only beginning to elaborate his conception of *mythe vécu*. Particularly in the section "La Nature Magique," M.L. uses the term "magic" loosely to describe what he would soon see as *"mythe, mode de connaissance."*

15. M.L., *Do Kamo*, pp. 297-98 (187-188).

16. B. Malinowski, "Confessions," pp. 404-5.

17. See Annette B. Weiner, *Women of Value, Men of Renown, New Perspectives in*

Trobriand Exchange (Austin and London, 1976), *passim*; and Chapter 5, pp. 88-91, above.

18. Quoted by M. Fortes, "On the Concept of the Person among the Tallensi," in *La Notion de personne en Afrique Noire*, C.N.R.S., Paris, 1973, p. 284.

19. Helen Codere, "Introduction," Franz Boas, *Kwakiutl Ethnography* (Chicago, 1966), p. xv; Dell Hymes, "Some North Pacific coast poems," *American Anthropologist*, 67 (1965), 316-41; see also E. Evans-Pritchard, "Preface," *Man and Woman Among the Azande* (New York, 1974).

20. "Textualization," as used here, is a process by which unwritten behavior, beliefs, oral tradition, ritual action, and so forth become "fixed" (as something meant), "autonomized" (separated from a specific authorial intention), made "relevant" (to a contextual world), and "opened" (to interpretation by a competent public). Behavior so transformed becomes susceptible to "reading," a process no longer dependent on interlocution with a present subject. These terms are proposed by Paul Ricoeur, "The Model of the Text: Meaningful Action Considered as a Text," *Social Research*, 38 (1971), 529-62.

21. From notes taken at a course in 1935-1936, Mauss Archives, Musée de l'Homme, kindly provided by C. Rugafiori.

22. This account of the three volumes as a whole, centered on the *Documents*, is based on M.L.'s own description contained in an extensive *curriculum vitae* prepared around 1950 (R.H.L.). For a helpful discussion of the trilogy, see P. Métais, "L'Oeuvre ethnologique et sociologique de Maurice Leenhardt," *Journal de la Société des Océanistes*, Dec. 1955, pp. 51-69.

23. M.L., *Documents*, pp. 334-36; *Do Kamo*, pp. 255-57 (158-59).

24. Clifford Geertz, *The Interpretation of Cultures* (New York, 1973), ch. 1. On page 19 Geertz discusses ethnography as the "inscription" of social discourse, the means by which (following Ricoeur) an event becomes an interpretable "text." But if, as Geertz implies in his famous analysis of a Balinese cockfight (p. 450), culture is always already interpreted, one may extrapolate that it is also already inscribed. (A ritual occasion is already a "text"? How does the phrase "oral literature" manage to mean anything?) In this perspective, ethnography is less a process of inscription, the passage of an oral event into textuality, than a procedure of *transcription*, of "writing over."

25. An important exception is Joseph Casagrande, ed., *In the Company of Men: Twenty Portraits of Anthropological Informants* (New York, 1960), though it is significant that these portraits found their place in a separate, "popular" collection rather than in the ethnographies made possible by these informants. A book that goes farther in implicitly questioning ethnographic authority is Marcel Griaule's *Conversations with Ogotemmêli* (Oxford, 1965). For an excellent recent example of a frankly co-authored book, see Ian Saem Majnep and Ralph Bulmer, *Mnmon yad Kalam yakt: Birds of my Kalam Country* (Auckland, 1977).

26. See R.H. Leenhardt, "Un Sociologue Canaque: le pasteur Boesoou Erijisi, 1866-1947," *Cahiers d'histoire du Pacifique*, 4 (1976), 19-53.

27. Personal communication; on the quality of M.L.'s informants as independent researchers, see Guiart, *Structure de la chefferie*, Introduction; see also Boesoou's critical insight into the process of individuation, discussed in Chapter 11, below.

28. M.L.—P., 3.4.15; M.L., *La Grande Terre* (Paris, 1922), p. 111.

29. J. Guiart, writing self-consciously in a Leenhardtian tradition of research in New Caledonia, has made some of these points in a polemical *prise de position*: "L'ethnologue et l'Océanien," *Journal de la Société des Océanistes*, 32 (1976), 267-69.

30. On this "full stop," see Vincent Crapanzano, "The Writing of Ethnography," *Dialectical Anthropology*, 2 (1977), 69-73.

CHAPTER IX

1. M.L.—Je., 30.5.24 (R.D.-L.).

2. One of the young people Leenhardt inspired at the C.M.J. summer camps was Jean Guiart, later to become a distinguished Oceanist; see his Introduction to *Structure de la chefferie en Mélanésie du sud* (Paris, 1963), p. 13.

3. *Propos*, 30 June 1927, p. 6.

4. *Propos*, April 1931, p. 78.

5. *Ibid.*

6. See Jean Poirier, "Maurice Leenhardt, océaniste et sociologue," *M.N.C.*, Jan.-March 1955, p. 80.

7. M.L. (Jean Caro), "Le Naturaliste et la légende," circa 1930, typescript (R.H.L.). M.L.'s contributions to the *Dépêche coloniale et maritime* span the years 1928-1933.

8. M.L., "L'âme créatrice des canaques" and "Beauté des jardins d'Océanie," *Dépêche*, 3 and 28 July 1932.

9. *Propos*, 15 August 1927, p. 7.

10. See M.L., *Do Kamo*, p. 114 (55).

11. See above, Chapter 7; p. 114.

12. Recounted by R.-H. Leenhardt at J.L.'s funeral service: Paris, 19 Nov. 1970, extracts mimeographed (R.H.L.), p. 3.

13. On Lévy-Bruhl's respect for fieldwork, see his exchange with Evans-Pritchard, *Revue philosophique*, Centenaire de Lucien Lévy-Bruhl, no. 4, 1957.

14. See Mauss, *Oeuvres* (Paris, 1968-1969), 1:491; on his interest in field techniques, *ibid*, p. 354; also G. Condominas, "Marcel Mauss et l'homme de terrain," *L'Arc*, no. 48, 1972.

15. Mauss, *Revue de Paris*, no. 20, 1913, pp. 815-37.

16. Lévi-Strauss, "Introduction à l'oeuvre de Marcel Mauss," Mauss, *Sociologie et anthropologie* (Paris, 1950).

17. M.L., "Marcel Mauss," *Annuaire*, E.P.H.E., 5e section, 1950-1951, pp. 19-23.

18. M.L.—President E.P.H.E., 1949 (R.H.L.).

19. *Sociologie et anthropologie*, pp. 333-62.

20. M.L., "Marcel Mauss," p. 19.

21. See Steven Lukes, *Emile Durkheim* (London, 1973), pp. 327-28; G. Condominas, "Marcel Mauss, père de l'ethnographie française," *Critique*, Feb. 1972, pp. 123-24.

22. M.L., "Marcel Mauss," p. 22.

23. Mauss, "Les techniques du corps," *Sociologie et anthropologie*, pp. 365-86; M.L., "L'Expression chez les primitifs," *L'Équipe*, March 1946.

24. Mauss, "Techniques," p. 368.

25. *Annuaire*, E.P.H.E., 1932-1933, 1933-1934.

26. E. Gilson, "Le Descartes de Lucien Lévy-Bruhl," *Revue philosophique*, no. 4, 1957, p. 433.

27. Poirier, "Maurice Leenhardt," p. 87.

28. *Ibid.*, p. 80.

29. Personal communication from Michel Leiris.

CHAPTER X

1. M.L., *Gens*, edition of 1952; see esp. the 1937 preface and conclusion, pp. 7 and 211.

2. For an account of Leenhardt's initial attempt to visit the performers, see R. Dousset, *Colonialisme et contradictions* (Paris, 1970), p. 16.

3. Published in *Travaux et mémoires de l'Institut d'Ethnologie*, vol. 46 (Paris, 1946).

4. This version departs somewhat from Leenhardt's French in an attempt to reproduce something of the song's repetitions and rhythm. Also, I am guessing at an interpretation: the taro shoot is associated with the child, and the *rocher*, perhaps a boulder or outcropping on a mountain, is certainly an ancestor. The uprooted child seems to be comforted finally by the *parole* of the clan, which, Orphic, evokes a reply from the mythic landscape; the world that had become soundless, motionless, without relationship, is brought back to life. M.L., *Langues et dialectes*, p. 180.

5. *Ibid.*, p. vii.

6. *Langues et dialectes*, pp. x-xiii; on the dangers of questionnaires see also M.L., "Sociologie religieuse."

7. Je.—children, 28.1.39 (R.H.L.).

8. Letter addressed to the Missionary Conference of New Caledonia, 7 May 1938; signed by Couve, Schloessing, and Paul Bernaud, original (R.H.L.). In fact, Leenhardt's stay on the Grande Terre was clouded by further recriminations and accusations of meddling associated with an ill-timed request by Rey-Lescure for reassignment to his old post.

9. J. Guiart, "Naissance et avortement d'un messianisme," *Archives de sociologie des religions*, Jan.-June 1959, pp. 3-44.

10. See M.L., *Notes*, pp. 247-49.

11. On the *doki* ("*toki*"), see E. Métais, *La Sorcellerie canaque actuelle* (Bordeaux, 1967), *passim*. On antisorcery divines, see her ch. 5.

12. M.L., *Vocabulaire*, p. 49; *Notes*, p. 238.

13. Je.—children, 28.1.39 (R.H.L.).

14. Je.—children, 1.2.39 (R.H.L.).

15. Guiart, "Naissance," p. 20.

16. *Notes*, p. 241.

17. Je.—Children, 4.2.39 (R.H.L.).

18. Guiart, "Naissance," p. 44.

19. Waia Gorode, *Les souvenirs d'un Néo-Calédonien ami de Maurice Leenhardt* (Paris, 1976), 66 pp., privately printed by R.H. Leenhardt, esp. pp. 57-58. Gorode's father was a pastor trained at Do Neva. His testimony is remarkable for its poetry and for the Messianic cast of its view of the Leenhardts.

20. M.L., "La Vieille Calédonie et le Musée de l'Homme," *Études mélanésiennes*, Noumea, no. 1, Dec. 1938, p. 14.

21. The following account of the Gondé meeting is drawn from M.L., "Lettre aux Pasteurs de Nouvelle-Calédonie, 10 octobre, 1939," *M.N.C.*, Oct.-Dec. 1963 (36 pp.), translated from the Houailou by R.-H. Leenhardt.

CHAPTER XI

1. M.L., *Do Kamo*, p. 263 (164). "Esprit" is here translated "spirit" because the context is religious. It could be rendered "mind," in opposition to "body" (in a European definition); for mythic "spirits," according to Leenhardt, constitute a valid "mode of knowledge."

2. *Ibid.*, "Introduction." For M.L.'s overview of religious evolution see "La Religion" and "Quelques éléments." On "cosmomorphism" see: "Totem et Identification," *Revue de l'histoire des religions*, Jan.-June 1944, pp. 5-17; *Do Kamo*, ch. 5; "Quelques éléments," pp. 88-90.

3. Lévi-Strauss, *Totemism* (Boston, 1963), p. 104.

4. The following five paragraphs are largely based on M.L., "Quelques éléments," pp. 88-100.

5. M.L., *Do Kamo*, p. 68 (21).

6. See esp. M.L., *Do Kamo*, ch. 5.

7. See below, Chapter 13.

8. M.L., *Do Kamo*, p. 134 (69-70).

9. Lévi-Strauss, *Totemism*, ch. 1; *The Savage Mind* (London, 1966), ch. 1.

10. Lévi-Strauss, *Totemism*, p. 71.

11. See, for example, Georges Gusdorf, "Situation de Maurice Leenhardt: ou l'ethnologie française de Lévy-Bruhl en Lévi-Strauss," *M.N.C.*, July-Dec. 1964, pp. 139-92.

12. J. Guiart, "Maurice Leenhardt entre deux mondes," *M.N.C.*, July-Dec. 1964, p. 195.

13. R. Bastide, "La Pensée obscure et confuse," *M.N.C.*, July-Dec. 1965, pp. 137-56.

14. This standpoint is best seen in M.L., "Sociologie religieuse."

15. M.L., *Do Kamo*, p. 130 (67).

16. M.L., *Notes*, pp. 179-212.

17. Bastide, "Pensée obscure," p. 150.

18. *Ibid.*

19. *La Sorcellerie canaque actuelle* (Bordeaux, 1967), p. 43.

20. *Ibid.*

21. M.L., *Do Kamo*, pp. 126-34 (64-70).

22. By the "Ouverture" to *Le Cru et le cuit* (Paris, 1964), Lévi-Strauss no longer accords a causal privilege to mental structures derived from those of

structural linguistics. Mythic thinking cannot be reduced to a code or system, but is presented as an open-ended process of interpretation or trans-coding. Lévi-Strauss seems to have abandoned his more reductionist prescriptions of *Structural Anthropology* (1958) and *Totemism* (1962). This development is, of course, part of a general evolution in the recent history of structuralism and semiology. A similar path may be observed in the career of Roland Barthes, who entertained a certain dream of structuralist scientificity [his *Elements of Semiology* (1962) can be conveniently paired with *Totemism*], but who by the late 1960s had moved into a clearly "post-structuralist" phase in which the closure of semiotic systems modeled on Saussurian "*langue*" was thrown in doubt.

23. Lévi-Strauss, *The Raw and the Cooked* (New York, 1969), p. 2; M.L., *Do Kamo*, p. 43 (2-3).

24. M.L., "La Religion," p. 64; Lévi-Strauss, *The Raw and the Cooked*, p. 11.

25. In the "Overture" to *The Raw and the Cooked*, Lévi-Strauss writes: "Since it has no interest in definite beginnings or endings, mythological thought never develops any theme to completion: there is always something left unfinished. Myths, like rites, are 'in-terminable.' And in seeking to imitate the spontaneous movement of mythological thought, this essay, which is both too brief and too long, has had to conform to the requirements of that thought and to respect its rhythm. It follows that this book on myths is itself a kind of myth" (p. 6). Roland Barthes goes farther in his *Fragments d'un discours amoureux* (1977). There, his emphasis on gestural "figures" recalls Leenhardt's notion of an esthetic mode of apprehension operating by pure juxtaposition in the creation of affective, mythic occasions. The *pensée obscure et confuse* that Barthes imitates in the form of his writing is introduced thus: "Throughout any love life, figures occur to the lover without any order, for on each occasion they depend on an (internal or external) accident. . . . No logic links the figures, determines their contiguity: the figures are non-syntagmatic, non-narrative; they are Erinyes; they stir, collide, subside, return, vanish with no more order than a flight of mosquitoes." Barthes, *A Lover's Discourse, Fragments* (New York, 1978), p. 6.

26. M.L., "Quelques éléments," pp. 100-101.

27. M.L., *Do Kamo*, pp. 183-84 (105-6); on ritual evolution see pp. 146-48 (79-81).

28. M.L., "Le Temps," p. 84; *Do Kamo*, ch. 6; p. 160 (89).

29. M.L., "Le Temps," p. 86; *Documents*, pp. 334-46.

30. M.L., *Notes*, pp. 56-105; summary statements, occasionally with original formulations: *Gens*, pp. 131-52; "Le Temps," pp. 88-89; "La Personne," pp. 95-96; *Do Kamo*, chs. 7 and 11. Leenhardt's "relational" model of social life has yet to be adequately assessed by anthropologists. See, however, J. Guiart, *Structure de la chefferie en Mélanésie du sud*, an extension and criticism of Leenhardt's work; also Guiart, "M.L. entre deux modes," esp. pp. 195-96.

31. M.L., "La Personne"; in somewhat shortened form, this essay appears as chapter 11 of *Do Kamo*.

32. M.L., "La Personne," pp. 93, 100, 101.

33. *Ibid.*, pp. 88-89, *Do Kamo*, pp. 182-83 (104-6). See Rodney Needham's important critique of the category of "kinship": *Remarks and Inventions* (London,

1974), esp. ch. 1. In this context, Leenhardt's suspicion of system—his portrayal of alliance and descent as categories constantly spilling over into religion, cosmology, ecology, and a wide range of collective activities—takes on a new significance. For a recent statement along these lines and with respect to Melanesia, see Annette Weiner, *Women of Value, Men of Renown* (Austin, 1976), pp. 243-44. She cites A.I. Hallowell, whose work is close to Leenhardt's in general orientation: *Culture and Experience* (Philadelphia, 1954); in this context it is also worth mentioning Godfrey Lienhardt's *Divinity and Experience* (Oxford, 1961).

34. M.L., *Do Kamo*, pp. 248-51 (153-55).

35. K.O.L. Burridge, "Missionary Occasions"; Boutilier, ed., *Mission, Church, and Sect in Oceania* (Ann Arbor, 1978), p. 15.

36. Jacques Lacan, "Réponse aux interventions: Actes du Congrès de Rome," *La Psychanalyse*, 1 (1956), 246. See also Lacan, *The Language of the Self* (New York, 1968), including commentaries by Anthony Wilden, pp. 80, 168, 181-82, 188.

37. R. Barthes, *Roland Barthes* (New York, 1977), pp. 129-30.

38. M.L., "La Religion," p. 70.

39. Leenhardt does not cite Heidegger, and it is unclear how much of his work Leenhardt had read. But he became familiar with the philosopher's ideas and vocabulary through regular, intense conversations with his son-in-law, the great Islamic scholar, phenomenologist, and translator of Heidegger, Henry Corbin. For an interesting, though fragmentary, discussion of the Heideggerian problematic in relation to Leenhardt's and especially Lacan's concern with the "authentic" subject, see Anthony Wilden, "Lacan and the Discourse of the Other," in Lacan, *The Language of the Self*, pp. 177-83. Leenhardt's conception of spatio-mythic habitat rhymes with Heidegger's vision of human "dwelling." See M. Heidegger, "Building, Dwelling, Thinking," *Poetry, Language, Thought* (New York, 1971), pp. 145-61.

40. M.L., "La Personne," p. 103; M. Mauss, "Une catégorie de l'esprit humain, la notion de personne, celle du 'moi'" (1938), *Anthropologie et sociologie* (Paris, 1950), p. 362.

41. Much of Africa, M.L. thought, was lodged in this impasse: see "La Religion," p. 79; *Structure*, pp. 66-67.

42. M.L., "La Personne," pp. 118-19; *Do Kamo*, pp. 270-71 (168-69).

43. *Ibid.*, and *Do Kamo*, ch. 12.

CHAPTER XII

1. His most extended comparative effort is found in "La Religion."

2. The lectures were entitled "Formes mythiques de la vie des Mélanésiens," Conférences Loubat, Collège de France, 1942.

3. I am, of course, speaking in general terms. The missionary and imperial endeavors have not always gone hand in hand. Nonetheless, the years marked off by M.L.'s lifetime may be seen as a distinct period of particularly close and potent collaboration between Western evangelical, educational, cultural, politi-

cal, and economic influences, all engaged in a project of world domination previously unprecedented and now significantly contested.

4. See O'Reilly, *Pèlerin du ciel* (Paris, 1952), ch. 10; Thompson and Adloff, *The French Pacific Islands* (Berkeley, 1971), chs. 21 and 22; and O'Reilly, *Calédoniens*, p. 157.

5. O'Reilly, *Calédoniens*, p. 49; Guiart, *Destin d'une église*, provides a partisan account of Raymond Charlemagne's eventual break with the Société des Missions Evangéliques, portraying it as a continuation of M.L.'s earlier struggles.

6. My account of these events is incomplete, but, I believe, essentially accurate. It is based on interviews; on the published account of Pierre Routhier, "Souvenirs sur Maurice Leenhardt, Premier Directeur de l'Institut Française d'Océanie," *M.N.C.*, Jan.-March 1955, pp. 113-20; and on documentary evidence in R.H.L., Dossier 43, including official correspondence.

7. R.H.L., Dossier 43; Combes to Governor of New Caledonia, 30 Aug. 1947.

8. R.H.L., Dossier 43, M.L. to [?], typescript; the context suggests that it is addressed to a high official in the Colonial Office, 10 Aug. 1946.

9. R.H.L., Dossier 43; M.L. to Soustelle, 14 June 1948; Routhier, "Souvenirs," p. 115.

10. R.H.L., Dossier 43; typescript, "Le Gr de NC a Mr Le Ministre de la France d'Outre-mer," dated "Nouméa, 28 février, 1948."

11. Routhier, "Souvenirs," pp. 114-15.

12. *Ibid.*, p. 116; R.H.L., Dossier 43; Jeanne Leenhardt to Raymond Leenhardt, no date.

13. Routhier, "Souvenirs," pp. 117, 119-20.

14. *Ibid.* Routhier underlines M.L.'s capacity for combining the perspective of an ethnologist with that of a naturalist.

15. Waia Gorode, *Les Souvenirs d'un Néo-Calédonien ami de Maurice Leenhardt* (Paris, 1976), pp. 63-66.

16. Académie des Sciences Colonjales, *Comptes rendus des séances*, séance du 17 décembre 1948, "Réception de M. le Pasteur Maurice Leenhardt," pp. 784-95. On M.L.'s views of the I.F.O., see also *Journal de la Société des Océanistes*, Dec. 1949, pp. 5-14; *Gens*, p. 223; "Institut Français d'Océanie et développement culturel de l'Océanie française," *Encyclopédie coloniale et maritime française*, Paris, Oct. 1950, 1:49-51.

17. "Réception," pp. 793-94.

18. Personal communication from J. Guiart.

19. M. Leiris, "L'ethnographe devant le colonialisme," a lecture, first published in *Les Temps modernes*, 6th year, 58 (1950); also, Leiris, *Cinq Études d'Ethnologie* (Paris, 1969); *Brisées* (Paris, 1966), pp. 125-45.

20. See, for example, M.L., "A Propos d'un centenaire: La Nouvelle Calédonie," *M.N.C.*, July-Sept. 1953, pp. 233-43.

21. "Réception," pp. 786, 792.

22. "L'ethnographe devant le colonialisme." For a further, incisive elaboration of Leiris's perspective, see "Folklore et culture vivante," in R. Jaulin, ed., *Le Livre blanc de l'ethnocide en Amérique* (Paris, 1973), pp. 357-75.

23. M.L., *Gens*, p. 210; "Deuxième Avant-Propos," p. 8.

24. *Ibid.*, pp. 221-23.

25. *Ibid.*, p. 8; for another strong statement of this position, see M.L. in *Journal de la Société des Océanistes*, 6 (1950): 258-59.

CHAPTER XIII

1. M.L., "Préface," Lévy-Bruhl, *Les Carnets de Lucien Lévy-Bruhl* (Paris, 1949), p. v; English translation by P. Rivière, *Notebooks on Primitive Mentality* (New York, 1975), p. xi. I have altered the translation here, as elsewhere, to bring it into agreement with stylistic decisions I have made in rendering M.L.'s thought.

2. See Rodney Needham, *Belief, Language and Experience* (Oxford, 1972), esp. ch. 9; also Jean Duvignaud, *Le Langage perdu* (Paris, 1973), ch. 3.

3. It has already been suggested that Leenhardt's thinking needed Lévy-Bruhl's in order to develop, for it could not comfortably take shape in the molds provided by the École Sociologique or functionalism. In any event, Leenhardt's criticism of Lévy-Bruhl took place through conversation, not polemic. A fruitful dialog requires initial acceptance of the other's presuppositions and vocabulary. Thus, when he was beginning to theorize, Leenhardt made use of Lévy-Bruhl's terminology. And in the *Carnets* we sometimes come upon the paradoxical situation of the philosopher criticizing Leenhardt for being too Lévy-Bruhlian. Thus Leenhardt's casual use of the term "prelogical" and his assertion that "contradiction" is absent in mythic consciousness seem unfortunate to Lévy-Bruhl, who is in the process of definitively abandoning the former term and replacing the latter with the less absolute notion of "incompatibility." (*Carnets*, p. 73; *Notebooks*, p. 57.) That Leenhardt was in no sense a vulgar Lévy-Bruhlian will be apparent in what follows; however, his writings are sprinkled with language drawn from the philosopher's early works.

4. M.L., "Le Mythe," unpublished typescript, reconstituted by Raymond Leenhardt, dating from 1953, p. 8 (R.H.L.). [Lévy-Bruhl cites this objection in *Carnets*, pp. 137, 220 (*Notebooks*, pp. 105, 168).]

5. See Lévy-Bruhl's late clarification of the term "mystical" in *L'Expérience mystique et les symboles chez les primitifs* (Paris, 1938), p. 3; M.L., "Préface," pp. xiii-xiv (*Notebooks*, p. xviii).

6. M.L., "Le Mythe," p. 8.

7. M.L., "Le Mythe," p. 9.

8. Gunnar Landtman, *The Folk-Tales of the Kiwi Papuans* (Helsingfors, 1917), Acta Societati Scientarum Fennicae, 47:495.

9. Lévy-Bruhl, *La Mythologie primitive* (Paris, 1935), pp. 232-36.

10. Lévy-Bruhl, *Carnets*, pp. xii-xiii (*Notebooks*, p. xvii; translation altered).

11. M.L., "La Religion," p. 58.

12. *Ibid.*

13. *Ibid.*, p. 64.

14. Lévy-Bruhl, *Carnets*, p. 74 (*Notebooks*, p. 58; translation altered), original emphasis.

15. *Ibid.*, p. 75 (*Notebooks*, p. 59; translation altered slightly).

16. *Ibid.*, pp. 250-51 (*Notebooks*, p. 192; altered), original emphasis.

17. *Ibid.*, p. xiii (*Notebooks*, p. xviii; altered).

18. *Ibid.*, p. xiv (*Notebooks*, p. xviii).

19. *Ibid.*, p. 252 (*Notebooks*, p. 194). In this context see Duvignaud's comparison of Lévy-Bruhl's struggle (with the language of the Other) to Freud's; in *Le Langage perdu*, pp. 123-27.

20. M.L., "La Religion," p. 58.

21. M.L., "Danses mélanésiennes," *Tropiques, revue des troupes coloniales*, no. 337, Dec. 1951, p. 73.

22. M.L.—Je., 1.11.23 (R.H.L.).

23. Leenhardt's writings on esthetics are scattered. See *Arts de l'Océanie* (Paris, 1948), translated as *Arts of the Oceanic Peoples* (London, 1950); *Gens*, pp. 97-120; *Notes*, ch. 1; *Structure*, p. 113; *Annuaire E.P.H.E.*, 5ᵉ section, 1945-1946; 1946-1947, pp. 23-26; also 1949-1950.

24. M.L., "Cours d'esthéque," lecture notes, dated 13.1.45, typescript (R.H.L.), p. 3. (Leenhardt's unpublished lecture notes contain much suggestive material. But their interpretation is risky, and I have based my discussion on publications wherever possible.)

25. The term "prior" has two possible meanings: first, in phenomenological reduction, perception is "prior" to cognition; second, evolutionarily, esthetics (cosmomorphic) is "prior" to myth (*mode de connaissance*). Leenhardt argues for both senses at times—inconsistently, and without positing rigid developmental stages.

26. M.L., *langues et dialectes*, p. xxxvii; also p. xxxix; and *Do Kamo*, p. 60 (15).

27. A paragraph from Landtman's introduction seems to confirm some of Leenhardt's ideas on the relation of "lived myth" to myth as narrative:

> One singularity common to many of my informants was their disposition at the beginning of a story to so to speak fumble about with the subject for a good while before coming to the plot. It sometimes happened, that when they began a story they compressed the whole argument into a few broken sentences, absolutely unintelligible, if the legend was not familiar to one before. In other cases the same uncertainty expressed itself in a long drawn-out introduction which for instance included a description of the people engaged in their everyday occupations, first in the home, and then in the plantations over and over again, till at length the action began. Once however the story was properly started it was pursued with good observance to coherency. Repetitions came about often, when certain episodes reoccurred in the same tale, and all the details were delineated each time with the same fullness.

Folk-Tales of the Kiwi-Papuans, p. 2. Getting into the mood of the story seems to require entering the space-time of the occurrence. This act involves refamiliarizing oneself with the smallest details of the setting. The narration appears to be nonlinear, dealing in juxtaposed events, and thus there is little idea of repetition. The beginning, in which a few broken sentences are juxtaposed prior to their elaboration and separation in narrative, gives a sense of the translation involved in moving from an experience of the myth as a rapid ensemble of feelings/events to the much different experience of storytelling. Landtman's evidence seems to confirm Leenhardt's belief that Melanesian myth exists primarily in localized experience and only secondarily as formulated narrative.

28. M.L., *Arts de l'Océanie*, esp. pp. 139-40.

29. Gaston Bachelard, *The Poetics of Space* (Boston, 1964), pp. xv-xvi.

30. M.L., *Do Kamo*, chs. 9 and 10; see also "Ethnologie de la parole," *Cahiers internationaux de sociologie* (1946), 2:82-105 (includes some points not in the fuller *Do Kamo* version).

31. *Do Kamo*, p. 238 (138). In my translation, I have not followed the English edition in rendering *parole* uniformly as "word" and *verbe* as "Word." In the present context the status of *parole* as "speech" is centrally at issue.

32. *Ibid.*, p. 232 (141). My translation.

33. Paul Valéry, "Première leçon du cours de poétique," 1937, *Oeuvres complètes* (Paris, 1957), pp. 1340-58.

34. *Do Kamo*, pp. 218, 219, 221 (131, 132, 133), translation slightly altered.

35. *Ibid.*, pp. 221-31 (133-40).

36. *Ibid.*, pp. 222-26, 235-43, 246 (134-36, 143-49, 151-52).

37. *Ibid.*, p. 235 (143). M.L. undertakes no systematic discussion of the Saussurian distinctions between *"parole," "langue,"* and *"langage."* His general attitude follows that expressed by Merleau-Ponty in 1951: a "return to speech." [Corporeal, situational, gestural—see "On the Phenomenology of Language," *Signs* (Evanston, 1964), pp. 84-97.] Leenhardt attempts to absorb much of *"langue"* into his expanded *"Parole." "Langage,"* the trans-cultural human capacity for speech, does not concern him. Leenhardt's general ethnographic approach to language, based on native categories, is more fully developed in G. Calame-Griaule, *Ethnologie et langage, la parole chez les Dogon* (Paris, 1965), a phenomenological elaboration of the Dogon term *sò*, a category similar to the Houailou *nō*.

38. *Do Kamo*, pp. 231-32 (140-41), translation altered.

39. *Ibid.*, p. 235 (143); also M.L., "L'Expression chez les primitifs," *L'Équipe*, 1946.

40. M.L., "In Memoriam, Gerardus Van der Leeuw," *Revue d'histoire et de philosophie religieuses*, 1951, no. 4, p. 498.

CHAPTER XIV

1. M.L., *Do Kamo*, p. 271.

2. "Sculpte ton masque," "Pourquoi se vêtir?", *Amour de l'Art*, nos. 49-51 (1951), pp. 53-58; nos. 58-60 (1952), pp. 3-14; "Langues Mélanésiennes," A. Meillet and M. Cohen, eds., *Les Langues du monde* (Paris, 1952), pp. 675-90; "Quelques éléments"; "Danses Mélanésiennes," *Tropiques, revue des troupes coloniales*, Dec. 1955, pp. 73-82; *Gens*, 1952, new Preface and Conclusion;" "Sociologie religieuse"; "La Condition missionnaire," *M.N.C.*, no. 24 (1952), pp. 448-63; no.

25 (1953), pp. 52-70; no. 26, pp. 160-72; "Kapéa (rêves et dessins d'un indigène de Nouvelle-Calédonie)," *M.N.C.*, no. 25 (1953), pp. 52-70.

3. On Leenhardt's affinity with Bachelard, see E. Métais, *La Sorcellerie canaque actuelle* (Bordeaux, 1967); her footnotes, which quote extensively from the two thinkers, form a sort of dialog. On Leenhardt's strong, but *laisser faire*, influence on Jean Guiart, see the latter's *Structure de la chefferie en Mélanésie*, Introduction.

4. M.L., "Travail apostolique et Alliance Evangélique Universelle," *M.N.C.*, Jan.-Mar. 1952, pp. 14-29.

5. M.L., "Mission structure de l'église," *M.N.C.*, Dec. 1947, pp. 406-25; see above, Chapter 11, p. 186.

6. M.L.—Soustelle, 22 Nov. 1947, copy (R.H.L., Dossier 43).

7. M.L., "In Memoriam, Gerardus Van der Leeuw," *Revue d'histoire et de philosophie religieuses*, no. 4 (1951), p. 498.

8. M.L., "Quelques éléments," p. 108.

9. *Ibid.*, p. 109.

10. See, for example, the article on "Religion" by Clifford Geertz in the *International Encyclopedia of the Social Sciences* (1968, vol. 13), which, after reviewing a variety of approaches to religious phenomena, concludes that religion is an explication of the cosmos and of daily life, overdetermined, and not yet susceptible to integrated theoretical explanation.

11. M.L., "Sociologie religieuse," p. 770.

12. It may clarify Leenhardt's point of view to juxtapose a recent definition, taken almost at random from the ethnohistorical literature on African religions:

> Religion, as we define it, is a system of symbols, beliefs, myths and rites experienced as profoundly significant or serious, primarily because it provides individuals, groups and societies with an orientation toward ultimate conditions of existence.

(W. De Craemer, J. Vansina, R. Fox, "Religious Movements in Central Africa," *Comparative Studies in Society and History*, 18 [1976], 459.) The collective, cosmological emphasis brings out aspects of religious experience neglected in Leenhardt's initial definitions—though not in his practical questionnaire. The cited definition is characteristic of a great many modern approaches. It is open to a number of "Leenhardtian" criticisms. The statement, typically, slides almost at once from a definition into an explanation. And with this definition it would be hard to distinguish religion from philosophy—an appropriate confusion in the case of archaic thought but more problematic in modern experience. It should, moreover, be possible for a person to experience religious realities without being particularly concerned with "ultimate conditions of existence." Elementary feelings of transcendence, with which Leenhardt begins, are here flattened into an experience of the "profoundly significant or serious." This formula is a survival of the Durkheimian notion of the "sacred," a transpersonal category that Leenhardt criticized on more than one occasion as being too generalized and ambiguous to do justice to what was properly religious. See M.L., "Sociologie religieuse," p. 770, fn.; *Annuaire*, E.P.H.E., 5ᵉ section, 1950-

1951, Course in the History of Religions, p. 29; *Do Kamo*, p. 237 (145); "La Religion," p. 64.

13. M.L., "Sociologie religieuse," p. 772.

14. See M.L., *Annuaire*, 1950-1951, p. 27.

15. See M.L.'s statement of this difficulty, "Sociologie religieuse," p. 768.

16. It may be objected that phenomenological perspectives themselves are infected by Judeo-Christian individualism connected with monotheism. In response, it is at least arguable that all cultures possess some category of personhood, however this locus of participations and symbolic functions may be defined. Certainly the concept of personhood as a primary reality is not limited to Christianity; see *La Notion de personne en Afrique noire* (Paris, 1973), C.N.R.S. colloquium.

AFTERWORD

1. Testimony of the Grand Chef Mus, Moméa tribe, Moindou District, 21 June 1978, *Centenaire Leenhardt, 1878-1954* (Noumea, 1978), pp. 39-41.

Bibliography of Works
By and About Maurice Leenhardt

THE PRINCIPAL PUBLICATIONS OF MAURICE LEENHARDT

Le mouvement éthiopien au Sud de l'Afrique, de 1896 à 1899. Cahors, 1902; reprinted, Académie des Sciences d'Outre-Mer, Paris, 1976.

"Correspondance missionnaire," *Journal des Missions évangéliques de Paris*: numerous letters and reports from M.L. in New Caledonia, from 1903, vol. 78 (I), pp. 130-34 until 1920 (II), pp. 346-53.

La Grande Terre. Société des Missions évangéliques, Paris, 1909.

"Note sur la fabrication des marmites canaques en Nouvelle-Calédonie," *Bulletins et mémoires de la Société d'Anthropologie de Paris*, Paris, 17 June 1909, pp. 268-70.

"Percuteurs et haches de Nouvelle-Calédonie," *ibid.*, 1 July 1909, pp. 270-72.

"Note sur quelques pierres-figures rapportées de Nouvelle-Calédonie," *Revue de l'École d'Anthropologie*, Paris, 19th year, vols. 8-9, August 1909, pp. 292-95, ill.

"Discours prononcé au culte d'Actions de Grâces à l'occasion de la Victoire dans le temple de Nouméa, le 1er décembre 1918," Nouméa, 1918.

"Calédonie et Loyalty," Paris, Société des Missions évangéliques, 1921.

"Expériences sociales en terre canaque," *Christianisme social*, Paris, no. 9, October-November 1921, pp. 96-114. (Republished, *M.N.C.*, no. 66, 1963.)

Peci arü, Vikibo ka dovo i Iesu Keriso, e pugewe ro verea sce Ajie. Paris, 1922. (Translation of the New Testament into Houailou.)

La Grande Terre, mission de la Nouvelle-Calédonie. Revised and expanded edition, Paris, Société des Missions évangéliques, 1922.

Le catéchumène canaque. Paris, Société des Missions évangéliques, 1922, *Les cahiers missionnaires*, no. 1.

De la mort à la vie, L'Evangile en Nouvelle-Calédonie. Paris, Société des Missions évangéliques, 1922, *Les cahiers missionnaires*, no. 3.

NOTE: For select bibliographies on New Caledonian ethnography and history, see Chapter 2, n. 4 and Chapter 3, n. 6.

"Notes sur la traduction du Nouveau Testament en langue primitive," *Revue d'histoire et de philosophie religieuse*, Strasbourg, May-June 1922, pp. 193-218.

"La monnaie néo-calédonienne," *Revue d'ethnographie et des traditions populaires*, Paris, vol. 3, 1922, pp. 326-33.

"La fête du pilou en Nouvelle-Calédonie," *L'Anthropologie*, Paris, vol. 32, 1922, pp. 221-63.

"La Mission des Loyalty et de Nouvelle-Calédonie," *Un siècle en Afrique et en Océanie, 1822-1922*, Paris, Société des Missions évangéliques, 1923, pp. 103-30.

"La société indigène en Nouvelle-Calédonie," *Océanie française*, Paris, March 1924, no. 74, pp. 45-48.

Propos missionnaires, no. 1, June 1927. (This review, edited by M.L., appeared every two months until August, 1940, including a total of 70 issues. Every number contains articles, comments, and reviews by M.L. Only the most important have been included here.)

"Tempérance et Mission," *Propos*, August 1927, pp. 8-9; February 1928, pp. 8-9; April 1928, pp. 12-13.

"Missionnaire et Administration," *Propos*, December 1927, p. 22.

Dépêche coloniale et maritime. Leenhardt published several articles in this revue, beginning in 1928, including stories under the pseudonym Jean Caro.

Étapes lumineuses, Visites aux chantiers missionnaires. Paris, Société des Missions évangéliques, 1928; *Cahiers missionnaires*, no. 12.

"Savoir Regarder," *Propos*, April 1928, pp. 18-20.

"La Dot," *Propos*, April 1929, pp. 52-56. (See also August 1929.)

"Le prestige du Blanc menacé," Paris, Société des Missions évangéliques, 1929; *Pages documentaires*, no. 2.

Notes d'ethnologie néo-calédonienne. Paris, 1930; *Université de Paris. Travaux et Mémoires de l'Institut d'Ethnologie*, vol. 8.

"Des Résistances dans le ministère missionnaire," *Propos*, February 1930, pp. 43-47; April 1930, pp. 53-54.

"Autour du Salaire: Don ou dû?," *Propos*, April 1930, pp. 57-59.

"Objection de conscience et le salut des païens," *Propos*, June 1930, pp. 5-12.

"Le Travail forcé," *Propos*, October 1930, pp. 31-38.

"Immoralité noire et angoisse missionnaire," *Propos*, April 1931, pp. 77-78.

"La place du missionnaire dans la mission, apostolat et pastorat," *Propos*, April 1931, pp. 78-82; June 1931, pp. 4-5.

"Le terme 'rédemption' dans les traductions," *Propos*, August 1931, pp. 15-18.

"L'art néo-calédonien," *Lyon universitaire*, Lyon, April-May 1931, pp. 11-15.

"L'habitation indigène dans les possessions françaises d'Océanie," *La Terre et la vie*, Paris, no. 8, September 1931, pp. 480-99.

"Exposition coloniale de Vincennes: Les Palais et les Pavillons. VI. La Nouvelle-Calédonie," *Revue des deux mondes*, Paris, 15 September 1931, pp. 364-80.

"L'art canaque à l'exposition coloniale de Vincennes," *Revue du Pacifique*, Paris, 1931, pp. 708-13.

Documents néo-calédoniens. Paris, 1932; *Travaux et mémoires de l'Institut d'Ethnologie*, vol. 9.

"Le prêt de la dot," *Propos*, April 1932, pp. 64-66.

"Deux points de la prédication des prophètes Africains: monothéisme et nationalisme," *Propos*, April 1933, pp. 59-61.

"Le masque calédonien." *Bulletin du Musée d'Ethnographie du Trocadéro*, Paris, July 1933, pp. 3-21.

"Comptes Rendus des Conférences," *Annuaire*, Ecole Pratique des Hautes Etudes, 5ᵉ section, Paris, 1934-1951. (Beginning in 1933-1934, M.L. taught part of Marcel Mauss's course on the "Religions des Peuples Non-civilisés." From *Annuaire* 1934-1935 on, rather extensive summaries of M.L.'s teaching appear, except for 1938-1939 and 1948-1949, when M.L. was in the Pacific.)

"La Bible en mission," *Evangile et Liberté*, 21 October 1934.

"Initiation coloniale des missions étrangères en Afrique et Océanie françaises," *Propos*, April 1935, pp. 65-72; June 1935, pp. 77-84; August 1935, pp. 90-96.

"Magie et religion," *Propos*, October-December 1935, pp. 103-05.

Vocabulaire et grammaire de la langue houaïlou. Paris, 1935; *Travaux et mémoires de l'Institut d'Ethnologie*, vol. 10.

"La Mythologie Primitive," *Propos*, April 1936, pp. 21-24.

"Le mariage," *Propos*, February 1937, pp. 3-6.

"Le Colonialisme," *Propos*, June 1937, pp. 50-56.

Gens de la Grande Terre: Nouvelle-Calédonie. Paris, 1937.

"Le temps et la personnalité chez les canaques de la Nouvelle-Calédonie," *Revue philosophique*, Paris, September-October 1937, pp. 43-58.

"Tranches de vie canaque: Suicide et vitalité dans les îles du Pacifique," *Monde colonial illustré*, Paris, October 1937, pp. 240-41.

Questionnaire linguistique: destiné à l'étude les langues de la Mélanésie du Sud. Nouméa, 1938.

"Le rite communiel et les Thongas," *Propos*, February 1938, pp. 7-11.

"Valeurs du Pacifique," *Propos*, August 1938, pp. 71-74.

"La Vieille Calédonie et le Musée de l'Homme," *Etudes mélanésiennes*, Nouméa, no. 1, December 1938, pp. 11-16.

"L'organisation de la recherche scientifique en Océanie française," *Congrès de la recherche scientifique dans les territoires d'outre-mer*, Paris, 1938, pp. 527-33.

Alfred Boegner, d'après son journal intime et sa correspondance, Paris, 1938.

Cahiers de Foi et Vie: Le Monde non chrétien. Seven numbers published between 1938 and 1945; M.L. is one of the directors.

"La fabrication de la perle, monnaie calédonienne," *Etudes mélanésiennes*, Nouméa, April 1939, pp. 5-7. (Republished 5 Jan. 1951.)

"L'archipel des Loyalty. Résumé." *L'Anthropologie*, Paris, vol. 49, 1940, pp. 833-34.

"Rectitude de langage et prédication," *Propos*, April 1940, pp. 3-5.

"Sur une plage des Nouvelles-Hébrides; Pasteurs indigènes et missionnaires," *Propos*, February 1940, pp. 6-10.

"Les chefferies océaniennes," *Comptes rendus des séances de l'Académie des Sciences coloniales*, Paris, 1941, pp. 359-76.

"Conique et marmites en Nouvelle-Calédonie: Problème de préhistoire,"

Comptes rendus des séances de l'Institut français d'Anthropologie, Paris, no. 7, 21 May 1941, p. 13.

"La personne mélanésienne," *Annuaire de l'Ecole pratique des Hautes Études*, section des sciences religieuses, 1941-1942, Melun, 1942, pp. 5-36.

"Totem et identification," *Revue de l'histoire des religions*, Paris, vol. 127, January-June 1944, pp. 5-17.

"Les missions protestantes françaises," Boegner and Siegfried, eds., *Protestantisme français*, Paris, 1945, pp. 372-405.

"La Société des Océanistes," *Journal de la Société des Océanistes*, Paris, 1945, vol. 1, no. 1, pp. 13-18.

"Mawaraba mapi. La signification du masque en Nouvelle-Calédonie," *Journal de la Société des Océanistes*, Paris, vol. 1, 1945, pp. 29-35.

Langues et dialectes de l'Austro-Mélanésie. Paris, 1946; *Travaux et mémoires de l'Institut d'Ethnologie*, vol. 46.

"Sir George Grey," Ch.-A. Julien, ed., *Les techniciens de la colonisation*. Paris, 1946, pp. 211-31.

"L'Expression chez les primitifs," *L'Equipe*, Paris, 1946.

"Ethnologie de la parole," *Cahiers internationaux de sociologie*, Paris, 1946, vol. 1, pp. 82-105.

"Le ti en Nouvelle-Calédonie," *Journal de la Société des Océanistes*, Paris, 1946, vol. 2, pp. 192-93.

Do Kamo, La personne et le mythe dans le monde mélanésien. Paris, 1947. (Republished, 1960, with preface by Maria Isaura Pereira de Queiroz, pp. 7-37.)

Le Monde Non-Chrétien. Paris, January 1947, no. 1. (Leenhardt founded *M.N.C.* in 1947 and edited it until his death. Nearly every issue contains articles, comments, and reviews from his pen. Only the most important are cited.)

"Mission, structure de l'Eglise," *M.N.C.*, Paris, no. 4, December 1947, pp. 406-25. (Also included in *Le Problème de l'Eglise*, Paris, 1947, pp. 123-39.)

"Sépultures néo-calédoniennes," *Journal de la Société des Océanistes*, Paris, 1947, vol. 3, pp. 110-12.

Arts de l'Océanie, Photographies prises par Emmanuel Sougez au Musée de l'Homme. Paris, 1948. (Collection *Arts du Monde*.)

"La religion des peuples archaïques actuels," *Histoire générale des religions*. Quillet, vol. 1, 1948, pp. 107-39. (Originally written in 1937.)

"La roussette," *Etudes mélanésiennes*, Nouméa, 1st year, n.s., 1948, pp. 9-13.

"Réception de M. le Pasteur Maurice Leenhardt. Discours de M. le Gouverneur général Delavignette. Réponse du Pasteur Leenhardt," *Académie des Sciences coloniales, comptes rendus des séances*, 27 December 1948, Paris, pp. 773-95.

"Préface" to *Carnets de Lucien Lévy-Bruhl*. Paris, 1949, pp. i-xxiv; included in Lévy-Bruhl, *The Notebooks on Primitive Mentality*, trans. P. Rivière, New York, 1976.

"Carnets posthumes de Lucien Lévy-Bruhl," *Cahiers internationaux de sociologie*, Paris, vol. 6, 1949, pp. 28-42.

"L'Institut français d'Océanie," *Journal de la Société des Océanistes*, Paris, December 1949, vol. 5, no. 5, pp. 5-14.

"Marcel Mauss (1872-1950)," *Annuaire*, Ecole pratique des hautes études, 5e section, 1950-1951, pp. 19-23.

Arts of the Oceanic Peoples. Photographs by Emmanuel Sougez. Translated from the French by Michael Heron. London, 1950. 150 pp., pl., carte, 8°.

"Institut français d'Océanie et développement culturel de l'Océanie française," *Encyclopédie coloniale et maritime française*, Paris, vol. 1, October 1950, pp. 49-51.

"L'art en Nouvelle-Calédonie," *Tropiques*, Paris, 48th year, December 1950, pp. 81-88, ill.

"Aspects juridiques du mariage chez les peuples archaïques; cérémonie et sceau du mariage," *M.N.C.*, no. 15, July-September 1950, pp. 321-35.

"Découverte des Eglises et de l'Eglise aux territoires d'outre-mer," *M.N.C.*, no. 18, April-June, 1951, pp. 170-94.

"Modes d'expression en sociologie et en ethnologie," Significal Summer Conference, *Synthèse*, vol. 10, n.d. [1951?], pp. 259-64.

"Notes on translating the New Testament into New Caledonian," *Bible Translator*, London, vol. 2, 1951, pp. 97-105, 145-52. (Translation, somewhat unreliable, of the 1922 article, shortened version.)

"L'expérience hébridaise," *M.N.C.*, no. 19, July-September 1951, pp. 304-15.

"Le problème des migrations en Nouvelle-Calédonie," *Etudes sur l'Océanie*, Bale, 1951, pp. 294-317.

"In memoriam. G. van der Leeuw," *Revue d'histoire et de philosophie religieuses*, Strasbourg, 1951, no. 4, pp. 497-99.

"Sculpte ton masque!," *Amour de l'Art*, Paris, 30th year, nos. 49-51, 1951, pp. 53-58.

"Primauté de l'esthétique," *Catalogue illustré. Arts de l'Océanie*, Paris, 1951, pp. 7-10.

"Danses mélanésiennes," *Tropiques*, Paris, 49th year, no. 337, December 1951, pp. 73-82.

"La condition missionnaire," *M.N.C.*, Paris, no. 24, 1952, pp. 448-63; no. 25, 1953, pp. 52-70; no. 26, pp. 160-72.

"Pourquoi se vêtir?," *Amour de l'Art*, Paris, 31st year, nos. 58-60, 1952, pp. 3-14.

"Das Verhältnis zwischen Religion und Recht im Lichte einiger Eigentamsbegriffe bei den Primitiven," *Religiöse Bindungen in frühen und in Orientalischen Rechten*. Wisbaden, 1952, pp. 9-17.

"La propriété et la personne dans les sociétés archaïques." *Journal de Psychologie normale et pathologique*, Paris, July-September 1952, pp. 278-92.

"Langues mélanésiennes," A. Meillet et M. Cohen, *Les langues du monde*, new edition, 1952, pp. 675-90.

"La fallacieuse ambiguité du terme mission," *M.N.C.*, no. 22, April-June 1952, pp. 150-68.

Gens de la Grande Terre. Revised, expanded edition, Paris, 1953.

De la mort à la vie: l'évangile en Nouvelle-Calédonie. Nouvelle edition: Centenaire de la Nouvelle-Calédonie. Paris, Société des Missions évangéliques, 1953 (the 1922 pamphlet, slightly revised).

"Quelques éléments communs aux formes inférieures de la religion," M. Brillant and R. Aigrain, eds., *Histoire des religions*, Paris, 1953, vol. 1, pp. 83-110.

"Kapéa rêves et dessins d'un indigène de Nouvelle-Calédonie," *M.N.C.*, Paris, no. 25, March 1953, pp. 52-70; includes commentaries by M.L.

"Sociologie religieuse: Questionnaire en vue de l'établissement d'une carte religieuse de l'A.O.F.," *Bulletin de l'Institut français d'Afrique noire*, Dakar, vol. 15, no. 2, April 1953, pp. 768-97.

"La Nouvelle-Calédonie: à propos d'un centenaire," *M.N.C.*, Paris, no. 27, July-September 1953, pp. 233-43.

"La Condition missionnaire: Madagascar," *M.N.C.*, no. 65, January-March 1963, pp. 9-38.

"Lettre aux Pasteurs de Nouvelle-Calédonie, 10 octobre 1939," *M.N.C.*, no. 68, October-December 1963; translated from the Houailou by R.-H. Leenhardt, original and French versions (36 pages).

Structure de la Personne en Mélanésie. S.T.O.A. Edizioni, Milan, 1970; a re-edition of various essays by C. Rugafiori and H.J. Maxwell; contains "Le masque calédonien," 1933; "Mawaraba Mapi," 1945; "Religion des peuples archaïques actuels," 1948 (omitting the opening sections); "Le temps et la personnalité," 1937; "La personne mélanésienne," 1942; "La propriété et la personne," 1952.

"La Réquisition des indigènes en Nouvelle-Calédonie (1918)," *Objets et Mondes, Revue du Musée de l'Homme*, summer 1977, pp. 85-89; issue contains other documents by M.L., circa 1918.

Centenaire Leenhardt, 1878-1954. Nouméa, 1978; contains unpublished documents by M.L. in New Caledonia.

Do Kamo: Person and Myth in the Melanesian World. Chicago, 1979, translated by Basia Miller Gulati.

"Notes sur le régime de l'engagement des indigènes en Nouvelle-Calédonie, mars 1914," *Journal de la Société des Océanistes*, Paris, vol. 34, nos. 58-59, March-June 1978, pp. 9-18.

Leenhardt also contributed minor articles to the following publications: *Almanach des Missions* (1923), *Almanach du tempérant* (1922, 1931, 1932), *Appel au monde païen* (1944), *Au service du Maître* (1932), *Bulletin de la France d'outre-mer* (1950), *La Cause* (1935), *Civisme* (1925), *L'Espérance* (1933), *Évangile et Liberté* (1932), *Feuille du bon missionnaire* (1931), *Journal des Écoles du Dimanche* (1932), *Le Lien* (1931), *Ligue Française* (1922), *Le Libérateur* (1931), *Missions des Iles* (1950), *Pour l'Étude et l'Action missionnaire* (1928), *Réforme* (1944), *Semeur* (1928), *La Vie de la France et de l'Union française* (1951), *World Dominion* (1935).

SECONDARY WORKS CONCERNING LEENHARDT

Collections

"Hommage à Maurice Leenhardt," *Journal de la Société des Océanistes*, Paris, vol. 10, no. 10, December 1954 (70 pages). (Essays by Jean Poirier, R. Becker, A. Sauvageot, R.-H. Leenhardt, Pierre Métais.)

"Maurice Leenhardt, 1878-1954," *Le Monde Non-Chrétien*, Paris, no. 33, January-March 1955, pp. 3-120. (Essays by A. Roux, Jean Guiart, Pierre Routhier, Jean Poirier, I. Meyerson, G. Le Bras, G. Gurvitch, A. Sauvageot.)

In *Le Monde Non-Chrétien*, Paris, nos. 71-72, 75-76, 1964, 1965, a series of re-assessments of Leenhardt in the light of structuralism: G. Gusdorf, "Situa-

tion de M.L., ou l'ethnologie française de Lévy-Bruhl en Lévi-Strauss"; J.
Guiart, "M.L. entre deux mondes"; J. Roumeguerre-Eberhardt, "Actualité
de Maurice Leenhardt pour les études africanistes"; R. Bastide, "Conclusion
d'un débat récent: la pensée obscure et confuse."

Objets et Mondes. Revue du Musée de l'Homme, Paris, summer 1977, special
Leenhardt edition, works by M.L., Guiart, and Clifford.

Centenaire Leenhardt, 1878-1954. Nouméa, 1978, contains analyses and recollec-
tions of M.L.'s work by 24 Melanesians and a historical introduction by
Dominique Bourret.

Le Courrier du Musée de l'Homme. Paris, January 1978, presents historical documents relating to M.L.'s career.

"Centenaire du Maurice Leenhardt," special issue of the *Journal de la Société des
Océanistes,* Paris, vol. 34, nos. 58-59, March-June 1978; includes evaluations of
Leenhardt's work by various hands and unpublished documents by M.L.

Individual Works

Becker, R. "Le missionnaire," *Journal de la Société des Océanistes,* Paris, December
1954, vol. 10, no. 10, pp. 11-27.

Clifford, James. "Maurice Leenhardt, Ethnologist and Missionary," 556 pp.
Dissertation, Harvard University, 1977.

Condominas, Georges. "Maurice Leenhardt, l'ethnologue de la Nouvelle-
Calédonie," *France-Asie,* Paris, April-May 1954, pp. 571-82.

Crapanzano, Vincent. "Introduction," *Do Kamo,* Chicago, 1979, pp. vii-xxix.

Danon, Hilda. "Lire Maurice Leenhardt aujourd'hui," *Objets et Mondes,* Paris,
vol. 16, no. 3, Autumn 1976, pp. 117-24.

Dousset-Leenhardt, Roselène. "Maurice Leenhardt," *L'Homme,* Paris, January-
March 1977, 17 (I), pp. 105-15.

―――. *La tête aux antipodes, récit autobiographique.* Paris, 1980.

Gorode, Waia. *Les Souvenirs d'un Néo-Calédonien ami de Maurice Leenhardt.* 66 pp.
Paris, 1977.

Guiart, Jean. Introduction, *Structure de la Chefferie en Mélanésie du Sud.* Paris, 1963.

―――. *Destin d'une église et d'un peuple, étude monographique d'une oeuvre missionnaire
protestante.* Paris, 1959.

―――. "Naissance et avortement d'un messianisme," *Archives de Sociologie de
Religion,* Paris, January-June 1959, pp. 3-44.

―――. "Les Conditions d'une enquête sur la mythologie du masque en
Nouvelle-Calédonie; dialogue avec Maurice Leenhardt," lecture, Musée de
l'Homme, 28 January 1972. Reprinted in *Journal de la Société des Océanistes,* vol.
30, nos. 42-43, March-June 1974, 111-116.

―――. "Maurice Leenhardt inconnu: l'homme d'action," *Objets et Mondes,* Paris,
summer 1977, pp. 75-85.

Leenardt, R.-H. "Linguiste, parce que missionnaire," *Journal de la Société des Océanistes,* Paris, December 1954, vol. 10, no. 10, pp. 33-40.

―――. "Figures Mélanésiennes," a series of monographs on M.L.'s New Caledonian collaborators: "Un sociologue Canaque: le pasteur Boesoou Erijisi,
1866-1947," *Cahiers d'Histoire du Pacifique,* Paris, no. 4, 1976, pp. 19-53; "Le

Pasteur Joané Nigoth (1866?-1919)," Paris, 1976, 43 pp.; "Trois pasteurs Lifou à Houailou: Weinith, Numera, Makonn," Paris, 1977, 36 pp.; "Le Grand Chef Amane des Poyes de 1898 à 1917," *Journal de la Société des Océanistes*, Paris, March-June 1978, vol. 34, nos. 58-59, pp. 23-36.

_____. "Témoignage: Un tournant de l'histoire de la Nouvelle Calédonie, Maurice Leenhardt (1878-1954)," *Revue français d'Histoire d'Outre-Mer*, Paris, vol. 65, 1978, no. 239, pp. 236-52.

Massé, Jean. "Maurice Leenhardt, une pédagogie libératrice," *Revue d'Histoire et de Philosophie religieuse*, no. 1 (1980), 67-80.

Métais, Pierre. "Sociologue parce que linguiste" and "L'Oeuvre ethnologique et sociologique de Maurice Leenhardt," *Journal de la Société des Océanistes*, Paris, December 1954, vol. 10, no. 10, pp. 40-50, 51-69.

Pagnoni, Ines. "Il contributo ethnologico di Maurice Leenhardt," doctoral Thesis, Catholic University of Brescia, 1975.

Pereira de Queiroz, Maria Isaura. "Préface," M.L., *Do Kamo*, 1971 edition, pp. 7-37.

Poirier, Jean. "Maurice Leenhardt, océaniste et sociologue," *M.N.C.*, Paris, no. 33, January-March 1955, pp. 72-95.

Routhier, Pierre. "Souvenirs sur Maurice Leenhardt, premier directeur de l'Institut Français d'Océanie," *M.N.C.*, Paris, no. 33, January-March 1955, pp. 113-20.

Roux, André. "Maurice Leenhardt, missionnaire," *M.N.C.*, Paris, no. 33, January-March 1955, pp. 12-51.

Sauvageot, Aurelien. "Maurice Leenhardt, linguiste," *Journal de la Société des Océanistes*, Paris, December 1954, vol. 10, no. 10, pp. 28-33.

Spindler, Marc. "Maurice Leenhardt et Madagascar," *M.N.C.*, January-March 1963, pp. 39-59.

Teisserenc, Pierre. "Maurice Leenhardt en Nouvelle Calédonie: Sciences sociales, politique coloniale, stratégies missionnaires," *Recherches de Science Religieuse*, Paris, 1977, pp. 3-56.

Wagner, Roy. Review of *Do Kamo, American Anthropologist*, no. 2 (1980), 690-91.

Index

Aekè (a language of the Koné region), lullaby quoted, 160
African Methodist Episcopal Church (founded 1896), 24
Ajië (a language of New Caledonia), 59. *See also* Houailou
Allegret, Elie, 117
Allier, Raoul, 236 n15
Almanach des Missions (edited by ML), 24
André-Michel, André, 72
André-Michel, Jeanne. *See* Leenhardt, Jeanne
Année Sociologique, 152
androgyny: *Bao* as feminine "life" and masculine "power," 90; and Jesus, 8, 221
anthropomorphism, described, opposite of cosmomorphism, 174
Aranda, 205
Atai (leader of rebellion of 1878), 124; appropriated by anthropology, 125; legacy of, 226
authenticity: cultural, 35, 65, 91; personal, 190; theme in ML's bachelor thesis, 24
authority: in ethnographic texts, 144; ML quoted on, 121

Bachelard, Gaston, 210, 219
bao: as Christian God (*Bao*), 80; defined, 87; meaning "spirit," "ancestor," or "corpse," 79; mediating masculine and feminine, 87-91
Barthes, Roland, 185; and *pensée obscure*, 181 n25; and post-structuralism, 180 n22
Bastide, Roger, 178-180
Bergeret, Etienne: conflicts with ML, 116, 118
Boas, Franz, 137, 173

body: Boesoou Erijisi quoted on, 172; in modern life, 185; lacking for personage, 185; ML quoted on, 176; and myth, 188
Boegner, Alfred (director of Paris Mission Society), 19; and Franz Leenhardt, 22; quoted, 148-149; ML critical of, 77
bougnas (food, ceremonial), 4
bricolage, 177
Brunet, Charles (Governor of New Caledonia), 53
Bulmer, Ralph, 141 n25
Burger, J.P., 241 n15
Burridge, K.O.L., 131 n3, 185
bwiri: meaning "spontaneous expression," 112; and *parole*, 214
Bwaxat, Chief (instigator of 1917 rebellion), 102

Calame-Griaule, Geneviève, 214 n37
Calvin, John, 27
Canala (site of *grand pilou*), 134
Caro, Jean (pseudonym of ML), 148
Casagrande, Joseph, 141 n25
Cassirer, Ernst, 202
Catala, René, 192
Césaire, Aimé, 197
Codere, Helen, 138
Codrington, R.H., 47, 134
Coillard, François, 23, 110, 238 n13
colonialism: and anthropology, 124, 196-198; and cultural disintegration, ML quoted on, 108; and *Do Kamo*, critique of, 189-190; and education, 38; as ideological constraint, 113; influence, diverse modes of, 125; and missionary work, 3, 113; "natural" status, 58; in New Caledonia, 46-55, 226; and

reciprocity, ML's view, 82; and traditional culture, 163
Commission Missionaire des Jeunes (C.M.J.), 145
Conrad, Joseph, 107
Corbin, Henry, 219
Corneille, Pierre, 21
cosmomorphism, 173, 176
Couve, Daniel (cousin of ML; a director of Paris Mission Society), 111, 118

Da Vinci, Leonardo, 22
Delacroix, Eugène, 22
Delord, Philadelphe, 26, 32, 77
Descartes, René, 178
do kamo: meaning "authentic person," 1, 129; as ideal for ML, 190, 198-199
Do Kamo: stylistic, ideological critique of, 189-191
doki, meaning "red god," "maleficent influence," 163-165
do neva, meaning "the true country," 59, 70
Do Neva (ML's mission station), description, 68-73
Durkheim, Emile, 2, 75, 92, 152, 172, 184, 190, 214
Duvignaud, Jean, 5
Dwane, James, 24
Ecole Pratique des Hautes Etudes, 2, 149; Mauss's chair at, 153; ML's teaching at, 154-157
Eliade, Mircea, 181
ensemble: in esthetic perception, 207-210; in Houailou language, distinguished from Western composites, 85, 209; in ML's cogito, 178; socio-mythic, 183-185; village as, 38
Erijisi, Boesoou, 63, 176; biographical sketch, 141; body, his notion of, 172, 186; as ethnographic informant, 141; as translator, 84
esthetics, 206-210; as access to pensée obscure, 208; in ML's apprehension of place, 38; New Caledonian, 186; participative and corporeal, 114; perception, as nascent logos, 210
ethnography, 62, Chapter 8 passim; and colonial roles, 126-127; Geertz's conception of, 140 n24; as indigenous interpretation of custom, 133; and

mission work, 130-135; ML's early activities, 75, Chapter 5 passim; as translation, 86; ML on method for study of religion, 222; as process of self-reflection for ML, 133; and reciprocity, 86, 142; as transcription, 140 n24; and construction of vernacular texts, 138
evangelical method. See missiology

Feillet, Paul (Governor of New Caledonia), 48
Fromentin, Eugène, 21
functionalism, 106, 135, 190

Gabon: ML's visit, quoted on esthetics of place, 114
Geertz, Clifford, 140, 222 n10, 245 n24
Gide, André, 107
Goethe, Johann Wolfgang von, 215
Gondé (village in Houailou Valley), 4, 36, 100, 171
Gorode, Waia, 170, 248 n19
Grande Terre. See New Caledonia
Griaule, Marcel, 2, 141 n25, 156
Guiart, Jean, 51, 95, 142, 163, 168, 170, 177, 196, 246 n29
Guillain, Charles (Governor of New Caledonia), 47
Gusdorf, Georges, 177 n11

habitat, 36, 38. See also landscape; esthetics
Heidegger, Martin, 187 and fn
Hermann, Charles, 109
Hmae, Apou, 97, 99, 168, 194
Horton, Robin, 237 n7
Houailou: ML's arrival at settlement, 34; as language of religious instruction, 117, 120; and totemism, 89-90; and ensembles, 85, 209
Hugo, Victor, 21
Hymes, Dell, 138
immanence, 91, 173; in Lévy-Bruhl, 205; in ML's Christianity, 3, 80, 81; in mythic experience, 90; of totems, 41, 90-91. See also transcendence
individual, 153; as ideological construct, 185; in Lévy-Bruhl, 205; and the person, 89; and the personage, 184; and phenomenology, 223 n16; secular, 188

Ingres, J. A. D., 22
Institut d'Ethnologie, 2, 149
Institut Française d'Océanie (I.F.O.), 2, 191

jau, meaning "divine," "healer," and "prophet," 43, 163
Jaurès, Jean, 151
Jopaipi (a traditional healer): his participatory experience, 149, 183
Journal des Missions Évangeliques, 27, 48, 60
Jung, C. G., 207
juxtaposition, in folktale, 210; of images in myth, 178, 204; in *mythe vécu*, 183

Kant, Immanuel, 178
Kapéa, 217
Kefeat (leader of rebellion of 1917), 99
Kruger, Hermann, 23, 107

Lacan, Jacques, 185
Laffay, Paul (schoolmaster at Do Neva), 53 n19
Lambaréné (Gabon), 109
Lamartine, Alphonse, 21
landscape: in cosmomorphic perception, 174; mediator of visible and invisible, 40; and myth, 7, 35-37, 40, 66, 101, 114-115, 169, 187-188. *See also* habitat; *maciri*
Landtman, Gunnar, 203; on mythic narratives, 210 n27
language: and *parole*, 214; ML contrasted to Saussure on, 254 n37
L'Anthropologie, 107, 135
LeCoeur, Charles, 2
Leenhardt, Aloyse, 14
Leenhardt, Amélie, 14
Leenhardt, Camille, 14
Leenhardt, Francine, 70
Leenhardt, Franz: death of, 105; and Lévy-Bruhl, 106, 202; life and thought, 13-16; on ML's education, 21
Leenhardt, Henri, 13
Leenhardt, Jeanne: on Boesoou Erijisi, quoted, 63; character of, 27-29, 114, 149-150, 165; life and work with ML, 70-72, 114, 156, 159, 161; quoted 166-169
Leenhardt, Maurice: Alliance Evangelique Universelle, president of, 219;

Almanach des Missions, editor of, 16; and art, early enthusiasm for, 19, 21-22; and *Les Arts de l'Océanie*, 210; Catholics, relations with, 56; and Coillard, 23; and Colonial Exhibition, 159; and Commission Missionnaire des Jeunes (1928), 145; and *Documents néo-calédoniennes*, 138-139; and *Do Kamo*, 1, 101, 172, 179, 181, 188, 189, 210-212; and Do Neva, 59-60, 70, 112-117; Ecole Pratique des Hautes Etudes, teaching at, 154-157; Boesoou Erijisi, ethnographic work with, 141-142; and esthetics, early thoughts on, 22; and esthetics, late theories of, 206-210; ethnographic work of, 40-41, 75, 129-144, 158-163; family history of, 13-15; father's influence on, 16-17, 35-36, 105-107; and France (patriotism), 92-94; and France, return to, 117, 145; in Gabon, 107-109; and *Gens de la Grande Terre*, 38, 158-159, 186, 197; government, attitude toward, 50-55, 96; and hermeneutic, cross-cultural, 54; illness, final, 224; as *indigènophile*, 50; Institut Française d'Océanie, director of, 191; Jeanne, engagement to, 26; Jeanne, relationship with, 149-150; Jeanne, work with in the field, 161, 165-166; Kruger, influenced by, 23; and *Langues et dialectes de l'Austro-Mélanésie*, 160; letters characterized, 72-73; and Lévy-Bruhl, 105, 159, 189-190, 200-206; life characterized, 216-217; and Malinowski, 136-137, 146-147; Mauss, friendship with, 153-154; missionary role model, 20, 23-24, 116; *Le Monde Non-Chrétien*, editor of, 217-218; nature, relation to, 18-19; New Caledonia, present reputation in, 2-3, 225-227; and *Notes d'ethnologie néo-calédonienne*, 132, 139, 172, 179; Nouméa, attitude towards, 31-32; ordination, 28; pastor in Paris, 145; person, theory of, applied to, 6, 216-217; "La Personne mélanésienne," 183, 187; physical characteristics, 72; in politics and religion, loyal opposition, 52-53; *Propos missionnaires*, founder, 156; pseudonym (Jean Caro), 148; Pwagach, relations with, 164;

"Quelques éléments communs aux formes inférieures de la religion," 220; rebellion of 1917, role in, 95-99, 102-104; religion, early thoughts on, 22; religion, late views of, 221-223; reports to mission society characterized, 77; and Rivet, 106, 159; schooling, 17-19; "Sociologie religieuse, questionnaire," 221-223; as student at Edinburgh, 26; as theology student, 24; thesis, bachelor's, 24-25; and *Vocabulaire et grammaire de la langue Houailou*, 138-139; World War I, role in, 92-94; in Zambeze mission field, 110-111

Leenhardt, Paul, 15, 21, 29, 150
Leenhardt, Raymond, 4-5, 70-71
Leenhardt, Renée, 70-71
Leenhardt, Roselène, 70
Leenhardt, Stella, 70-71
Leiris, Michel, 156, 157; on ethnography and colonialism, 196-197
Lengereau, François, 32
Lenormand, M.-H., 191
LeSotho, 23, 111
Leuba, James, 92
Lévy-Bruhl, 7, 92, 138, 146, 155, 176, 181, 189, 190, 200-206, 208, 237 n3
—— and ML: collaboration with, 159; contrasted, 210; importance for, 75, 151; influence on, 201; meeting with, 105; psychological relationships with, 106, 202; support for, 113
Lévi-Strauss, Claude, 2, 152, 173, 185; compared with ML, 176-181; on Western personality, 89
Ligue de la Moralité Publique, 145
London Missionary Society, 43
Loyalty Islands: history, 43; Protestantism on, 116; conflict with New Caledonia, 115-121
maciri, meaning "peaceful abode," 36, 90, 194. *See also* habitat: ensemble
mai, meaning "Protestant festival," 100
Majnep, Ian Saem, 141 n25
Malinowski, Bronislaw, 106, 173, 180, 244 n14; and ethnographic texts, 140; functionalism, 136, 190; and ML compared, 136-137; *Sexual Life of Savages*, reviewed by ML, 146
Mathaia, 59

Mauss, Marcel, 2, 138, 139; on ethnology, quoted, 137; distinction between *personnage* and *personne*, 187
—— and ML: discussions with, 153; importance to, 151; meeting, 106; similarity to, 154; religion, phenomenological interest in, 152-153
Melanesia. *See* New Caledonia
Merleau-Ponty, Maurice, 129, 214 n37
Métais, Eliane, 179-180
Métraux, Alfred, 2
Michel, Louise, 47
missiology: conversion process, 77-78; paternalism and colonialism, ML on, 121; difficulty, ML on, 67; distinction between missionary and pastor, 20, 116; and ethnography, 107, 126-127, 133-136; evangelical method, 24-26, 63, 68, 79-91, 109-113, 115-121; and liberation theology, 52 n17, 235 n17; translation in, 76-91
Mokone, Manghena, 24
Moméa, 225
Monod, Théodore, 218, 221
Montauban, 14
Musée de l'Homme, 2
Musset, Alfred de, 21
myth, archaic, 202; in casual gesture, 182; Christianization of, 48; as condition of newness, 181; defined by ML, 137 n14, 222; as ensemble, 210 n27; as landscape, 7, 40, 90, 169, 174; Lévi-Strauss quoted on, 181 n25; lived, ML quoted on, 203-204; as Malinowski's "magic," 136; as mode of knowledge, 7, 202-206; and narrative, 209; opposed to Lévy-Bruhl's *mystique*, 202; as patterned events, 184; Van der Leeuw, 137 n14. *See also mythe vécu*
—— totemic: as feminine, 175; as religious experience, 176; versus magic, 89
mythe vécu, 7, 209; and acculturation, 187; contrasted with practical activity (Malinowski), 137; and folktale, 203; and Lévi-Strauss's *bricolage*, 177

narrative: "de-narrated" story, 204; patterns implicit in ML's theories, 173; and personal structure, 7
natas, meaning "messenger," Melanesian

pastors, 32, 42-44, 55, 59-66, 76, 87, 89, 118, 165, 168, 171
Néa, role in 1917 rebellion, 99, 102
Nebay, Eleisha, 8, 97, 99, 194; on conversion experience, 78
Needham, Rodney: on ethnographic experience, 62; critique of "kinship," 249 n33
Néja Mindia, 34, 59; as ethnographic informant, 130-133
New Caledonia: and colonialism today, 226; colonial politics, 45-57, 191-195; commerce and industry 1950s, 196; cultural development, ML's ideal, 195-199; geographical characteristics, 31, 33; *La Grande Terre*, 26; history, 26, 29, 31, 45-55, 191; population, 45; Protestantism today, 91; racism, 196; rebellion of 1917, 95-103; religious history, 59-60; and World War I, 92-94; and World War II, 191
Nida, Eugene, 85 n34
Nigoth, Joané, 63, 82, 103
nô, meaning "*parole*," "speech," "word," 85, 210-215
Nouméa: described, 30-32; development, 47

Ortigues, Edmond, 218
Ouvéa, Loyalty Island, 40, 50

Pandey, Triloki, 134
Paris Anthropological Society, 106, 124
Paris Evangelical Mission Society, 18; and colonial missions, 110; misunderstanding of ML, 77, 111, 115-121; New Caledonia, 74-75, 117; ML's disagreements with, 74-77, 111, 115-121; ML's training by, 22-29
Paris Institute of Ethnology, 2, 113, 138
Parisot (Governor of New Caledonia), 193
parole (speech, the Word), 84-85, 131, 135, 185, 208, 210-215
participation, 40, 89, 200-215; and cosmomorphism, 174; defined, 222; in ML's experience, 107; Lévy-Bruhl, 204-205; and two dimensionality, 182
Pasteur, Paul, 112, 115
Peci Arii (Houailou New Testament), 90
pensée claire et distincte, 178

pensée obscure et confuse, 178; and authenticity, 188; and lived myth, 180; and mythic structure, 178; and parole, 213
person, 172-188; authentic, 187; and biography, 7, 216-217; in conversion, 79; and discontinuous socio-mythic time, 7; and individual, ML quoted on, 216; as locus of dual relations, 38; Mauss on, 153; as mediation, 187; personage, emergence from, 67-68; ML's Christian notion of, 66, 101-102; ML quoted on, 186; and *parole*, 213; and socio-mythic ensemble, 183-187; in structuralism, 185; structure of, in New Caledonia, 175
personage: in archaic participation, 187; distinguished from person, 68; as multi-relational, 184-187; structured by myth, 174; traditional Melanesian, 40
phenomenology, 208 n25; esthetic, 114; in ML's method, 172-173; and individualism, 223 n16; and landscape, 177; and research, ML's approach, 2, 214; of Melanesian art, 22
pilou (traditional ceremony), 41-42, 61-62, 100, 107, 135-136
place: defined by ML, 182; as superimposition, 7; esthetic of, 114, 175. *See also* habitat; landscape
Paetou, Maurice, 99
Poirier, Jean, 155-156
Popular Front, 151
post-structuralism, 2, 173, 180
Pound, Ezra, 141
Propos missionnaires, 145-147
Protestantism: and Catholicism, in New Caledonia, 56-57, 59; and colonialism, 43-44; French, 13-29; history in New Caledonia, 59-60, 104, 161; liberal, 4; on Loyalty Islands, 116; and neo-paganism, 170; and rebellion of 1917, 99; today in New Caledonia, 4-5, 91, 226-227
Pwagach, 163-171

Quine, W.V., 66 n18

Revue de Métaphysique et de Morale, 155
Rey-Lescure, Philippe: ideas of cultural

authenticity, 120; and missionary conflicts, 118-121; ML's nephew, 115; influenced by ML, 117

rhë (totem or life force), 88

Ricoeur, Paul, 138 n20

Rimbaud, Arthur, 183

Rivet, Paul, 106, 113, 138, 159

Rousseau, Jean-Jacques, 82

Rusillon, Henry, 111

Ryle, Gilbert, 140

Saussure, Ferdinand, 173, 214

Schmidt, Pater, 175

Schweitzer, Albert, 107

Siegfried, André, 13

Société des Missions Evangeliques. *See* Paris Evangelical Mission Society

Société des Océanistes, 2

Soustelle, Jacques, 220

speech. See *parole*

stone, 5; Jesus as, 65; and memory of ML, 225-227; in mythic landscape, 169, 226-227; in Old Testament, 68

structuralism, 177, 181, 185, 214

Sundkler, B. M. G., 26

Temala, 58 and ML's method of transcription, 140; as translation, 141; textualization defined, 138 n20; and "thick description," 140

totemism, 221; Christianity's recovery of, 80; and divinities, 175; and Lévi-Strauss, 173; maternal source, 87; in ML's New Testament translation, 90; Melanesian, 179; as myth, 176

transcendence: male association, 173; ML's dilemma, 81; and person-God couple, 22. *See also* immanence

transcription, in ethnography, 139

translation, 74-91; in conversion, 79; "deep," 83-84; and de-narration, 204; as dialectical process, 140; and dynamic equivalence theory, 85 n34; and ethnography, collective, 139; intercultural, Gospel "primitivized," 84; ML's commitment to, 23; ML's dynamic theory of, 86; of moral reasoning, 111; of *nō*, 210-12; and reciprocity, 142

Tylor, E. B., 173

Valéry, Paul, 213

Van der Leeuw, Gerardus, 181, 218, 220; definition of myth, 137 n14

Van Gennep, Arnold, 2

Vincent, Emile, 116

Westphal, Louise, 14

Whitehead, Alfred North, 66

Wilden, Anthony, 187 n39

Zambeze, mission field, 23, 110-111

Designer:	Barbara Llewellyn
Compositor:	In-House Composition
Printer:	Thomson-Shore, Inc.
Binder:	John H. Dekker & Sons
Text:	10/12 Andover
Display:	Andover